Jesse Leon

I'M
NOT
BROKEN

Jesse Leon is a social-impact consultant to foundations, impact investors, nonprofits, and real estate
developers on ways to address affordable housing,
substance abuse, LGBTQ issues, and educational
opportunities for young adults. Since receiving a
master's degree from the Harvard Kennedy School,
Jesse has managed multimillion dollar philanthropic
grantmaking for various foundations and banking
institutions, managed over $1 billion in public sector
investments for affordable housing, and built thousands of units of mixed-income housing as a real
estate developer for Bank of America. Jesse recently
moved to San Diego to be closer to his mother and
to pursue his dream of publishing this book. He is
a native Spanish speaker and fluent in English and
Portuguese.

I'M
NOT
BROKEN

I'M
NOT
BROKEN

A MEMOIR

Jesse Leon

VINTAGE BOOKS

A DIVISION OF PENGUIN RANDOM HOUSE LLC

NEW YORK

A VINTAGE BOOKS ORIGINAL 2022

Library of Congress Cataloging-in-Publication Data
Names: Leon, Jesse, [date] author.
Title: I'm not broken : a memoir / Jesse Leon.
Description: First edition. | New York : Vintage Books, 2022.
Identifiers: LCCN 2021056633 (print) | LCCN 2021056634 (ebook)
Classification: LCC HQ75.8.L465 A3 2022 (print) |
LCC HQ75.8.L465 (ebook) | DDC 360.76/62092 B—dc23
LC record available at https://lccn.loc.gov/2021056633
LC ebook record available at https://lccn.loc.gov/2021056634

Vintage Books Trade Paperback ISBN: 978-0-593-46651-3
eBook ISBN: 978-0-593-46652-0

Book design by Nicholas Alguire

vintagebooks.com

Printed in the United States of America
10   9   8   7   6   5   4   3   2   1

This book is dedicated to my Amá, Linda Sierra,
Ricardo Rosario, and my ancestors who paved the way.

Let's fast-forward to the end.

I am in the middle of Harvard Yard proudly sitting on a plastic folding chair, wearing my black cap and gown, surrounded by classmates seated in neat rows and columns.

I hear a loud, familiar whisper from behind me. "Hey, Nerd! Turn around, Nerd!"

Why am I hearing my brother call me Nerd? I think to myself without even turning around. Here I am, sweating under my cap and gown on this scorching-hot June day, sitting in the middle of Harvard Yard listening to the commencement speaker, on the day of my own graduation, and I am hearing my brother's voice in my head calling me Nerd? Damn, I must be going crazy!

The truth is, that nickname, which eventually became a term of endearment from my brother and my closest friends, started out as one of my brother's many forms of bullying me for being a smart nerdy kid. My friend sitting behind me taps me on the shoulder. I turn around to find my brother slouched down at the end of the row where I am sitting. He's wearing creased-out slacks and his nicest short-sleeve guayabera shirt. He's waving at me with his tattoo-covered arm.

My brother is not unassuming. He is five feet, ten inches tall, muscular, and covered in tattoos from his neck down. He tends to get noticed wherever he goes and whether he wants the attention or not. I'm sure people are wondering about the buff, tatted, gangster-looking guy creeping along the rows of chairs on the plush green lawn surrounded by classic brick buildings. Thousands of graduates, family members, alumni, and faculty are gathered to celebrate Harvard's 350th graduation-day ceremonies for the college and all the university's graduate schools, and there's my brother, taunting me. "Nerd," he calls me.

"What the fuck are you doing?" I hiss back.

I can't believe this is happening. I feel the tension of breaking etiquette tightening around me. Everyone else is adhering to the rules of decorum. I feel embarrassed yet protective. Despite the years of angst between us, I want to guard my brother and my family against any judgment that might be cast their way, any glares that would show others we are out of place.

"Hey, Nerd! Amá's not feeling well. She feels dizzy, her feet are swollen, and there is nowhere for her to sit in the shade. It's way too hot out here. She doesn't want to leave, but I'm taking her somewhere cool where she can sit before she passes out." His voice quivers with nervousness. He points in the direction where they'll be, as if he actually knows where he's going. "We'll see you at the apartment before the afternoon ceremonies."

The students around me give him confused looks as the

tassels on their caps wave around with the movements of their heads. It is clear no one can believe that my family would leave just because it is too hot. This is *the* day, and my brother and mother are leaving.

I can't help but laugh bitterly at the situation. Only *my* family. Only *my* brother would not give a fuck about protocol or etiquette, not even for our commencement speaker. Family always comes first. And our mom's health always takes precedence. "Okay," I say, "I'll see you all later."

I put my head down. I feel disappointed, and a few tears escape my eyes and roll down my cheeks. The student sitting next to me puts his hand on my lap to comfort me as I wipe my face dry.

Getting into and graduating from Harvard is a big deal to me. But I understood. My mom, who I call Amá, had survived two heart attacks and struggled with high blood pressure and severe diabetes. I remind myself that she and my brother had come all the way across the country, from San Diego, to be with me, and that is what matters most. And yet, the disappointment wells in my chest and in my eyes as I lift my head back up to look forward and face the rest of my big day alone. My best friend, Ariyel, and her mom, Joy, are here, too, but my family leaving still cuts deep.

"Two tears in a bucket, fuck it," I tell myself in a whisper.

I took out a loan for $2,500 to fly my family out to see me graduate, because otherwise they wouldn't have made it. My mother at first wasn't planning to come because she had already seen me graduate from community college and UC Berkeley. Those graduations were enough, she'd said, and to her it didn't make sense for me to incur additional fees on her behalf for yet another ceremony. She didn't understand how significant it was for me, and she didn't want to be a burden; she didn't want to make my load any heavier.

In the end, I just paid. I wanted Amá, my brother, my little sister, my brother's wife, and my two nephews to be here so that they could watch a poor, sexually abused, drug-addicted Chicano kid get his master's degree from Harvard, of all places. Dad was too frail to make the trip because of his age and his early onset of dementia. My sister stayed back to care for him. Getting the others here, in many ways, had felt like pulling teeth. But here they were, on my day, and I was glad for that. For this day meant the world to me. I was twenty-six years old and had been through hell to get here. Ultimately, I was proud, and I was proud for my family to be here.

This is my story, the story of the pains and the miracles that led me to this day on the Harvard Yard, where I felt the hot sun on my face and, for the first time, felt my life was laid out boundlessly before me. As for so many others like me, this was not what was supposed to happen. And yet here I was. I survived. I was not broken. This was me, and I had made it here. But, to get to where we are, we have to come from somewhere. So this is also the story of my family.

△▽△

Esperanza, or Espi, who I call Amá, didn't stay in school past fifth grade in Mexico, where she grew up. Since arriving in the United States, she had spent most of her life working periodically as a nanny, a farm laborer, and a dishwasher. She didn't even know what Harvard was. But when I was four years old, she made sure to place me in Head Start, an early education program for low-income families, where she volunteered between her two jobs. When I was in elementary school, she was PTA president. She cared so much about our education that she got a part-time job at the school's cafeteria serving lunch. She became known as the Lunch Mom. During the two hours between her breakfast and lunch shifts, she volunteered at the school, doing whatever she could to make it a better place. She stayed there as I progressed to middle school and high school.

When I was a kid, I never thought twice about the types of jobs my mom worked because so many of my friends' parents were farmworkers and dishwashers. I was happy when my mom got a job at the school cafeteria, because it made her happy. It gave her, and us, stability. At least, that's what I overheard her tell the neighbors.

For me, though, that job became a thorn in the side. Every time I'd get into trouble, the teachers or other students would tattle to my mom. And my mom didn't talk quietly; she talked by yelling. So every time she heard I was up to no good, she would find me in class, pull me hard by the arm, and shout at me to behave. In front of other students and teachers, I would be filled with shame. It felt like my mom always had eyes on me. She was there to pressure me, to make sure I did well in school. I didn't like Amá yelling at me. Although she never told me this herself, I felt I was making her look bad in front of people, especially the teachers. So I tried my best to not disappoint my mom.

Amá was a healthy, solidly built woman standing at five feet, five inches tall with a round face and glasses. I remember she had wavy black hair that flowed down her back. But at some point, while I was still a young kid, she cut it short for practical reasons. It was too thick to maintain while raising kids and was especially inconvenient when working in kitchens. She was working too much to care for her physical appearance. I've never known her to get a manicure or a pedicure. My father, who was fiercely Catholic, never allowed her to wear lipstick, makeup, or nail polish. So she looked like a simple Mexican immigrant with olive skin, big lips and cheeks, and a smile that lit up any room she walked in. As the years passed, she gained weight. She became diabetic and had high blood pressure. But she always maintained her joyful spirit, and she loved making other people happy. Most of all, she was never ashamed of being poor.

When I got accepted to Harvard, I called Amá from my tiny apartment in Berkeley, where I was living at the time, to share the good news. I was giddy with excitement.

"¿Y qué es eso?" she asked. *And what's that?* "Ay, mijo, pero, ¿por qué Boston? Está muy lejos. Tienen muy buenas universidades aquí en San Diego. Y en las noticias dicen que hace mucho frío allá y te puedes enfermar. ¿Por qué no mejor te regresas a casa y vienes a la escuela acá?"

Immediately my spirits fell. I had disappointed Amá, who had never heard of Harvard or Cambridge. And I was angry at our life's circumstances. To my mom, Boston was a far-off place at the other end of the country. She hadn't heard of UC Berkeley, where I did my undergrad, my car-rera, either. But she knew it was in California, and close by. She understood what that carrera was. In her mind, a bachelor's degree was all I needed to be successful in the United States. She reasoned that I simply didn't want to move back home.

Even though she had little formal education, Amá learned the names of the local colleges and universities because these were places the teachers she worked with talked about. San Diego State University (SDSU) was the best of the best, and she dreamed that I would attend there. She didn't realize that there could be better opportunities elsewhere.

"Okay, Mom," I told her, "thanks. I love you. I gotta go. I have a class that I need to get to." I lied just to get off the phone.

"I am super proud of you," she assured me.

I didn't doubt her pride in me, but I cried tears of anger and sadness when I hung up the phone. I was angry that we were poor. I was angry that my mom worked so hard and still she didn't have the luxury of knowing what I knew. I was angry at the injustice of it all.

The day before I was to leave for Harvard, I was picking up my mom from work when the secretary of the elementary school explained to me how Amá had finally accepted that I would be leaving. Amá had been sitting in the school cafeteria during her break between the breakfast and lunch shifts when the secretary walked in. Amá was wearing her hairnet and a work apron over her usual flower-patterned blouse. She sat on a plastic school lunch bench in the middle of the cold, drab concrete room. She was crying, all alone, with her head between her hands. Shocked, the secretary asked my mom, "Espi, why are you crying? Are you okay?"

"Mi hijo. Primero lo perdí a las drogas. Luego se me fue para Berkeley. Y ahora se me va a una escuela en Boston que se llama *Harr-varrd*. ¿Por qué no se regresa aquí a estudiar para estar cerca de la familia? Aquí está la mejor universidad en San Diego," Amá pleaded in Spanish. Why didn't I come home and go to school close to my family? The best university was here in San Diego!

The secretary hugged Amá while she sobbed and asked her, "What school did you just say your son is going to?"

"Se llama *Harr-varrd*. En Boston. Solo Dios sabe dónde queda Boston. Me dicen que está muy lejos, hasta allá cerca de Nueva York. ¿Usted se imagina? ¡Nueva York!"

The secretary held her by the shoulders, looked at her tear-covered face and directly into her eyes, and said, "Are you kidding? It's Harvard!"

She then went directly to the teachers' lounge and wrote on the board: *Please congratulate Espi. Her son just got accepted to Harvard!*

And so everyone did. Teacher after teacher, and even the principal, came by to congratulate Amá that day. Her tears of sadness turned into tears of joy. She looked up to these teachers, and she finally began to understand that Harvard was one of the best and most prestigious schools in the world. And her son, who she had sacrificed so much for, was going to be attending Harvard.

PART
1

In the early years of the 1900s, my father's family owned ranchland, horses, cattle, and gold mines. They lived in the Sierra Madre region of Durango, Mexico. The Mexican Revolution was just beginning. These gold mines, and my family's wealth, helped fund the revolution—a long and bloody ten-year civil war that overthrew a dictator, established the separation between church and state in Mexico's government, and changed the country's landownership policies.

My father, Ricardo Leon, passed away in 2013 believing he was 103 years old. It may be true. According to family lore, he was born between 1909 and 1919—he couldn't say for certain. His mother, Lola, insisted it was 1909. His older sister, Victoria, said 1914. And my dad said he was born in 1919, not realizing that would leave him much younger than 103. Back then, in the Sierra Madre of Durango, Mexico, his parents would have had to wait until they were visiting the closest city to register a child and receive a birth certificate.

Ricardo was born in a tiny village named Cebollitas ("Small Onions"), far up in the mountains above a small town named Canelas ("Cinnamon"), Durango. His own education ended with the third grade. When he died, my father was the last of his generation. He took many family stories with him. He had rarely talked about his life. He was a guarded, private, machista man. Though he cared in his own contradictory ways, he trusted no one.

Some of our family legends endured, however, and have come down to me. The Sierra Madre in Durango was a very dangerous place, especially at that time. Trips down the mountains and into the city were few and far between. My paternal grandfather, Roberto Leon Vizcarra, was a very tall Mexican of Basque descent, from Northern Spain. He, his brothers, and his cousins were all high-ranking revolutionary soldiers who fought alongside Pancho Villa. One of my grandpa's cousins was a general named Domingo Arrieta Leon. These men passed down their strong sense of machismo to my father.

△▽△

Rewind. It's 1983. I am nine years old.

We each had our own garbage bag but no gloves. We hit the tourist areas of Shelter Island, Mission Beach, Seaport Village, La Jolla, fishing piers, and public parks in San Diego in pursuit of aluminum cans. How my mom and dad made this fun, I do not know, but they did.

White people would walk by, stare, and sometimes make derisive comments under their breath, such as "That's disgusting, they should just go back to Mexico" or "I can't believe these parents are encouraging that vile behavior." I didn't pay them any mind. To me, this was family time.

While out collecting cans, we didn't fight. My brother wouldn't be picking on me. My dad wouldn't be criticizing me for not being like my older brother or belittling my mom as an excuse to go hook up with one of his many mistresses. On these trips, I felt like I belonged in this family, and I was proud that I was contributing to our income.

As each garbage bag filled, my septuagenarian, semi-bald, gray-haired dad would carry it to our tiny, blue, beat-up '70s pickup and bring us back a fresh bag. Sometimes my mom would help him, but he often preferred to do this himself. My dad was very machista like that. He often refused physical help from women. My brother and I, meanwhile, ran from trash can to trash can, laughing. We peered under picnic tables as if we were looking for Easter eggs. Some cans still had beer or soda in them, so we'd empty them, the liquid splashing around our feet. We had no hand sanitizer. To speed up the process and avoid having to do the work later, I dropped each empty can onto the ground, then stomped on it, first crushing the middle part and then stepping on each side to flatten the whole can like an envelope.

Once we had filled enough bags—an average of two each, for a total of eight—we drove home and the real work began. My mom helped my dad unload the bags from the back of the truck as my dad carried them to the alley behind our apartment. He poured the cans onto the pavement for us to begin crushing the ones not already flattened. I can still hear that loud sound of aluminum clanging onto the concrete. We'd lift our knees high and stomp on them, our own form of exercise. When a can got stuck around my mom's or dad's shoe, we'd laugh uncontrollably before we pulled the can free. Those days were fun and innocent, when we were all together laughing like that under the San Diego sun.

Recycling was one of my father's many ways to earn extra money. My father was an entrepreneur, he just wasn't a successful one. In the 1950s or '60s, he was working at the El Cortez Hotel in downtown San Diego, setting up for an event, when a pile of tables fell on him. The accident left him disabled with an injured back. Occasionally, when he was in pain, he needed to use a cane to help him walk. As he got older, he limped as he walked, bent over and slouched.

To contribute financially to the family, he bought old cars and fixed them, selling them for a meager profit. He was also known to some as El Señor de los Huevos, the Egg Man. He would drive an hour out of San Diego, to farms in Ramona, California, to buy eggs at low prices. Then he'd return in his little truck and drive around the city, selling those eggs. He tried to buy a house once. He put twenty thousand down on a rent-to-own home in Logan Heights, a low-income Latino neighborhood in the southeast of the city. But the "seller" turned out to be someone who had never owned the home, didn't have the authority to rent it out, and, after collecting payments from my dad for a few months, disappeared with our money. He was a fraud.

We lived there until one day when the police showed up with the actual owner and we had to vacate the premises immediately. Luckily, a good friend of my father's did land-scaping for a family who owned apartments in Little Italy, a working-class Latino and Italian neighborhood where we had previously lived. My father never wanted to buy a house again, and he convinced my mom to agree with him.

△▽△

My parents, Ricardo and Espi, were married in 1970. She was twenty-eight years old. He was sixty.

I was born in 1974 in San Diego. During my mom's pregnancy, both my parents believed they were going to have a girl, who they would name after their second child, my older sister, who had died in Tijuana two years before from a rare anorectal malformation. The night I was born, it was raining. On the way to the hospital my dad asked my mom, "What are we going to name the baby if it's a boy?"

Amá responded, "I don't know."

Right at that moment, a car that was entering the highway from the on-ramp spun out of control, skidding and spiraling toward them. They almost crashed. Amá screamed, "Jesus, Maria y Jose!" Later that night, the first name that came to her mind was Jesus Maria Jose.

A few hours after giving birth to me, my mother held me in her arms as my dad stood by her side. A heavyset woman with glasses and blond hair pulled back in a ponytail walked into my mom's room without knocking. A Spanish-speaking nurse was in tow to help translate. The blond woman, as if in a bad mood, said to my mom in English, "I was told you want to name the baby Jesus Maria Jose. That doesn't even include yours or your husband's last names. That's just too long. I don't understand why you Mexicans are always giving your babies such long names. You need to drop one of them."

The other nurse apologetically translated what the woman said. My mom, exhausted, cheeks still flushed, looked up at my dad with an expression that told him she did not want to argue and asked him, "¿Viejo, qué nombre le quitamos?" *Viejo, what name do we drop?*

"Pues quítale Jose ya para que la pinche vieja se vaya a la chingada y te deje descansar," said my dad. In other words: *Take off Jose so this lousy woman can go to hell and let you rest.*

The nurse translated selectively. Thus Jose was dropped and I was stuck with Jesus Maria.

The San Diego I was born into was not the "America's Finest City" that most people imagine. The downtown area of San Diego I grew up in, during the late '70s to the early '90s, was predominantly Mexican, Italian, and African American, with pockets of people from the Philippines, Vietnam, Laos, Samoa, and Guam. There was no Gaslamp Quarter or the gentrified downtown that exists today. Those of us who lived in and around downtown saw the daily juxtaposition of the city—business district by day and red-light district by night, when the adult movie theaters, strip clubs, tattoo parlors, sex workers, military personnel cruising for entertainment, pimps, and drugs became active. If you didn't belong, you knew not to be downtown after dark. But for the many of us who lived there day and night, it was just home.

Back then, there were also no luxury condominiums and fancy restaurants. Beautifully restored Victorian houses were run-down old homes where we poor Mexicans lived. My family lived on one side of an old, unkempt Victorian divided into a duplex, in a tiny single-story apartment on the right side of a dark hallway. My dad and the neighbor's dad would repair the place themselves. They didn't want to ask the landlord for help with the leaking pipes or chipped paint for fear of the rent being raised. Gone now are the swinging tires hanging from long ropes on big trees in front yards. And even though we lived in the downtown of an urban area, people kept chickens, goats, roosters, and rabbits in the yards behind their apartments. The animals filled the air with farmyard noises. Corn, squash, tomatoes, and chilies grew in my dad's front garden, and we too kept chickens in a small coop.

My dad liked to pick vegetables while my mom prepared a chicken for dinner. She would grab the chicken by the head and swing it around to snap its neck. Other times she would cut its head off with a big butcher knife, letting its body run free, until it finally dropped dead, to scare us kids. She would laugh while we screamed. The soup she made was always flavored with a chicken's head and feet.

I was happy then when the family ate together. We shared everything. We helped one another set the table with mismatching plates, cups, and utensils while my mom warmed up tortillas to accompany our meals, which mostly consisted of beans, rice, tortillas, and a protein. In between meals, I loved making Mexican hot dogs—wienies attached to a fork cooked over the flame on a gas stove and then wrapped in a hot tortilla and dressed with either sour cream or ketchup. Most of all, I loved helping my mom tend to the chickens and helping my dad trim vegetables in the garden. I remember that he'd have me pick a few extra tomatoes, chilies, or squash and put them into a separate bag to take to our neighbors. Every week we'd receive bags of bread, tortillas, and eggs that neighbors shared with us. The community knew and supported one another. We never went without.

△▽△

I was four years old when my mom dropped me off for my first day at Head Start. I was terrified. The program was based in Little Italy, abutting downtown, in a large community room at what was called Bayside Settlement House. Bayside housed social programs for low-income immigrant families, seniors in the community, and after-school programs for the kids that went to Washington Elementary School, one of the oldest elementary schools in San Diego, directly across the street.

I wore plaid pants with a plaid shirt that didn't match and bulky black shoes. I looked around at the large posters of alphabet letters taped on the yellow-painted concrete walls of what looked like a cafeteria turned classroom. Some kids sat quietly on colored rug mats, nervously staring at me. Other kids were running around together. Clearly, those had already formed bonds. The minute Amá left, a choking fear arose in me. I was terrified she wasn't going to come back to pick me up. I ran to the window and watched her walk away as I screamed and cried out to her, "AMÁAAA!" I cried the entire day, looking out the window, waiting for her to return. No one could have pulled me away from that window.

At the end of the day, I was still sitting at my post, cross-legged, exhausted from crying, when I saw my mom walking toward the building. I jumped up and screamed, "Amá! Amá!" with my hands plastered against the pane. When she walked into the room, I ran to her, wrapping my arms around her waist and crying even harder, overcome with joy and relief. "Ya, ya, Jesse, aquí estoy, mijo," she said repeatedly. I can still hear her voice comforting me. "Aquí estoy." *I am here.*

The next year, I attended Washington Elementary. My kindergarten teacher, the happy Mrs. Kay, had long straight silver hair. She was very tall and wore flowy skirts with high black leather boots. She always smelled like flowers and herbs, and she always made me feel welcomed. She'd call on me for answers, inspiring me to learn, and told me I could be anyone or anything I wanted to be. It was the first time I'd ever heard that, and she reminded me frequently that I was smart. As the weeks passed, I joyfully admired the shiny star stickers I received for my homework assignments and my name on the chalkboard with stars drawn beside it for good behavior.

That same year, however, I started to get bad headaches when reading books or writing on paper. The school nurse told my mom to take me to the eye doctor. I needed glasses. We were on welfare and Medi-Cal. At the optometrist's office, the only pair covered by our plan had ugly thick black or brown frames. It turned out that I had twenty-twenty vision in my right eye and twenty-fifty in my left. So one lens was thick while the other was thin. On my face, the glasses leaned to one side and looked lopsided.

That's when the bullying started.

My older brother, who was three years ahead of me, began the trend, calling me a nerd, a dork, four-eyes, and cyclops. The slurs tickled him senseless and made his face red with laughter. Because I also had allergies and severe asthma attacks, he called me bubble boy and told me I was better off living in a plastic bubble every time Amá brought me home from the hospital or the doctor's office. The other kids took his lead, and *Nerd* stuck. Suddenly I became the Mexican nerd who wore thick, lopsided welfare glasses like a goofy cyclops. To make matters worse, my mom liked to part my hair on the side with a greasy hair lotion called Wildroot, or sometimes a pomade called Three Flowers, which added to the overall dorky effect.

Both my mom and my dad wore glasses, and they made sure I kept mine on. My dad started calling me campamo-cha tuerta (one-eyed praying mantis) because the prescription lenses made my left eye look enlarged. Campamocha never bothered me, though. Nicknames are common in Mexico. That my dad would have one for me filled me with joy. It was his way of showing me love. And I felt accepted by him.

Until third grade I was among the smartest kids in class. I finished math quizzes first, scored the highest, and was among the best readers. But that year, I was sent to my brother's sixth-grade class for reading, English, and math. He ignored me the entire time.

My brother was my complete opposite. He was light skinned with golden brown hair and a muscular body. He loved sports. All the girls in the neighborhood had a crush on him. I thought he would be proud to have me in his class, but he saw me as a burden. I might have become accustomed to being bullied by him, but I was still hurt that he wouldn't acknowledge me. Being smart was the only advantage I thought I had over my brother. It didn't matter. He was bigger and stronger, and hung out with the cool guys; he had my dad's attention for all the manly things he was into—making our father prouder than he could ever be of his nerdy son who loved to spend time with his amá in the kitchen.

At home, the only moments when I felt acceptance from my father came in the evenings, when he would force me to finish a series of math problems, which I would labor over for hours. Then, before bed, he would sit me down for a game of chess. All the while, my brother liked to bully me until I cried, forcing me to study alone in my room just to be rid of his taunting voice. I disappeared into my love of learning. This, of course, made my mom, my dad, and my teachers proud of me. I was their smart kid, their good kid. Yet at home, my mom was my one protector. "¡Déjamelo en paz!" she would scream at my brother when she overheard him bullying me. *Leave him alone!* My dad didn't step in. To me, it was as if in his silence he agreed with my brother's treatment of me. It was as if he needed me to toughen up.

One day I was pulled out of class along with one other student to take a test in the school cafeteria. Afterward the school administrators told my mother that my scores were high. They recommended I transfer to a magnet school with a gifted program, because it would be good for my future. The magnet school was in another part of San Diego. The white part.

△▽△

School was the one thing in my life that I felt I was good at. Being uprooted and made to start over somewhere else made me feel like I was being punished for being smart. "Why do I have to go to a school where I don't know anyone?" I cried to my amá. Even though I was being bullied and tormented at that school, it was familiar to me, and I knew how to function there.

At the new school, getting picked on went to a whole new level. I was constantly treated like an outcast for being different. The white kids, none of whom were bused in as they all lived in the neighborhood and either walked to school or were dropped off in their parents' expensive shiny cars, picked on me for riding the big yellow bus for the poor dumb kids from the hood. I went from being the smart nerd at my old school to being called beaner, wetback, and dumbass.

The school, Sunset View Elementary, was in one of the richest neighborhoods in San Diego, with some of the most amazing views of both the ocean and the city's skyline. Sunset Cliffs in Point Loma was a neighborhood where the poor kids would go trick-or-treating because they'd get real American candy that was rarely handed out in the barrio. Here, I was an average fourth grader and no longer felt smart. "Jesse has a lot of potential, but he just doesn't apply himself"—I heard this during a parent-teacher meeting. My mother scolded me in front of the teacher. I'd made her look bad. I'd embarrassed her. I'd disappointed her. I was not living up to the school's or the teacher's expectations, which in turn meant I wasn't living up to my mom and dad's expectations as well.

Amá grounded me when we got home after that meeting. It was the first time I recall answering her disrespectfully. We walked into our small apartment's tiny living room with off-white walls on which hung three family pictures, our large painting of the Virgen de Guadalupe, and a painting of Jesus Christ as a shepherd on a hillside with two sheep at his side. I went to turn on the TV, and Amá grabbed me by the arm, sat me on our yellow-stained hand-me-down couch, and yelled at me that there would be no TV for me until I improved my grades.

"No vas a ver televisión y le voy a decir a tu papá que te haga hacer más matemáticas hasta que mejores tus calificaciones," she yelled at me.

"¡Pues yo no tengo la culpa! ¡La culpa la tienes tú!" I screamed at her. *It's all your fault! Those people don't want me. And no matter how hard I try, I'll never be enough. That's what you get for listening to those teachers and sending me to that school in the first place!*

She lifted her hand to slap me but stopped herself. I cowered in fear as she yelled, "¡Soy tu madre y a mí se me respeta, cabrón! ¡Vete a tu pinche cama y ahí te quedas hasta que yo te deje salir!" *You're not coming out of your room until I say you can, for disrespecting me as your mother, you little shit!* She shoved me into the small bedroom with bunk beds that I shared with my brother.

I blamed my mom for making me embarrassed. I resented Amá for encouraging me to read and my father for making me do daily math assignments. I knew I was testing well and was considered smart precisely because my parents pushed me to learn and to practice. Even though I grew to love playing chess, reading, and solving my math problems, I refused to do any of it anymore. My parents couldn't see how cruel the other kids were, and I didn't understand it, this line between two worlds that I was forced to straddle.

△▽△

At my new all-white school, after-school pool parties for our class were occasionally held at a rich white kid's home. I was excited because no one in my neighborhood had a backyard swimming pool. We didn't even have lawns. I was looking forward to my first backyard pool party, and I could barely contain myself when my mom took an old pair of my brother's hand-me-down jeans and cut them into shorts. I was proud of wearing them, proud of how I looked. It never occurred to me to feel self-conscious about not having proper swim shorts. We made do with what we had, and my mom's creativity made me happy, and proud.

The day of the party, our teacher walked us to the house of the hosts. I was awestruck by the house, which appeared like a palace to me. We walked through the side entrance, leading to the immaculately landscaped, immense backyard with lush green plants and multicolored inflatable beach balls for us kids to play with while two other adults tended to a large barbecue grill. Some of the other nine- and ten-year-old kids jumped in the pool screaming and laughing as if this was all normal for them, and it was. They were unfazed by the grandeur around us. Kids ran for the balls and started throwing them back and forth.

I stayed back, not far from the teacher, looking around at the beauty of the house, the manicured backyard, the pool, and the laughing, playing kids. I took off my shirt, laid it on a chair, and slid my huaraches neatly underneath. Here I was, at a private pool in someone's backyard for the first time in my life, and I couldn't wait to join in on the fun.

But as I walked up and before I could jump into the pool, some of my classmates and the girl whose family owned the house began yelling at me, "You can't come in here! Stop! If you come in, you'll get our pool dirty with your dirty skin. Besides, you're already wet—you wetback!"

They were calling me a dirty Mexican; they were reminding me of how much I didn't belong there. I felt those stabs in my chest, twisting like a knife, and tears started bubbling up in my eyes.

"Look at his shorts!" yelled another kid as they all seemed to laugh at me in unison. I stood at the edge of the pool with my head down, tears flowing down my cheeks, while the others joined the laughing and taunting. The teacher pulled me to her side, but I pushed her away and ran and cried. I tried to disappear behind a large palm tree—praying for God to remove me from this evil place. I thought of my mom and how she'd forced me to enroll in this school. I hated her for it. The teacher came to grab me. She had my T-shirt and huaraches and escorted me back to the school to wait for my dad to pick me up.

I never told my mom what happened, and I was never again invited to these after-school pool parties. Instead I was sent to the office to do homework until it was time to get on the yellow bus to go home. Being excluded from activities was painful and made me feel like even more of an outcast. I often wondered if the school staff saw what was happening, and if they did, why they were not able to help. Or maybe they did know what was happening and considered keeping me away from the taunting to be the more humane option. Either way, I was left on my own.

During Christmas break when I was in fourth grade, my family took a twenty-five-hour road trip from San Diego to Mazatlán to visit my mom's family. My dad packed us into his large fixer-upper 1970s Dodge Tradesman van with carpeted interior and a poorly installed eight-track tape player. I couldn't read in the van because I would get carsick, so I had no option but to join the family in singing norteño music. The only other music was "Funkytown," which was featured on the one English-language eight-track tape that my brother owned. Admittedly, it was a fun drive—that is, until the radiator gave out along a hot desert road thirty minutes outside Culiacán, less than three hours from our destination. Luckily, someone gave my dad a ride into Culiacán, where he found a mechanic to tow the van. We slept in the van for two days, until the radiator could get fixed.

When we finally made it to Mazatlán, we all needed showers. I expected to take a warm shower in a regular US-style bathroom, but instead of a clean tiled room, I was greeted by a toilet that was a cement opening into a giant hole in the ground, in a wooden shack with a metal roof set toward the very back of the property. The shower, which was closer to the outdoor palapa-style kitchen, was a solitary pipe carrying water up from an underground reservoir and into an outdoor corrugated-metal shower. The water was too cold for me. My aunt, laughing because I wasn't used to their living conditions, had me wait, standing naked in the makeshift shower, while my cousins brought a metal bath bucket. They filled it from the shower as I stood awkwardly trying to cover my private parts and while my aunt boiled a pot of water to warm the bathwater for me.

When my aunt came with the boiling water, she also handed me a metal cup and a brick-size bar of yellow-brown soap. The culture and class shock was evident in the look I gave her. We stayed there for two weeks, celebrating an extremely large Mexican Christmas, New Year's, and Three Kings Day with my aunt, her eighteen kids, and their families.

When we got back to San Diego, I became fatigued. My muscles ached. I was jaundiced, my skin and the white parts of my eyes yellow. It turned out, we learned after we visited the doctor, that I'd contracted hepatitis A. I was quarantined to my bedroom for three months, and the rest of my family had to get hepatitis shots. For the first time, I had my own room and was forced to use my own plate, cup, spoon, and fork. I had never had anything be mine before. I didn't like it. I had become accustomed to sharing. It was what was natural to me.

Every time I used the toilet, I had to lay wax paper over the toilet seat and afterward spray it down with bleach. I felt contaminated. I was allowed to stay in school and complete my assignments remotely. My parents would pick up and drop off my assignments every week. But, during those three months I had no formal teaching other than the instructions in my weekly packets. Because my mom and dad couldn't read English, they couldn't help me with my work. In spite of it all, I passed every assignment with flying colors.

As I got better, I noticed my amá worried over me still. During one of my weekly doctor visits, I overheard the doctor tell her that I could suffer long-term liver damage. She looked at me and then asked the doctor, who spoke Spanish, to speak privately. They left me in the exam room. When they walked back in, I noticed my mom's eyes were red and puffy as if she'd been crying. On the way home, I asked her if she was okay.

"When you were born, mijo, your aorta vein in your heart was narrow and not fully open. You would turn blue every time you cried. We thought you were going to need heart surgery, but instead the doctors kept you under observation for a few weeks, hoping your aorta would widen on its own, which it did. But every time something happens, I can't help but get overwhelmed with fear that I'm going to lose you like I did your older sister," she said, crying as she hugged me close.

I didn't know what to say and allowed her to hug me and kiss me all over. When we got home, she made me my favorite snack—a wienie on a tortilla with ketchup. That day, I learned that I could manipulate Amá into thinking I was sicker than I actually was and that I could use it to not have to go to school and be bullied by the white kids or hear teachers tell me that I wasn't applying myself.

Once I was cleared to return to school, I would fake being sick at least one day a week; if I was at school, I would spend chunks of time in the nurse's office until I'd convinced her to send me home. No teachers, no administrators, not a single school psychologist stepped in to find out the real story or why I seemed to be perpetually sick. All the while, my poor mom took me to see countless specialists. Each doctor only added to her worry by recommending new tests such as X-rays, MRIs, CT scans, blood work, and allergy testing. Asthma, however, I didn't fake, and it was a constant in my life. My father would blame Amá's genes for me getting sick all the time since her mother had suffered from asthma until old age. He blamed Amá for everything.

Being at home and lying on the living room floor with books, the encyclopedia, and *National Geographic* magazines all around me or watching *Wild Kingdom* on TV gave me the only happy moments I experienced in those days. I loved reading the encyclopedia, looking up words in the dictionary, coloring, doing puzzles, watching documentaries, and learning about the people and places of the world. Learning allowed me to escape into worlds that were different, better, than mine.

I found my other escape in household chores. While my brother was out with kids in the neighborhood—riding bikes and changing flat tires, playing baseball or football in the street—I helped Amá around the house. I'd wake up Saturday mornings and help her make our meals for the day, sifting through pinto beans to pick out pebbles and bad beans. Once done, we'd leave the beans soaking in water while I helped cut vegetables for salsa, fry up chorizo with eggs, and make flour tortillas.

My father would occasionally throw out a sarcastic comment to my mom, "Lo vas a convertir en mariposa." *You're going to turn him into a butterfly*.

My mother would shush him with a pleading look, and he would stop, sucking his teeth before turning back to whatever fight was playing on the TV. At that age, I didn't understand his disapproval. I thought butterflies were beautiful, and so I took his derisive comments with pride. I figured what I was doing was okay. I didn't realize that he was accusing my amá of making me gay by having me do girlie things as opposed to the macho things my brother did.

By the time I was nine years old, my father gave up trying to show me how to fix cars or bikes. Invariably he lost patience, screaming at me in Spanish, "Just forget it. Go help your mom in the kitchen. That's all you're good for. Bueno para nada." *Good for nothing*.

I preferred helping Amá around the apartment. I also

enjoyed watching my family eat the food that Amá and I prepared. When done with the kitchen, I would help Amá do the laundry. I'd help her separate the dark colors, light colors, and the whites, placing them in separate piles. After every load the wet clothes would go in a plastic hamper and be carried outside our apartment complex. With a giant bag of wooden clothespins, we'd hang the clothes on the clotheslines. Usually, by the time we were done hanging one load, the other load would be done in the washer. All the while, I'd enjoy listening to and laughing at Amá's childhood stories, how her mom would get mad at her for playing marbles with the boys in the neighborhood because she loved being a tomboy, which I felt was her way of reassuring me to be me.

When we were done with the laundry, she would clean the kitchen and I'd clean the bathroom. I'd pour Ajax all over the bathtub and scrub the shower and the tiles, then move on to the toilet, the sink, and finally the floor. I felt helpful. I enjoyed serving a familial purpose.

With the chores done, my dad encouraged me to go play, but I was afraid to go out if my brother was around because he'd find a way to make me feel unwanted, as if I were a burden or an embarrassment to him. He'd force me to play dodgeball with rocks, pounding me with chunks of limestone. When we played darts in the back alley, he'd sometimes try to shoot me with an extra dart he "forgot" he had in his hand. Sometimes he'd shoot at me with a BB gun after a game of shooting soda cans. He taunted me for being sick. I never understood why he hated me so much.

Then one day, when I was nine, I had the bright idea of

taking a swig from my father's bottle of brandy before going out to play with the other kids. My father kept the bottle under the kitchen sink for the occasional guest. Drinking from it became a habit. Forced to play with the other kids, I would sneak into the kitchen and grab my dad's bottle of Don Pedro. I relished the light burning sensation of alcohol flowing down my throat and through my body, warming my chest. Fortified, I would run out to play.

Although my dad stomped around the house barking orders and criticizing my mom about every little thing—the dinner wasn't ready on time, the tortillas weren't hot enough or crispy enough, the creases in his slacks weren't ironed correctly—my mom never reacted. One day she painted her fingernails with a neighbor who sold Avon products. She bought a soft pinkish-red-toned lipstick. My mom proudly showed me her painted nails, put on her new lipstick, and said, "I hope your father likes it. I think it looks pretty. What do you think, mijo?"

I grabbed her hand, examining her nails, and smiled. "I love it, Amá. You look beautiful. Apá's going to love it, too!"

She went into the bathroom and did her hair, hoping to look pretty for my dad. When he walked in and saw her, he flew into a rage, accusing Amá of being a puta (a whore). "Only putas wear makeup and nail polish, when they are trying to trap a man. Go take that fuckin shit off your face and hands!" he yelled. "My wife will not look like a fuckin whore." My mom, to avoid a fight, took off her lipstick and threw the tube in the trash. She removed the nail polish quietly and then went into the kitchen to serve Apá his dinner.

I secretly pulled the lipstick out of the trash and showed it to her that night when she came to my bed for my nightly prayers. "Amá, I grabbed it and am going to hide it here under my mattress for you to put on whenever you want."

"No, mijo, si tu papá se entera se va a encabronar, mejor tíralo," she said. *No, my son, better to throw it away.*

I went to sleep confused. Everything Amá did, she did for him and the family, so why did he react so angrily? But from that day forward, something changed. The fights between my amá and apá grew worse. My father's criticisms were met with wrath. She'd yell back, accusing him of being a cheating, womanizing asshole and a bully. One day he raised his hand, threatening to hit her. My brother and I leaped off the couch, where we'd been trying to ignore the fracas, and stood between them. My brother pushed my dad toward the door and out of the house, screaming at him to get out as I tried to hold my mom back. She pushed me aside like I was a rag doll and charged at my dad, who ran out of the apartment, slamming the door behind him before she could get at him. My brother and I, both scared, tried consoling my mom. She was in a rage, breaking dishes in the kitchen.

"¡Pinche viejo, hijo de su chingada madre! Cómo se le ocurre intentar levantarme la mano. Le parto su pinche puta madre antes de que me toque, pinche viejo cabrón. ¿Qué se cree? ¿Que me voy a dejar pegar porque siempre me quedo callada? ¡Me quedo callada para evitar pleitos y mantener a la familia unida, pero ya! ¡Ya no puedo más!" Amá screamed. *Fuckin old son of a bitch! How dare he try to raise a hand at me. I'll fuck his ass up before he lays a hand on me, fuckin old motherfucker. Who does he think he is? Enough is enough!*

From that day on, my amá didn't stay quiet anymore. Yelling and screaming became a constant. But my dad never tried raising his hand at her again.

CHAPTER 2

It was a small gift shop, its shelves and walls lined with soda bottles and greeting cards.

"Excuse me. Do you have water balloons?" I asked the shopkeeper.

"We just received a shipment. There's a box in the storage room. I'll be with you in a minute."

The shopkeeper was about six feet tall with a slim waist and an average body. He wore faded jeans, black boots, a white T-shirt, and a black belt, and he had black hair and a thick black mustache. He looked like Freddie Mercury.

Today was one of the hottest days on record in San Diego and certainly the hottest of that summer in 1985. All the kids from the apartment buildings were getting together for a water-bucket fight. We rarely had any extra money to spend on such a luxury as balloons. Instead, we filled buckets with water from the hose and chased one another, carrying the heavy buckets of water to throw. But eventually everyone grew tired of lifting buckets and the older kids put their money together. My brother handed the money to me, since I was one of the youngest and often the one ordered around.

"Hey, Nerd," he barked, "take your bike up to Safeway and grab a few bags of balloons."

Safeway didn't sell balloons, so here I was at a small neighborhood gift shop a few blocks away. I walked around and noticed a section of adult gift cards at the rear of the store. Naturally enough, I sneaked a peek. I was eleven and a half years old and going through puberty. My heart beat fast and my palms were sweaty. I knew I wasn't supposed to be there, and I was afraid of getting caught. The farther I went down the aisle, the more explicit and risqué the cards became.

I had never seen cards like these. These were not your typical bi-panel cards, but rather double-folded with nude women along the entire length. I'd seen naked women on TV because my older brother and I would wait for my mom and dad to go to sleep and then tap into the Playboy channel by positioning the wire hanger we used as an antenna to try to get the best view of boobs through the squiggly lines.

The more I looked at the pornographic cards, the more immersed I became. It was as if everything around me went silent. I was a hard-core Catholic kid who served as an altar boy twice every Sunday. Looking at those adult cards put me through a roller coaster, physically and emotionally. Physically, I was turned on. Emotionally, I felt the shame and the guilt that came with doing something wrong. A part of me knew I should put those cards down, get the hell out of that store, and ask God for forgiveness the entire bike ride home. The other part of me wanted to stay right where I was.

The cards farther down the aisle featured images of men and women in sexual poses. I had never seen another guy's penis. My heart rate became even faster and my palms got sweatier. Was I feeling admiration for or attraction to the men? A part of me awakened in that moment, I think.

I was lost in my thoughts when I felt a hand press on my shoulder. Quickly turning, I saw the shopkeeper standing there between me and the front door.

He laughed as he bent over to pick up the card, which I had dropped in my surprise. He opened it, held it in his hands, and said, "That's a big dick, isn't it?"

I was caught. I stayed quiet and put my head down, wondering if any other customers had seen me.

He laughed again. "So how can I help you?"

I looked around the store. There were no other customers. With my head still down, I said, "I'm sorry. I came looking for water balloons for a water balloon fight, but you were busy, and . . ."

"Don't worry about it. Feel free to grab them. The door is right there. The box they're in is on the floor." He pointed to a door and then walked back toward the front of the store.

When I opened the storage-room door, I saw the sealed box on the floor. I turned to go out and let him know the box was sealed, but there he was, standing in the doorway. I was so innocent and naive; the only thought that crossed my mind was to ask him for permission to open the box. But before I could open my mouth, he punched me in the face. Flames of pain radiated through my head. I fell to the floor. He picked me up by my neck and threw me against the shelves that lined the room. Again I fell to the floor, a terrified lump of pain. Had he changed his mind and become angry that I'd gone back there? Did he think I was going to steal from him? I had never stolen in my life. Crazy thoughts came into my mind as I tried to understand. *What did I do wrong?*

I had been in a few fights in the neighborhood and with my brother but had never been punched and thrown around by a grown man like that. I was still a child.

The shopkeeper picked me up and slammed me against the wall, put one forearm across my neck, and used his free hand to pull down my shorts and underwear. "Keep your mouth shut!" he growled in my ear. "You yell or move an inch and I'll really give you something to feel hurt about."

He kneeled and wrapped his mouth around my private parts. I was paralyzed by shock and fear—and confusion, so much confusion. He pushed me harder against the wall as I whimpered. He came up for air and told me to relax and to enjoy it or he would show me what true pain was. Not knowing what to do, I shut my eyes tight and shut all sound from my ears. Tears rolled down my face. I disconnected my soul and my emotions from my body.

When he was done, he let me go, telling me that I had better come back in a few days or he would find out where I lived and kill me and my family. He stood and buttoned up his jeans as I stood frozen against the wall with my shorts around my ankles.

Glaring at me, he yelled, "Pull your fuckin shorts up!"

I pulled them up and tried to run to the front door. Laughing, he grabbed me by my T-shirt and half dragged me to the door. I realized it was locked. He unlocked the door but held it shut, telling me to walk out calmly and act like nothing happened. He handed me two bags of balloons that he'd pulled out of his back pocket. "See you soon," he said with a jaunty wave of his hand as he opened the door and let me out.

In a daze, I walked out slowly and got on my bike, afraid to look back for fear that he was watching. When I got home, everyone could see I was beat up. Amá panicked. I told them I'd fallen off my bike and hit my face on the curb.

That night, I couldn't sleep. I buried my face in the pillow so my brother, sleeping in the bunk above mine, wouldn't hear me crying. I felt ashamed, and I was terrified. I kept thinking, *Will he really find me if I don't go back?* I believed the man would kill me. I believed he would kill my family. My innocence had been stolen from me.

It took me years to understand that I was a child victim of a violent sexual predator and that I had been raped. I blamed myself. Why did I have to go to *that* store to buy water balloons? I was angry at myself for being naive. I was angry at myself for not telling my mom. I was angry at myself for not fighting back. I felt weak, lying there that night. I made the decision to change.

Everything about me, everything about little nerdy Jesse, was going to change. Never again would I let anyone see the fear or the sadness that I felt inside. From that night on, I would hide and protect that scared little boy. I resolved never to be hurt like that again.

CHAPTER 3

During that summer, after the incident in the gift store, I lived in complete and utter fear. Every morning I'd wake up with my heart racing, terrified at the idea of seeing the shopkeeper's face in my bedroom window, and every night I went to bed in terror of what the next day could hold. Tomorrow could be the day he'd kill my mother. I went back to the store again and again, palms sweaty and heart racing, like the scared kid that I was.

"Wait here until I call you to come out," he'd say each time after finishing getting himself off while performing oral sex on me. Often he'd slap me hard with the back of his hand when I least expected it and I'd fall to the floor. Every time, it took me by surprise. Five minutes later, he'd call me out: "Get out and make sure you come back in two days. If you try to tell, no one will believe you. You know what I've promised to do. Understand?"

Every time he walked out of the room as if nothing had happened, I felt a range of confusing and conflicting emotions—relief that he was done and it was over, numbness and disconnection from my emotions, shock that I was calm. I lived in a state of perpetual disbelief, questioning if this was really happening to me and why. And above all, I blamed myself. God was punishing me for the thoughts that had raced through my mind when I looked at those nudie cards that first day.

Afterward, on the way home, I'd repeat to myself in my head that it was my fault, that I was a good-for-nothing kid just like my dad always said, and that I deserved it. All of it. Maybe it wouldn't have happened to me if I knew how to fight or if I did manly things like my brother did.

I kept my molestation secret. Fear made me return to the store every two to three days after school. The occasions and the severity of the beatings fluctuated. Sometimes the shopkeeper was even friendly and kind. I never knew what to expect. I'd wince and jump at sudden movements, which made him grimace with satisfaction.

One day he pulled out a pipe from his back pocket along with a baggie. He packed the pipe with some bright lime-green weed and took a hit from it.

"Here. You're too fuckin jumpy. This'll relax you," he ordered.

"No thank you," I pleaded.

"Chill the fuck out and take a hit. Nothing's going to happen to you. Seriously, it'll help you relax," he said as he put the pipe to my lips and held it there.

I stared into his dark brown eyes as my lips wrapped around the pipe, which tasted different than cigarettes. *So this is what marijuana tastes like,* I thought. I looked around nervously, imagining and hoping that my mom would barge through the door and slap the pipe from between my lips. I looked at him nervously as I inhaled and immediately started coughing.

"I said *slowly*." He laughed. "I have an idea. Pull your pants down and relax."

I did what he said, letting my pants and boxers rest around my ankles as I leaned back against the wall.

"Close your eyes, try to relax, inhale slowly. I'll give you a sign when to exhale."

I did what he said. When I had a good amount of smoke in my mouth and lungs, he pulled the pipe out of my mouth. He went down and wrapped his mouth around my flaccidness. With his hands he squeezed my buttocks twice, giving me a sign to exhale. I did. The feeling was unlike anything I'd ever experienced. I felt a peace and a serenity take over my body so that, for an instant, it didn't matter where I was or what was happening to me.

Laughing, he said while looking up at me, "There now, that wasn't so bad, right? Now pull your pants up. I got a lot of work to do."

Once my pants were back on, and before we walked out of the back room, he put the pipe up to my face again and said, "Here, take another hit. Stop being so damn jumpy."

I did as he told me, and I loved the feeling it gave me.

He squeezed my arm and said, "Now remember: don't say shit, you little motherfucker, or I *will* kill you."

That was the first time I got high.

I lived in constant fear, but getting high helped take the edge off, helped make it more bearable. I learned to detach myself spiritually and emotionally from my body and my thoughts. I learned how to create a psychological barrier that prevented my feeling pain. The beatings hurt, but the pain was manageable when I shut down. I'd leave my body and imagine myself floating above, watching what was happening as if it were a movie.

Every time, as soon as I heard the door latch behind him, that clicking sound was like a switch that turned off my humanity and allowed my spirit to elevate from my body and float near the ceiling. His hand, touching my shoulders and moving to the back of my neck, didn't feel good or bad—it just was. My hands hung by my sides as he unbuckled my belt and pulled down my pants and boxers. If he placed my hand on top of his head or on his shoulder, my movements were robotic. If he hit me or slapped me or pushed my head around, I'd watch from above as if I were a rag doll devoid of life.

After a few of these visits, I found that my body responded to the indescribable feeling of the oral sex. This development was terrifying to me. Our bodies are made to react to stimuli without regard to our emotional state, but I was eleven, and I didn't know any better. All I knew was the deep shame, remorse, and guilt I felt upon enjoying these brutal, forced encounters.

It was now impossible to even think of telling anyone what was going on in that back room. I felt complicit. I didn't want anyone to say that I was looking for it. I was afraid that if my family found out, my dad and brother would disown me for not being manly enough. The thought of disappointing my amá was unbearable. She had been through so much. I didn't want to add to her suffering. In my silence, I believed I was protecting them from ridicule and shame.

After I'd been going to the store for two months, the shopkeeper started letting other men join and touch me. He charged them money. It dawned on me that I was being pimped out.

The sexual abuse changed me. I loathed being in my skin. I was ashamed and felt dirty. I was confused about who and what I was before the abuse even started. As a young child, I found myself staring at good-looking older guys playing football and basketball in the neighborhood, and I didn't know if I was admiring these men because I wanted to be like them or if I was attracted to them. A part deep inside me just wanted to keep looking at them. I didn't understand what I felt. The sexual abuse complicated my sense of self. It made my self-blame and self-hatred worse, like an ache that never lessened. Rather than having an opportunity to explore my sexuality and my gender identity, the abuse thwarted my sexual development. After each visit to the gift shop, I'd go home and shower. I scrubbed my skin until it hurt, as if trying to eradicate my disgust. I never could. Often I'd crouch in the shower, holding my knees close to my chest, crying while the water rolled down my back.

What if I hadn't agreed to go to the shop and buy water balloons? What if I'd gone straight home after I found that the first store was out of balloons? Would things have turned out differently in my life if I hadn't walked into a rapist's store? Did I deserve what was happening to me?

The questions swirled. More and more, I dulled myself and my reality by getting high. Gone were the days of taking swigs from my dad's stash; I'd moved on to something harder. At home, the fighting between my mom and dad no longer bothered me. The noise in my own head was louder than any yelling in our home. Still, I found comfort in the familiar chaos of home because I understood my place in it and knew what to expect when I was there.

△▽△

My anxiety attacks began a few months after the shopkeeper began molesting me. It's not easy growing up with anxiety attacks in a Latino immigrant family. The attacks started with nightmares, yelling in my ears that drowned out the noise around me. I would get a taste of metal in my mouth and be overwhelmed with feeling, like I was trying to hold tiny silver balls between my fingers that would evade my grasp, slipping out of my hand. The yelling would grow louder in my ears and my breathing would get heavier. I'd start to sweat and feel claustrophobic with an exaggerated desire to move faster and faster, as if everything around me was in hyperspeed. Sometimes the anxiety attacks would come on when I'd be reading books or magazines and my perspective would shift. I'd sit there rapidly turning pages as if I were a speed-reader. I wasn't. I'd pull out of the attacks by shutting my eyes, taking deep long breaths, and clenching my fists until the sensations passed. And just as quickly as they'd come on, they would go away.

I learned to trust no one. I had adopted my dad's mottoes: *There are no friends in this world* and *Trust no man*. How could I trust when the world had shown me what it was capable of? I'd trusted my mom when she told me that God loved me and would protect me, but that God had failed me. I no longer believed that other people were good. If the world and God were good, then why would He have allowed this to happen to me? No words could describe the amount of anger I felt toward God, my family, and the world.

I felt abandoned by God, like I had been placed in this world by mistake. I couldn't confide in anyone about the pain I was living with. So I hated God for giving me life, my mom for bringing me into this world, and my dad for giving up on teaching me how to be a man. *Maybe if he hadn't given up on me, I would have learned to defend myself,* I always thought. But my father did give up on me, and that could mean only that I was a complete failure. I believed this to my very core. I didn't want to live anymore. But I was too Catholic to kill myself.

CHAPTER 4

As I approached seventh grade, it was suggested to Amá that I go to a magnet school named Gompers for junior high. After months of enduring sexual abuse in the back of the store, I had no fight left in me. I didn't want to argue with Amá even though I desperately wanted to be allowed to go to my neighborhood school, so I could be with the few friends I had. I did what I was told. Once again I would have to go to a school where I didn't know anyone and where I didn't want to be.

Gompers was a school for seventh through twelfth graders, and the large student body made it easy for me to get lost in the crowd. During lunch I would eat alone behind the building at the end of the playground. One day while I was out there, a group of ninth- and tenth-grade cholos showed up to smoke weed. Seeing me there, one of them said, "What's up, ese?"

The others didn't pay me any mind. They lit their joints. When they were done and had started to walk away, the one who'd said hello turned to me and nodded his head, as if to say, *See you later.* His acknowledgment made me smile.

The next day the same thing happened, and the next day. On the fourth day, the teenager walked up to me and said, "Why you eat lunch here all alone every day?"

I shrugged. "I guess I like to be alone."

"Come on, get up. Let me introduce you to the homeys."

As we walked over to the others, he asked my name, telling me his name was Guillermo but that everyone called him Willy. His homeboys introduced themselves, giving me the homeboy handshake and offering me some weed. "Nah, I don't wanna smoke," I told them.

I still wore my nerdy glasses and hair part, so they didn't seem shocked that I declined. One of them offered me his 7-Eleven Slurpee cup. "Here, try this. You do at least drink, right, little homey?"

"Hell yeah, I drink," I said, and I chugged whatever was in the cup. They were surprised at how quickly I drank it down and seemed proud of me.

That year, Willy and his friends became my get-fucked-up-during-lunch-behind-the-building homeboys. Eventually I started getting high with them, too. Their friendship and our lunches were the one thing I enjoyed about Gompers. They looked out for me, especially Willy. They came to my rescue when some older kids were bullying the nerdy seventh graders. Once Willy pointed me out and said, "Don't mess with that one or we'll fuck you up." Quickly I came to enjoy a sense of camaraderie and protection. I felt liked. I felt empowered. I found some courage. All I had to do was get drunk and get high.

I never understood why Willy took a liking to me or why he protected me. *Maybe I remind him of a little brother? Maybe he was once bullied?* I thought. The truth was that I'd never felt for anyone else as I did for Willy. Being around him was like being surrounded by hummingbirds and like the noises of the world were being blocked out by the rhythmic sound of waves breaking against the shore. *Am I gay?* I thought. The bromance was real, and it scared the fuck out of me. I'd think, *What the fuck is wrong with me?! Why is this happening?*

The only thing I was sure of was that it wasn't because Willy and his homeys were cholos or because I was starting to feel like a part of a group of masculine guys. Homeboys, cholos, vatos, eses, and gangsters were nothing new. My brother hung out with the cholos in the neighborhood. They were all part of my reality. Sure, I'd stare at a few of them, with their muscular tattooed arms bulging out of their white tank tops, when they walked by, but I always thought it was admiration that I felt. This was different. I knew I had a boy crush, and nowhere in my community, in society, on TV, nor anywhere else was I told that this was okay. My head was telling me this wasn't right. Yet it felt perfectly right. It felt wonderful when I'd see him smile at me. What I was feeling for Willy scared me, and I made a point of pushing it down as far as possible inside me and vowed to myself to never let it be known.

I was afraid that Willy would find out I had a crush on him and that it would end our friendship—or even worse, that the homeboys would fuck me up and jump me for being gay. I mean, homeboys are not gay. And I wasn't willing to be the first.

A few weeks into seventh grade, about four months after my sexual abuse had started, fueled by the courage I'd gained by having new friends, I decided to stop going to the molester's store. I decided I no longer believed his threats. I figured, *Fuck him. He ain't gonna do shit.*

I was wrong.

One evening a group of us kids were playing outside. It was past sundown and getting dark. As I was running toward the front of the apartments, I stopped dead in my tracks. The shopkeeper was standing across the street with his foot on a fire hydrant. It felt like I'd been punched hard in the stomach and had the wind knocked out of me. I froze in place. There was no mistake; it was him, the tall white man with black hair and a thick Freddie Mercury mustache. He had on blue jeans, a white T-shirt, and a baseball cap. He pointed to his watch. The message was very clear. He knew where I lived. The threat was real.

The next day, defeated, I went back to the store. That familiar feeling of powerlessness returned. When I walked through the door, the man was nice. He put his arm around my shoulders as he walked me to the back, making small talk. "It's so good to see you . . . I've missed you . . . You had me worried about you . . ." Anyone looking on might have thought we were old buddies, old pals. But I, of course, knew better.

As soon as we stepped into the back room, he moved his hand from my shoulder to the back of my neck, squeezed hard, and pushed me forward with brute force, slamming my face against the wall. I felt the familiar radiation of pain throughout my body, my nose throbbing, then bleeding. He let go and I slid down the wall. He lifted me up and slammed me a few more times against the wall. I didn't even cry.

"I know where you live. I've spoken to your mother. I will kill her first," he breathed with menace into my ear.

"Don't talk about my mom like that, you faggot mother-fucker. Just do what the fuck you gotta do," I spit back. At the mention of my amá, for the first time, I tried to stick up for myself. Wrong move.

He unbuttoned his jeans; the sound of the zipper felt loud. He lifted me up by the back of my shirt like he was grabbing a puppy by the scruff of its neck and said, "I'll show you who the faggot is here." He grabbed the back of my neck and pushed my face against the wall, and it began all over again. Only this time it was worse. I couldn't hold back the tears like I thought I would. The ripping of my insides was unbearable. This was the first time I experienced anal rape. I had never felt so humiliated and emasculated in all my life. I'd never felt so low, so dominated and weak. I wished I had some alcohol or weed to numb the pain.

When he was done, he stood there, watching me lie on the floor. For a fleeting moment, I entertained the thought that the man was going to let me go for good. He told me to get up, go into the bathroom, clean up. I struggled even to get to my feet. He pushed me into the bathroom, looming over me from behind. In the mirror, I could see the menace of his reflected face. I was afraid even to wash up, thinking he was going to bang my face against the sink or the mirror.

He turned on the water and put his hand on my shoulder. Again, his demeanor changed.

"Don't cry. You have no reason to be scared," he said. "You really hurt my feelings when you didn't come back to see me. I love you. Please don't do that to me again. Don't make me angry. It hurts me to hurt you."

Shaking all over, I took the paper towels he handed me. I wept, but I was too afraid to let out a sound when I saw my blood as I cleaned myself.

△▽△

I didn't go straight home. I walked to Balboa Park, one of San Diego's oldest urban destination parks, where I'd spent many happy summer days. I leaned against a tree and stared blankly at the place that at one time had seemed fun and familiar to me. Now it seemed like part of an unknown world, an abyss of darkness and nothingness, where I felt insignificant and worthless.

The child inside me was dead.

Once it got dark, I set off for home. I walked like a robot, a zombie, unaware of my surroundings. When I got home, lying was not difficult. I told my mom and dad that a few guys had jumped me while I was waiting for the bus downtown. My mother reached for the phone. My father pulled it from her hands, screaming, "Don't be ridiculous. The cops aren't going to do shit. He needs to learn how to fight and defend himself like a man. I'm tired of him being a little sissy."

I wanted so much for my mom to call the cops, but I said nothing, filled with terror I could not show that the shopkeeper would kill her if she did report the incident. I was quickly stripped of my hope and fear, however. I deflated.

"But, Apá, I fought back! I may have gotten my ass kicked, but I fought back," I cried.

"Eso es, mijo. ¡Qué bueno! ¡Aprende a ser hombre, chingado!" said Apá. *That's it, my boy. Learn how to be a man, dammit!*

"Let me pour you some brandy to celebrate, Apá," I told him, praying he'd let me get the bottle so I could take a swig of the brandy with him.

My ploy worked. As I went to grab the bottle, my mom shook her head in disapproval. "No lo puedo creer," she said loudly. *I can't believe this.* And she walked out the back door. I opened the bottle, served my dad and myself each a glass of brandy.

"Ten, Apá. Brindemos por ser hombres," I told him. *Here, Dad. Let's toast to being men.*

He looked at me, hesitating, but took the glass from my hand. We toasted. The light burning sensation from my swig of brandy felt like holy water cleansing me from the inside. My father watched. He had taken only a sip of his drink while I chugged mine in one gulp. I laughed and hugged him, then went to shower. Even the hot water pouring over my body couldn't wash away my sense of nothingness.

In Mexico, my father had grown up in a world that was

kill or be killed. I could only guess where he got his pow-
ers of verbal abuse. I never expected my father to protect
me. All of my need for protection fell onto my mother. Like
the image of the Virgen de Guadalupe, left to protect all
Indigenous people with no man around, that was my mom's
role. And when she failed, she was horribly criticized. I
don't know what Amá would have done differently had she
known what was happening to me. I'm sure that if I had
confided in her, she would have tried her hardest to protect
and save me. But who was there to protect her against the
wrath of my father?

Amá did the best she could to manage the reality of
being married to an old-school machista man decades her
senior. He was physically disabled and unable to work, yet
every other word that came out of his mouth was a cuss-
word. She had three children to raise. Me, my older brother,
and my little sister were a handful. But I was her nerd, the
good kid, and I was changing rapidly. She didn't understand
why, and this added to her sense of powerlessness. I wanted
to protect her—not just from the shopkeeper but from my
father. I sensed he was capable of hurting her. While she
was at work, he would beat my brother and me with belts
and broken car antennae. I was afraid he would one day
beat her up like he did us.

I didn't want to disappoint my amá or add to her bur-
dens. So I did my best to hide it all from her. She woke up
at four thirty every morning to catch the five-thirty bus and
get to work in time to serve breakfast at school—my father
refused to give her a ride so early in the morning. She'd get
out at 3:00 p.m., go to her second job for a few hours, and

then rush home to cook dinner for the family. She did the best she could. Like for so many immigrant parents who had no one to turn to when their kids were recruited by gangs or started using—Amá didn't know where to turn to other than church, where oftentimes people didn't know what to do, either. At least she never gave up hope.

CHAPTER 5

On one of my visits to the gift shop, a few months after I had returned home badly beaten, there were two guys I hadn't seen before. At first I thought they were customers. One was a tall, slim, very light-skinned Black man with a thick mustache like the shopkeeper's and a short 'fro. He watched the front of the store while I was led to the back with the shopkeeper and the other man. From that point forward, he would be there occasionally, standing guard. Sometimes he would come to the back room and watch. Sometimes he would join in.

One day when I walked into the store, the Black man nodded his head, signaling me toward the storage room. Instead of the shopkeeper, I found a fat older white man. I waited for a few minutes with that strange man until the Black guy walked in and asked him, "Do you like what you see?"

The white man responded, "Yes. Yes, I do."

"Go ahead. Do whatever you want," the Black guy responded. When the fat guy walked toward me, the Black guy grabbed his arm. "First give me the money." The fat guy handed him a wad of bills, his eyes on me.

I stared at the Black guy as he stood by the door, watching. He smirked as I was raped. I was overwhelmed with hatred for him and the shopkeeper. I wanted to cry and scream, *Leave me the fuck alone, you sick motherfucker! Please!* I couldn't.

When the fat guy had finished and left, I was getting dressed. While I tied my sneakers, the Black guy said to me, "We're going to make some serious money with you," and threw a five-dollar bill at my face. "This is yours. Don't get used to it. Go buy your little girlfriend something." Then he laughed. I rushed home to wash his nastiness off me. I felt used, far more than I ever had before. I was terrified, yet resigned to the fact that I was going to be pimped out.

I was right.

So began my career as a sex worker. For the next two years, until I was fourteen, I would have a few hundred sex partners. Fifty-two weeks in a year and two visits to the store per week makes 104 men. Multiplying that by three years brings the total to around 312. But this does not include the shopkeeper and his friend, nor the fact that often there were two men waiting for me.

△▽△

In order to maintain my detachment from myself and escape from reality, I spent most of seventh grade drunk, high, and ditching class. How I made it through, I have no idea. Teachers and staff never called me out over my spotty attendance and poor grades. Maybe the teachers were too overwhelmed themselves to get involved or to pay attention. My seventh-grade teachers had no impact on my life other than being examples of disengaged and uncaring adults. Every time I asked for a pass to the bathroom or to the nurse's office, they would hand it to me. When I would return to class half an hour later smelling like weed or alcohol, they never asked questions.

The following summer, before eighth grade, everything changed. I didn't want to be the glasses-wearing, hair-parted-on-the-side nerd that I was. I transformed. I went on shoplifting sprees and got myself some baggy Dickies, black belts with silver buckles, black Kmart corduroy slippers (roach stompers), jerseys, and striped Charlie Brown–style polo shirts. I combed my hair back and wore hairnets to train it to stay in place like the other cholos did. I spent hours ironing creases into my clothes with starch. My white T-shirts had one crease down the front and three down the back, and my pant creases were even sharper.

My mom and dad noticed I was changing. My mom begged me to dress as I used to so I could look respectable, but I refused. I convinced my parents that the problem was Gompers, my school. I lied to them, saying that I was being picked on by gang members in the neighborhood surrounding the school because we lived in a different neighborhood, so I had to look and act tougher than I had before, otherwise I would keep getting jumped. My father encouraged me to fight. "Maybe that will help him gain respect and make friends," he said.

Gang violence in San Diego in the mid-'80s was escalating, and Amá eventually agreed that it would be preferable for me to attend a school closer to home. I transferred to Roosevelt Junior High in eighth grade, and this offered me a new start. At my new school, I wasn't going to be the smart nerdy kid. I was going to be a wannabe cholo.

I didn't want to be a mama's boy anymore. I was tired of being different from others and feeling defenseless. I was tired of feeling like I was on the outside looking in. My mom's love, which once made me feel protected, was what I now rebelled against the most. Her teachings had prompted my brother to pick on me and my father to not accept me. I wanted to distance myself from those qualities and from my true self. I lashed out. I told myself, *If only she hadn't watched over me so much. If only she didn't love me so much. If only she hadn't worked at my elementary school. Then maybe I could have been a normal kid.*

I believed that being a good little boy had led to my being bullied, beaten up, bossed around, molested, and raped. I believed my father when he said Amá was turning me into a mariposa. I believed it was that softness that the shopkeeper had smelled on me and that made him want to abuse me. Maybe if my mother had forced me to play with other boys like my father wanted me to, instead of letting me help her in the kitchen or encouraging me to draw and read, I wouldn't have been ordered by my brother to go to the store that day to buy water balloons. Maybe I would have been more like my brother. I blamed my mom's love for turning me into a sissy, and I didn't want to be a sissy anymore.

It took years for me to understand that I, just like my father, was placing the expectation on her—on mothers—to protect and take care of me while my father was exempt from the responsibility.

I grew handsome and stylish in my stolen clothing. I refused to wear glasses even though it meant I had to suffer headaches and blurred vision. Everything about me changed, including how I walked, stood, sat, and crossed my legs. I was a wannabe gangster. I went to "ditching" parties (house parties) during school hours. This new attention helped take some of my pain away.

I drank and got high regularly. My tolerance was high, and I could outdrink most of my friends, including my brother and his older homeboys. This transformation helped me win some acceptance from my brother—not a lot, but some was better than nothing. He'd ask me to iron his shirts. He approved of my new machismo. He probably felt like he didn't have to be embarrassed by me anymore.

△▽△

Since we had family that had moved to Tijuana (TJ), just thirty minutes south of San Diego, we spent many of our weekends there. All my male cousins in TJ were much older and worked on La Revolución, also known as La Revo, as managers and bartenders. La Revo was a long street with nightclubs and bars lined up one after the other on both sides. My cousin asked my mom to leave me in TJ for a few days to keep him company since his wife had gone down to Mazatlán to visit family. He was an older cousin, and he was my godfather, so my mom trusted him.

He took me with him to work on a Saturday night. It was my first time at a club in Tijuana. I was not yet thirteen years old. The club was packed with people dancing to late '80s music on a huge dance floor. A balcony overlooked the dance floor below. It felt exhilarating to me to be there.

My cousin first gave me a Shirley Temple and then a virgin margarita, so I asked one of my cousin's friends, also a bartender, to get me a real margarita. He did. Next he poured me a Long Island iced tea and then a Midori sour and then another Long Island. I didn't know the names of any of these drinks until he pushed them toward me. "Here try this one, it's called . . . ," he'd say each time he handed me another, laughing. My cousin didn't know what was happening until I was hopelessly drunk. I can't even imagine what I looked like, a twelve-year-old hanging out in a nightclub in Tijuana, drunk.

I saw my cousin whisper something to a beautiful woman in her mid-twenties with big breasts, a big fake-blond perm, a short tight turquoise-green bodycon dress, and knee-high black suede boots. She walked up to me, grabbed my hand, and led me to the dance floor. I looked around, surprised, as my cousin, the bartenders, and the security guards all laughed, watching me. The woman grabbed my chin with one of her hands, and I saw her makeup-caked face come toward me. Then—*bam*. Her mouth pressed against mine, her tongue parting my lips. I heard loud cheers over the music. Her hand moved down to my crotch, and she started to rub me through my jeans. Embarrassed, I wiggled out of her embrace and ran.

My cousin found me outside the front door, holding on to the wall and gasping as people stood in line waiting to be let in and music blasted onto the street. "What's wrong with you? She's the finest one in there. Go for it. It's all taken care of," he said loudly as he walked around the doorman and paused next to me.

He handed me a cigarette and, with his hand on my shoulder, led me back into the loud club to where the woman was standing by the bar, rocking to the beat.

"Oh, how cute," she said, "he's nervous. It's okay. Just relax, baby."

She kissed my neck and my mouth and lifted my shirt, and I felt her long nails graze my abs and my chest. I figured I might as well go along with it. I so desperately wanted the approval of my cousins and to appear macho.

Once she decided she was done making out with me, she kissed me goodbye. Before she walked away, I saw my cousin hand her something. The guys all came up and patted me on the back and shoulders, congratulating me.

"You better not say shit to your mom!" my cousin told me. "*Here* is where you'll learn how to be a man!"

I smiled, lit a cigarette, and drank another Long Island iced tea. I was one of the guys now.

△▽△

My partying days began that night. Almost every other weekend, I'd beg my mom to let me visit family in Tijuana. Amá had no idea I was clubbing with my cousin. In Tijuana, I also learned how to drive. My cousin taught me, and we would drive around his neighborhood every day before he took me with him to work. "I might need you to drive one night if I'm too drunk to drive myself. Better to be safe than sorry." After I drove him home once, it became routine. I drove him home from the bar every time I visited Tijuana.

I learned all the ins and outs of TJ, from the red-light-district bars in the neighborhood known as La Coahuila to the clubs on the strip of La Revolución. Everyone knew my cousins, so I felt safe. I never once paid for a cover or a drink.

My fuck-it attitude worsened the more popular I became. Partying was fun, something I'd never been able to experience before, so it took center stage. Breaking the rules was fun, so why go back to being a nerd? To getting picked on? To being punished and ostracized for being smart? To being boring? To having girls reject me because I wasn't cool? In eighth grade, I became the class clown, cracking jokes and being a smart-ass at the teachers' expense. I signed up at a local nonprofit boxing gym to learn how to fight, to the delight of my father. My mother said nothing. But still, I couldn't find the courage to stand up to the shopkeeper.

The person I pushed away most was the only person who did her best to love me. When Amá asked me to help her prepare vegetables in the kitchen, I'd refuse. I'd leave the house to go nowhere in particular. She'd come into my bedroom at night to make the sign of the cross over me, and I'd push her hand away and turn to face the wall. "Leave me alone," I'd say.

I didn't care about the pain my rejection must have caused her. I'd see her carry heavy laundry bags to the laundry room and I wouldn't offer to help. "Mijo, can you please help me? These bags are heavy," she'd ask.

"Man, fuck that. Go ask my brother or my dad to help you. Oh yeah—they're never around because you drove them away," I'd scream and storm out of the house. When I'd come home, my laundry would be neatly folded on my bed. I'd criticize how she folded my clothes.

"Mijo, why are you being so mean? I'm only trying to help. What did I do to you?"

"Yeah, that's the fuckin problem, you never know what the fuck you did. Just get the fuck out of my room," I'd snap.

"Don't speak to me like that, and don't disrespect me!"

"Or what? What the fuck are you going to do? Don't you get the hint?! My father don't want to be here. My brother's always out. So what, huh? What the fuck you going to do? Hit me? Go on, hit me. Shit! You don't even stand up to my dad," I'd yell.

"What did I do? Please, not you, mijo. I have enough to deal with, with your dad. Not you too," she'd cry.

"Why not me?" And I'd walk past her and out the front door.

Years later, I learned that forced sex workers in life-threatening situations do not self-identify as victims. We are so traumatized that we eventually believe we are making the only choice we have. In order to achieve a sense of normalcy, we are forced to live in an altered reality.

I wanted to be a kid and to experience life like a normal boy growing up, but I didn't know how. Since most guys and girls I knew in eighth grade were already having sex, I figured I should, too. But each time I hooked up with someone, I'd hear my mom in the back of my mind telling me, "All women must be respected."

My first exposure to sex was by force and pain, and with a man. I would be filled with anxiety when a girl or a woman approached me. I hated myself for this. I felt broken. I hated myself for not being able to live like all the other teenage boys who were experiencing puberty in a healthy way.

I started to read books at the public library on psychology, sexual anxiety, identity crises, and sexual performance improvement. I read the Kama Sutra, *The Art of Sex*, and learned about natural aphrodisiacs and sexual performance remedies like yohimbe, shark fin, and oysters.

I knew how to have sex with guys. It was a job. And I knew that I had been attracted to men before the sexual abuse because I would catch myself staring at the bodies and faces of men in the neighborhood. But that didn't feel sexual to me. I admired them. They were boyhood crushes from afar. I shoved those feelings deep inside, refusing to acknowledge them for fear that maybe I *was* gay. I blamed my budding curiosity as I grew older on my sexual abuse. I equated being gay with that pervert, and I thought all gay men were pedophilic predators. Even though I never heard my father or brother being overtly homophobic, I didn't know any openly gay people.

I wanted to experience being with girls in a normal-kid kind of way. I committed to trying my hardest to hook up with girls to get the gayness out of me. I made out with as many girls as possible and gained the reputation of being a great kisser. So much so that many of the ninth-grade girls would stop me between classes and ask me to kiss them. One was a girl named Brandy, a ninth grader with a cute cheerleader-type body and long sandy-brown hair. We became regular after-school make-out buddies. I liked being seen with her. Having Brandy's attention made me feel more important, because she was a white girl and popular. Sadly, she was a trophy of success for a young, confused, sexually abused boy trying awkwardly to find his way and make sense of the world. Brandy kept pressuring me to sleep with her, but I had never had sex with a girl. I wasn't ready, but I was too ashamed to tell her that. I had an image to uphold, yet every time she tried to undo my zipper, I would become filled with anxiety and push her away. I was overwhelmed with a sense of being violated and pressured to do something I didn't want to do.

At a house party one night, Brandy pulled me into a bedroom. She shut the door behind us and, while standing against the bed, started desperately kissing me. I could smell the alcohol on her breath. Aggressively she tore off my clothes. She quickly pulled my T-shirt over my head and unbuckled my belt. I didn't have a chance to offer my consent, and it made me uncomfortable. As I stood there in only my boxers, she took off her own clothes while kissing me. I tried to delay the inevitable, but she fell backward onto the bed, pulling me on top of her.

I reluctantly played along. My heart pounded in my

chest. I badly wanted to beg her to stop. But I was a cool kid now, and this was what everyone else was doing, I thought.

I had heard eighth-grade girls laughing at school about how they would fake orgasms just to make their boyfriends think they were good. I didn't want that to happen to me. I had never been naked with a girl before, and her body touching mine felt awkward. I was so nervous that I couldn't even get hard, which made my mind race faster. *Why?* The more I focused on not getting hard, the more I fumbled. The more aggressive she became in wanting to have sex, the more afraid I became. She exhaled in frustration as if I was letting her down. I tried to clear my mind and relax. Everything had functioned well at the bar in Tijuana when I'd made out with the older lady, so why not here?

I took a deep breath and I went down on her. She arched her back in pleasure and moaned loudly. Her hands pulled and squeezed the sheets. Her back arched even more. Her knees grabbed me in a headlock. I gasped for air and had to stop. She was mad.

"Why the fuck did you stop?! I was about to come . . . Fuck! Keep going," she ordered.

I thought I could feel safe with girls, but in this moment I was proven wrong. So I went on autopilot. It was as if I were back in the store. I was just doing what was expected of me. I learned to put myself second to everyone, which is tragically common behavior for the bullied and the sexually abused. I became a people pleaser, willing to do anything, especially sexually, to keep others from getting to know the true me. I could endure any unpleasantness myself as long as I knew my partner was enjoying herself.

Brandy insisted that I penetrate her. She threw me onto my back. She climbed on top of me. I saw the look of pain in her face and felt her hand squeeze my chest and her nails dig into my skin. I was suffocating; I was so afraid I was hurting her that I pushed her from me onto the bed. I jumped off the bed and quickly started putting my clothes on again.

"What are you doing? Why did you stop?" she yelled.

"I thought it was hurting you," I admitted.

"Yeah, it hurt a bit, but it also felt good. Come on. I didn't want you to stop."

"No," I said as I finished getting dressed. In a flash I left the room and walked through the party to find my home-boy Rudy, who I'd come with. I found him getting a blow job from a girl while leaning on a car.

"Hurry the fuck up, dude. Let's go!" I yelled at him.

He pushed the girl away and zipped up his pants. "Fuck it. Let's go. She can't suck dick anyway."

As we walked down the street, Rudy asked me, "What's wrong with you? I thought you were getting laid!"

I told him the whole story as our sneakers slapped the pavement in the night. He couldn't stop laughing, and the anxiety that had been welling up in my chest turned to embarrassment. I felt stupid, but his laughing became contagious, and I started to laugh, too. Rudy was the playboy who all the girls found attractive. Even high school girls would occasionally pick him up after school to give him a ride home. He never dressed like a gangster. He had a *GQ* magazine, pretty-boy style, and he hated me dressing like a cholo. He would tell me, "Man, that is the number one way to draw attention to yourself. Why do you think I am never in trouble? If you dress like a cholo, they'll target you and treat you like a thug."

Now he said, "Look, man, it'll take a while, but you'll get the hang of it. Trust me," he said, giving me a playful nudge.

"Dude, I didn't like it," I said, feeling stupid.

"Look, man. Pussy is an acquired taste," Rudy said.

"'Acquired'? Whatchu mean 'acquired'?"

"It means you'll grow to like it the more you do it, fool."

"Órale, holmes" was all I could say as I thought to myself that I wished my brother was teaching me this shit and not my homeboy in the middle of a long walk home at night. Rudy gave me some other pointers on sex with girls as I listened intently.

Brandy told all her friends that I loved to go down on her, and the news spread fast. Girls would come up to me in secret or pass me notes asking to "hang out." After I'd read the notes and look over at them, they'd giggle and I'd wink. The homeboys started to crack jokes, saying that the welfare cheese and peanut butter didn't last long in my house because I was always hungry. My ego grew. I felt like a little player.

△▽△

Yet even though Brandy and I continued to make out after school and I eventually got the hang of having sex with her—I did get used to it, as Rudy said I would—I also felt like less of a man for running out and not even saying goodbye to her the night of the party. It never occurred to me that she probably felt the same shame and embarrassment because of the disregard we had for each other. It didn't occur to me that I'd probably made her feel like less of a person, but I just couldn't fully trust her. Without that trust, I went on autopilot. I didn't realize that she was probably having sex with me because she thought it was what *I* wanted. I believed that if I told her the truth—that it wasn't at all what I wanted—she would think I was gay and spread rumors about me, destroying the reputation I'd created for myself. Luckily for me, I was able to maintain my facade.

All the while going to the gift shop a few days a week after school.

△▽△

One cool October evening in 1987, when I was almost thirteen years old, Rudy convinced me to join him and a group of guy friends who were going to a San Diego High School football game. The older brother of one of the guys was playing, and so was my older brother. My brother never invited me or the family to his games, but I figured, *Fuck it, why not?* I'd never been to a football game before. Besides, I knew my brother would be annoyed if he saw me. Rudy, the group, and I rode the bus together, everyone paying their own way. A friendly, bubbly blond white woman worked the ticket booth. I went along with the excitement of the game as if I understood what was happening, enjoying the rhythmic cheers and the acrobatics of the cheerleaders.

During halftime, while Rudy and I hung out near the concession stand, we saw a cute white girl with long blond hair and a caramel-skinned Latina with curly hair staring at us, giggling, as if they were trying to find the courage to come over and say hello. The Latina grabbed the white girl's hand and pulled her in our direction. The Latina girl said, "Hi! My name's Ariyel. This is my friend Melissa. You're in my Spanish class, but I don't think you remember me. My friend Melissa thinks your friend Rudy is cute and wanted to say hello . . . so hi!"

Rudy and I laughed. "That's cool. I'm Jesse, and this, as you know, is Rudy." Rudy had put his arm around Melissa as soon as he heard she liked him. In unison, Ariyel and I rolled our eyes, laughing. "So we're in Spanish class together?" I asked.

"Yeah. You're always pissing off the teacher. But you're funny. I sit in the very front toward the corner."

While Melissa and Rudy walked off together, Ariyel and I clicked immediately. She was half white, half Mexican with an innocent demeanor and a sweet fashion style—she wore a pink-and-white scrunchie in her hair, with pink-and-white double socks and pink-and-white Reeboks that had gills on the sides. She was funny yet quiet, quick-witted and observant. While we laughed and talked, the woman who had been working the ticket booth walked up to us and interrupted our conversation.

"Hi, honey. Who's your friend? And where's Melissa?"

she asked Ariyel, looking directly at me with a fake, forced smile. I squirmed with awkward nervousness. Her hands were manicured with beautiful red nail polish and adorned with rings and bracelets.

"Hi, Mom. This is my friend from Spanish class, Jesse. Melissa went to use the bathroom, but there's a long line like always, I'm sure."

"Hi. I'm Jesse Leon. Nice to meet you, Ariyel's mom," I said, smiling with my hand out.

"Leon? Is your brother playing on the football team?" she asked.

"Yup. That's my brother. But don't worry, we're nothing alike. I can't throw a ball to save my life," I said, shocking myself with my own charm.

"I'm Joy. I volunteer at the football games. I just don't like it when my daughter disappears."

"I didn't disappear, Mom," said Ariyel, rolling her eyes, annoyed and embarrassed at her mother's protectiveness.

"Well, I'm glad to see Ariyel made a new friend. I'm sure your brother is a good influence. Maybe you should come over on a Sunday for one of my barbecues. And, you—make sure you stay where I can see you," Joy said to Ariyel, her fake smile now authentic and friendly.

When Rudy and Melissa came back, Rudy whispered to me in Spanish, "Dude, this girl's annoying. Let's go." He walked off, waving at me to follow him.

PART
2

CHAPTER 6

The women on my father's side of the family were well known in their region for being good with rifles. My grandma and her cousins knew the Sierras like the backs of their hands. The family owned ranchlands with livestock—cows, goats, pigs, roosters, chickens, horses, pet owls, pet hawks, and a pet deer. At eleven years old, my father was an expert horse tamer who broke horses to make money for the family. While the men were out fighting in the Mexican Revolution, the women and children protected the ranches and towns.

Lola, my grandma, was half Tarahumara and half Tepehuan Indian. Both are native tribes of the region. The Tarahumara, also known as Raramuri, are known for their long-distance-running prowess. Lola taught Ricardo and his sister, Victoria, to be connected to nature and to learn the ways of the Sierra. They watched the movement of the wind and the birds' flight patterns. They listened to the birds chirping and paid close attention to the behaviors of dogs, deer, and other animals. They also knew how to listen to the silence. Because of this, they could spot when antirevolutionaries, bandits, or friends were approaching.

*Lola would teach them, "Drop to the ground. Put your
ears to the earth to listen for approaching steps. Listen
closely, and you will know how many people are coming." If
my grandma Lola suspected a sinister group lurked nearby,
she would gather the children and hide them in secret alcoves
underneath the pig and goat corrals. She'd lift the concealed
doors, throw the children in, and cover the trapdoors with
hay. Her biggest fears were that her daughter, my aunt Victoria, would be kidnapped and raped and that Ricardo would
be forced to fight in the war. After hiding the children, she
would stand in front of the house, rifle in hand and four
trained attack dogs at her side.*

*That region of Durango gave birth to many Mexican revo-
lutionary heroes in the second decade of the 1900s. As I grew
up, Mama Lola constantly reminded my siblings and me that
rebellion ran in our blood. "Jesse, mijito, we are people who
fight for justice," she said. "Don't ever forget that."*

△▽△

Throughout eighth grade and the beginning of ninth grade,
I watched the shopkeeper and his Black friend smoke weed
and the occasional joint laced with cocaine, which they
called Primos. I had just started ninth grade and was thirteen
going on fourteen when they first had me smoke a Primo
with them in the storage room. The first time I smoked one,
I felt like I could conquer the world. I felt invincible, which

was obviously absurd because I was trapped, forced into being a sex worker.

"Oh my god! This shit is fuckin good!" I told them. They laughed. Having sex with them both seemed easier while I was high on Primo. I was able to relax, and I lost my inhibitions. I would do things without being told to, disassociating myself from the acts I was engaged in. Primo became my escape.

Sometimes they'd give me some to take with me, which I would smoke or sell at school. Occasionally I'd get an additional twenty-dollar bill as opposed to the usual five, teaching me that having sex while high and uninhibited could be financially beneficial. I put the money away to buy a car. The shopkeeper didn't beat me up as often anymore. We'd laugh about shit after sex. I thought my life was getting better. I was at a new school. I had new friends, like Ariyel, who quickly became my bestie. I was cute. I was cool. No one remembered the old Jesse anymore. Then, once again, it all changed.

△▽△

A new kid transferred to our school, a white, wannabe Black, tall, and muscular gangster kid. He wore his long blond hair in cornrows under his baseball cap with long white T-shirts, sharply creased-out Dickies, and Nike Cortez sneakers.

At first I didn't pay him any mind; we had a lot of gang

kids at our school, so he didn't stand out except that he was white. But one morning after first period, I heard that the new kid had bullied and beaten up a friend of mine and Rudy's from computer class. The news brought up strong waves of anger in me—feelings I'd never been able to express when I was in that situation myself. I was overcome with rage. Why would this big guy beat up on someone who didn't bother anyone? This question kept flashing across my mind, filling me with that rage over and over again. As the morning unfolded, the new kid became the focal point of all my past years of anger. During lunchtime, I sat with a group of friends at a hard beige plastic table under the canopy of the outdoor cafeteria where all the students gathered to eat. Rudy wasn't there. The group talked loudly amid the chaos of a junior high school lunchroom.

"Yeah, that's some fucked-up shit, what that white puto did. Why don't he fuck with someone his own size? Someone needs to fuck his ass up," I said angrily.

"So whatchu gon do, holmes?" said a ninth-grade cholita girl of the group with raccoon-eye makeup and long feathered black hair.

"Yeah, whatchu gon do, homeboy? Go fuck him up, ey!" said one of the other guys in the group, who had a shaved head, a white T-shirt, and Dickies, as the rest of the group chimed in.

Inside I was scared, but I couldn't show them that. I wanted someone to defend our friend, but I didn't think the task was going to fall on my shoulders. The rage I'd felt all morning had slightly faded, and now I was angry at myself for opening my mouth. I didn't want to get in a fight and risk being suspended.

The girl with the chola raccoon-eye makeup said, "Or what? You scared? Why you actin like a chavala, ey? I think you're scared."

"I ain't no fuckin chavala," I told her with an angry look.

"Then go do something about it and quit talkin shit, ey," she said.

And then the group started egging me on. "Yeah, go fuck him up, Jesse. Go fuck him up!"

I felt backed up against a wall with no way out. For a moment I wished Rudy were there. He'd have gotten them off my case. But Rudy wasn't around. "Man," I said, "fuck all of you, I ain't no fuckin punk. I ain't no chavala. Fuck that puto. Watch, I'll fuck him up."

I was being called a pussy for not stepping up to fuck up this dude who I felt had picked on someone innocent just to prove a point. So what if I was afraid? This fuckin white boy was not going to take away my new reputation. And in a flash he became the focus of all my rage. *How dare he fuck with someone so small? Fuck him! Fuck him! Fuck him!* I repeated over and over in my head as I walked to where he was sitting with five or six Black guys I knew. *Oh, this motherfucker beat up my friend only to make a point and to make friends, that's why he's not by himself now,* I thought, which made me even more mad. He had taken advantage of someone else for his own gain.

"Get the fuck up, puto! Why you fuckin with my little homeboy? Fuck wit me, mufucker!" I yelled at him with my fists clenched, ready to fight.

He stood up from the bench he'd been straddling and quickly tried to swing at me. I dodged his punch and punched him so hard in the cheek that he fell backward over the bench and onto the ground. People gathered, and everyone spread out and encircled us, whooping and cheering. I jumped over the bench, and with one of my knees on top of his chest, I started punching his face. I could feel all that rage balling up in my fists, years of it coming down on him.

Then I stood up and began to kick him in the head. His cap fell off, and his do-rag was halfway off his head. I grabbed him by his blond cornrows and dragged him over to the hard and jagged stucco wall, screaming, "You think you're a badass, motherfucker?" I slammed his head hard against the wall, over and over again, his blood spurting everywhere. I couldn't stop myself. I blacked out. I no longer heard anyone screaming. I didn't feel anyone try to pull me off him. All I could see were images of the shopkeeper molesting me, slamming my head against the wall and beating me up, along with the faces of the countless men I'd been forced to have sex with.

After what seemed like forever, a school police officer—Officer Lopez—and a few security guards yanked me off the guy. Officer Lopez, a muscular mid-forties Latino with a salt-and-pepper goatee and hair combed backward, knew me well, and we had a rapport. He was kind to the students, always available to us and there with a helping hand. I came back to reality when I felt my face slam hard against the ground and a pair of handcuffs squeeze around my wrists. In a daze, I had no idea what was going on other than that I had just gotten into a fight and was covered in blood. I didn't understand why I was in handcuffs or why I was being pushed by the officer who I thought was a friend to me.

Before I knew it, I was sitting in the principal's office alone with my wrists behind my back. I looked around the office calmly, resigned to the facts of what happened and wondering what I'd done. What was going to happen now?

I could hear conversations outside the office but couldn't make out what people were saying. When Officer Lopez walked in, he said they'd called the other boy's mother, the only parent he had, and that the kid had been rushed to the ICU. He told me that the boy's mom wanted to press charges and that I had to wait there until they knew whether or not I was going to be arrested and charged.

"You might be looking at attempted murder, Jesse. What is wrong with you?" Officer Lopez yelled. "I never thought I'd have to worry about you doing this kind of stupid shit. You might get locked up for this! You better pray his mom doesn't press charges. You better pray that kid doesn't die. What's happening with you, Jesse?" I could feel genuine concern throbbing off him. Yet I sat there stoically, looking straight forward, breathing with a fuck-it-I-don't-give-a-fuck attitude. I didn't care that I was covered in blood. I didn't care about his concern.

Then, like a far-off echo in my head, I heard Officer Lopez say again, "Talk to me, Jesse. I'm trying to help you." He was kneeling beside me.

At that, a tear welled up and rolled down my face. Then another one, and another still. But I kept staring at the wall directly in front of me. In a soft voice, I said, "I couldn't stop. I blacked out. All I could see was that guy from the store."

"What? What guy? What store?" Again, his voice was a far-off echo.

"That white motherfucker from the store," I said again in a matter-of-fact yet shaky voice.

"What guy, Jesse? I don't understand."

Then, all of a sudden, uncontrollably, my breathing became heavy. My chest was heaving, up and down, up and down. "*Him!* That white motherfucker forcing me to suck his dick and sucking my dick. All I could see was the white shopkeeper's face and then I saw the faces of all them other white men."

The dam finally burst and I broke down, crying a flood of tears. "I'm sorry! I'm sorry. It had nothing to do with that white kid. I blacked out. I'm sorry. I didn't mean to hurt him like that. I was only protecting my friend. I wanted to make sure that kid didn't hurt anyone else. I am sorry. I blacked out."

Then, as if snapping out of a bad dream, I clearly saw Officer Lopez sitting directly in front of me. "What did you just say, Jesse?" he asked me carefully, concern thick in his voice. "Is someone forcing you to engage in sexual acts with them? Is that what you're saying, Jesse? Is some man sexually harassing you?"

Tears kept flowing down my face like a waterfall as I gasped for air. I thought I was having an asthma attack. "Yes." I was barely able to get out the word through my sobs.

Officer Lopez quietly told me to hold on and walked out of the office.

Twenty minutes later he came back in with the principal. They said they were going to wait for the school's social worker before they asked me any more questions. We sat there quietly. A few minutes later there was a knock on the door, and in walked a skinny, tall white woman I'd never seen before. She pulled up a chair and sat down next to me while the officer went over the details of the fight and then repeated everything I had said to him about the abuse.

She tried to make eye contact with me. "Jesse, now you know these are some very serious allegations you are making, right?"

I looked directly at her and said, "Bitch. I ain't making this shit up! Fuck you. That's why I didn't want to say nothing. He told me no one would believe me! But if it were some white little motherfuckin kid saying this shit to you, you'd believe what he was telling you. Wouldn't you?"

"Hey, hey, hey," the principal tried to break in.

I ignored him. "You fuckin white bitch." I could hear myself yelling now. I looked at Officer Lopez and asked, "So am I in trouble for beating up the white kid or what? Get this shit over with and get this bitch outta my face. Just take me to juvie and forget I said shit."

I had never snapped at an adult before. The social worker kept her voice level. "Jesse, I know you're upset. But I'm not the person you need to be upset with. I am here to help you. I need you to start from the beginning. Please try to pull yourself together and tell me what has been going on with you. When did the sexual abuse start? Is it someone in your family?"

"Was it a family member?" I snapped. "Bitch, what the

fuck is wrong with you? Ain't no one in my family gonna do this shit to me. We may be poor and fucked up, but not like that. Man, get her the fuck outta here," I told the cop.

Officer Lopez bent down in front of me, put his hand on my shoulder, and looked right at me. "Please, Jesse, I need you to cooperate. No one is blaming you or accusing you of being a liar. We need to know what is happening to figure out the best way to help you. You almost killed a kid today. If there is anything we can do to help you, then we will, but please, you have to let us help you first."

I desperately wanted my mom, my amá, there with me but was too afraid to ask them to call her because I didn't want to appear weak or like I needed Mommy by my side. I focused on Officer Lopez and told him the whole story. I started with the day of the water balloon fight.

As I talked, I was afraid Officer Lopez was going to judge me because he was a Latino man. He understood the machismo of the culture, and what I was saying definitely didn't make me seem macho. Also, I thought he was cool, and I didn't want him to be disgusted by or disappointed in me. I couldn't bear to feel the shame of that judgment on top of it all. He was the first person I'd ever told what happened, and tears flowed down my face. I'd reached my breaking point, the point I'd needed to hit for it to all come spilling out.

When I was done, Officer Lopez told the social worker and the principal that I was a good kid and that he knew something must be going on because I normally didn't get into this type of trouble. He asked if he could talk to them privately. They left me in the room alone, still handcuffed. I completely lost my sense of self. I no longer knew who I was. A part of me was scared, a ball of anxiety, while another part of me didn't care what could or would happen to me.

When they walked back in, the principal told me that they'd explained to the boy's mom what was going on with me without going into details and had begged her not to press charges. He told me that the boy's mom had agreed as long as they could find me some court-ordered help. A sense of relief washed over me. I didn't want the boy's mother to see me as a villain. I was begging for help.

△▽△

The rest is all a blur. I don't remember the handcuffs being removed. I don't remember cleaning up. All I remember is the three of them walking in and out of the office and waiting for long intervals until the social worker came back with Officer Lopez, holding a stack of forms.

No one contacted my mom.

"We have a lot of work to do," the social worker said, "and I'm going to need you to do your part if you don't want to get incarcerated. We need you to first tell us where this gift shop is exactly, so we can make sure the guy doesn't do this to any other children. And we need to tell your parents and explain to them what is happening, because they have to fill out these forms so we can get you some help from the state."

The part about telling my parents freaked me out. "Please," I begged, "*don't* tell them! They won't understand. Just tell them I got into a fight and have to deal with anger issues. Please don't tell them," I pleaded and pleaded. I was more and more freaked out every second as it dawned on me what my parents would learn about me. I was hysterical, regretful for having revealed my secret. I was afraid, angry, and I hated myself. I was talking to myself in my head like Gollum to Smeagol in *Lord of the Rings*. *Why did you tell them, dumbass?* I kept asking myself even as I was screaming at the social worker and the police officer not to tell my parents.

"I will give you until tomorrow to tell your mom what is going on," the social worker said. "You don't have to tell your father. I only need the signature of one parent. If I don't hear from her by tomorrow evening, I will be forced to call her and tell her what is going on myself. We need her signature to put you in the state's victim witness program and to get you some help."

It was the first time I had heard the term *victim witness program*. I didn't like the sound of it. I hated the word *victim*. It left a sour taste in my mouth, and I thought it made me sound weak.

The social worker said the boy's mom wouldn't press charges only if they showed documented proof that I was getting help. Those words rang in my ears.

Officer Lopez drove me home in the back of his cop car. The principal had called my mom to let her know, and when we got there, Amá was pacing back and forth in the driveway outside the apartments. When the officer opened my door, she rushed over to hug me. "¿Ay, Jesse, qué fue lo que hiciste?" *What did you do?*

"Remain calm, and please be patient with your son," Officer Lopez told my mom in Spanish as she hugged me close to her, rubbing my head with one hand. "He has a lot he needs to talk to you about. Jesse has to be in school tomorrow to meet with the principal, so he's not being suspended just yet."

The look of disappointment and hurt in her eyes shot through me. I could hardly look my amá in the face, and I was glad that Officer Lopez had done the talking thus far on my behalf.

"What time do I need to be there to meet with the principal?" asked Amá.

"You don't need to be there. We will handle it and let you know," Officer Lopez responded.

"Are you sure? My son just got into a fight. I want to know what's going on and what's going to happen?"

"Please, let us figure it out. We will be in touch," said Officer Lopez as he got back into his car. My mom, accustomed to respecting authority, resigned herself. The police and the principal would know what was best.

I had been hoping that Officer Lopez wouldn't go. I didn't want to tell my mom everything by myself. When we walked inside, my dad was sitting on the couch watching a boxing match on TV. When he saw the blood, he didn't even greet me; he just said, "Pues vale más que te lo hayas chingado, eh. O si no, soy yo quien te va partir la madre, cabrón." *You better have fucked him up. If not, I'll beat your ass.*

"I did. I beat his ass, Dad. I fucked him up so bad so that

you'd be proud of me," I snapped as I walked through the living room, passing him and heading to my bedroom. I saw him nod his head in approval.

I took off my clothes and brought them to the laundry room to wash the blood off, then I washed the blood off me. In the shower, I laid my head against the cold blue tiles and let the water flow over my head and down my back. I couldn't stop thinking, *How the hell am I gonna tell my mom?*

After the shower, I walked into the kitchen as my mom was coming from the laundry room. "¿Qué haces?" I asked her. *What are you doing?*

"Le puse Suavitel a tu ropa." *I put fabric softener on your clothes.*

"Oh, okay. Well, we need to go outside. I need to talk to you in private about what happened today."

It was around 5:30 p.m., so it was still light outside when we went out. We walked to the front of the apartment complex and sat down on a small brick wall. I had no clue what I was going to say, especially in Spanish. I grew up bilingual, but I spoke broken slang Spanish.

Before I could start, she asked, "¿Qué es lo que está pasando?" *What is happening?*

"Amá, no sé cómo decirte, pero necesito que por favor no le digas nada a nadie," I told her. *Please don't make a big scene, and I beg you to never tell anyone what I am about to tell you.*

"¿Qué pasa? Dime," she said with an inquisitive look on her face.

Then I told her, "Me están molestando."

In Spanish we have no word that translates directly to "molest." *Molestar* in Spanish means "to bother." *Molestando* means "bothering." So obviously my mom asked, "Who is bothering you and why?"

I took a deep breath and finally managed to eke out, "Me están molestando sexualmente."

"What do you mean, bothering you sexually?" she asked, confused. She was trying to make sense of what I was saying. Then I could see the light bulb go off in her head; her expression changed instantly from confusion to shock to disbelief to anger.

"Who is sexually abusing you? What is going on?" she said in Spanish, standing up.

I told her about the fight and how I blacked out. I told her all I could see while I was beating up that boy was the face of the man who was sexually abusing me. I didn't tell her about all the other men.

"¿Pero quién? ¿Dónde chingados está? Dime adónde está para ir a matar al hijo de su chingada madre," she said in a now-angry voice. "¡Lo voy a matar! ¡Llévame adonde está el cabrón!" *Tell me where he is so I can go kill that motherfucker. I'm going to kill him!*

She was stomping around now, with her hands rolled into fists as if ready to clobber him if only given the chance. "You're a child. I'm going to kill the motherfucker!" she continued in Spanish. I just went on, telling her that because I beat up the guy so bad in school, they were going to lock me up, but that the boy's mom had agreed not to press charges if I got help.

This was the most difficult conversation I'd ever had in

my life. I saw the way it changed my mother. And I was left to have it alone, with no guidance or coaching or support. There was no one there to help my mom process what I was telling her, either.

I explained to her that she needed to fill out paperwork so I could attend counseling for my anger and trauma. The counseling would be paid for by the state because I was the victim of a crime. When I said the words *victim of a crime* in Spanish, she grabbed me and pulled me close into her arms. She sobbed as she squeezed me tighter, as if she was afraid to let me go. I held her while she cried. I didn't shed a tear.

I told her that the police were already looking for my abuser, so she had nothing to worry about. "What the fuck you mean I have nothing to worry about?" she said. "All your life I have worked hard to make sure you were protected and had a good life, a life better than mine. And I failed. It's my fault for not taking better care of you. It's my fault! I failed you. I didn't protect you. I'm sorry for failing you. For working so much that I couldn't keep a better eye on you! I'm fuckin stupid! Stupid for not taking better care of you!" She yelled over and over as she pounded herself hard in the chest. "¡Soy una estúpida! Soy una pinche estúpida por no haber cuidado bien de ti. ¡Chingada madre!"

That is when I started to cry. This angry grief that made my mother beat at herself had me even more scared than I already was. I had never caused her this much anguish before. "It's not your fault, Mommy," I cried. "Please don't say that. It's not your fault. I didn't want to tell you, but I didn't want to go to jail. I should have just shut the fuck up. I should have just shut the fuck up!"

We held each other, weeping.

God bless my mom. I destroyed her world. I tried to hold her as she said, "How could you not tell me that someone put his hands on you? Why? Why didn't you come to me sooner?"

Those words pushed me over the edge. It wasn't her intention, but I felt she was blaming me, and it filled me with rage. I interpreted her words as "This is all your fault, Jesse, for not coming to me sooner." The agony of hurting my mother like this was too much for me to bear. My despairing mind turned my love for her into anger. I exploded like a pressure cooker.

I went off on her in Spanish. "Fuck you. I didn't want some stranger touching me. All I wanted was water balloons. But we were too poor to have water balloons in the house. This all happened because we are poor. Fuck you. I hate you. It's your fault they sent me to that all-white school where I was picked on for being poor and not as smart as the other kids. I hate you for bringing me into this world."

Her facial expression morphed into one of pain and despair as she pulled me close and I tried to pull away. I knew she could sense my sadness. I knew in my soul that she understood how these feelings could turn into anger. I wanted to hug her back, to wrap myself in her arms and bury myself in her thick embrace and feel safe with her as I once had, but instead I pushed her so hard that she lost her footing and fell. I wanted to help her up, to hug her, to be held by her. I wanted to say, *Mommy. I'm sorry. Amá, it's not your fault. I am so sorry, Mommy. I love you.*

But I didn't. I never said those words.

I couldn't grasp that I was most angry with myself for feeling like I'd let her down. She'd sacrificed so much for her family. She worked for peanuts and busted her ass off to support the family pretty much by herself because her selfish, womanizing husband was more a freeloader who demanded to be waited on hand and foot than a partner to her. How could I add to her pain when all she wanted was the best for me? But nothing could stand in the face of my anger.

"Just sign the fuckin papers," I yelled in her direction in Spanish as I ran away. It had grown dark, and I ran into the night to be alone.

When I came back about an hour later, she was still there, crying. When she saw me, she ran to me and hugged me. I stood with my arms limp at my sides. She said, "I'll sign whatever papers I need to sign to protect you and help you where I failed. I don't want your anger to take over your life." Over and over, she repeated through her sobs, "Perdóname, perdóname, perdóname, mijo." *Forgive me, forgive me, forgive me, my son.*

I pulled away from her and left her out in the cold as I went inside to my room, crawled into bed, and stared at the wall in silence.

△▽△

The next day, I was the talk of the school. I got props from guys who'd never spoken to me before the fight. The fight had only made me more popular than ever; fist pumps and back claps rained down on me all day. The praise from the other students only made me feel worse. It didn't feel right. The social worker pulled me out of fourth period and asked if I'd told my mom. I said, "Yes." Then I told her that I wanted to go home early because it was too difficult for me to be in school. I didn't want to deal with the other students, and I didn't want to think about the fight or the argument with my mom. I wanted the world to stop turning and let me off. I wanted to stop thinking.

I returned the papers that my mom had signed, and then I was sent home. There was no call to my mom. Nothing.

When I arrived, no one was there. Mom was at work. I pulled out a coloring book and crayons. I lay on the floor, as I had done so many times as a kid, and colored.

CHAPTER 7

Three or four days after the fight, the principal came to my third-period classroom with two detectives, one male and one female. They had on dark suits and sunglasses even though it was around 10:00 a.m. They waited by the door as the principal walked into the room. All the students went silent at the sight of the two detectives by the door; even Rudy, who sat near me, stared. All heads moved in unison, following the principal as he walked across the room to speak with the teacher and then looking back at the detectives.

The principal whispered something into the teacher's ear and then turned to me and said, "Jesse, please come with me."

All the students stared at me in silence at first, then started catcalling. "Oooooh, you are in trouble! You're gonna get it!"

I thought for a second that they'd decided to press charges against me, and this thought repeated itself over and over again as I followed them through the school campus to the principal's drab office. When we got there, the principal went to sit in the large leather chair behind his bulky wooden desk, but one of the detectives told him, "We want to speak with him alone. You can wait for us outside." The principal looked at me, confused by their request, and hesitantly walked out without protest.

They sat me in one of two wooden chairs facing the principal's desk. I was nervously hunched over with my elbows resting on my knees, holding my sweaty hands together while fidgeting with my thumbs, as the female detective leaned against the desk and the male detective leaned against the door, arms crossed. I wanted my mom. I wanted Officer Lopez.

Breaking the silence, I asked shakily, "Am I being arrested?"

Ignoring my question, they introduced themselves briefly and immediately launched into asking me questions about my sexual abuse. I don't remember their names. I don't remember all their questions. I do, however, remember how heartless, cold, and unemotional they were. They showed no compassion, no sign that they cared about what had happened to me. They didn't even ask me if I preferred to be called Jesse or Jesus, how my day was going, or if I wanted my parents present while I was being questioned.

The woman detective asked, "If we ask you to take us to the location of the supposed crime scene, could you take us?"

"'*Supposed* crime scene'? *Why would I make this up?*" I yelled. "If this gets out, I'm in deep shit! Why are you acting as if *I'm* the fuckin criminal?"

"Well, you did beat up an innocent kid. You could be lying to get yourself out of trouble," the female detective said, cocking her head to the side.

"Innocent? That motherfucker beat up someone way smaller than him. Did you know that? Did you even bother asking? That punk had it coming. And what? You think I'm a liar? Is it a bother for you to be here? Did I ruin your day or something by making you really work instead of eat doughnuts, motherfucker?" I seethed in anger.

They ignored me. "We need you to accompany us and point out the location."

"Nah, I ain't goin anywhere with you. You're crazy. He said he'd kill me and my family. He knows where I live. I'm not going with you," I said.

"You have no choice. You have to come with us." The female detective threatened me with handcuffs if I didn't comply. Shaking my head in disbelief, I forced myself to calm down, trying to push my fear and anger back and to focus on what was in front of me. The male detective squeezed my shoulder hard, lifting me from the chair, and led me out of the office and into their car. I slouched in the back seat. I answered their questions with one-word responses. There were no door handles or window cranks in the back of the car. For a second I thought they had lied to me and that they were taking me to Juvenile Hall.

We drove by the gift shop and I pointed it out to them. They drove around the block one more time, and as we slowly moved in front of the store, they asked me if the guy behind the counter was the guy who'd been abusing me.

I said, "No, he's not there." But he was there. He looked right at me, and my throat was immediately gripped in a paralyzing fear—a fear that overwhelmed even my anger at these cops and how they'd treated me.

The female detective asked again, "Did you see him? Was that him?"

"I said no."

The panic I felt when the shopkeeper saw me, coupled with the belief that the cops were not going to help me, kept me silent. The detectives took me back to school and dropped me off. They said they would return to get me if they needed anything else. They didn't walk me to the office or back to class. They just left me there at the gate. I felt vulnerable. I was disappointed in myself for opening my mouth the day of the fight.

As I stood there in front of the school, wondering what I was going to do, my homeboy Rudy walked by. Nodding my head at him, I said, "Sup, ey. What you gonna do? Let's ditch and go to your crib. I don't wanna be here today, homeboy. And I really don't wanna hang out with other people during lunch, so let's go."

"Fuck it, ey. Let's bounce. Are you okay?" Rudy asked, giving me a handshake and bumping shoulders with a one-armed hug. He could see the fear and confusion in my eyes as I stood there fidgeting.

"Yup, I'm good. I just have to walk to my house and grab something," I lied. He put his hand on my shoulder, leading me toward the street, leaving the school behind us.

I took him to the gift shop instead.

I stopped in front of the shop and looked in. The shop-keeper was still there, looking right out at me; that mustache was unmistakable. I remember standing there frozen, just staring at him and him staring right back at me. Rudy kept on walking and then stopped when he realized I wasn't by his side. He walked back toward me. "What's up, man?"

But I just kept staring at the guy in the store. I told Rudy, "That man is the reason the detectives came looking for me today." My voice was stoic and unemotional. "My life is fucked up now. That puto destroyed my life."

"Whatcha mean?" His face was growing thick with protective anger. "Him?"

Rudy reached for the door to walk into the store, ready to beat the guy up, but I pulled him away hard and said, "Nah, man. The detectives are all over it. We'll only get in trouble at this point. Besides, he has a bat and a gun behind the counter. I can't afford to do anything stupid. I hope he gets his. Let's just go."

"Fuck that, holmes. Let me handle it! Why is that punk fucking with you? You owe him money or something?"

"Let's go, man. I'll explain later."

We didn't go to my house. We walked to Rudy's house instead. Rudy kept asking me, "What happened? What happened?" I stayed quiet, lit a joint, and smoked it with my head down, staring at the crease in my jeans and at my black Vans with white soles as we walked.

When we got to Rudy's, I told him the whole story, including the many different men I'd been pimped out to, which I had not even told the detectives about. "I'm a prostitute, dude," I told him as I took more weed and papers out of my pocket to roll a joint. He put his hand on top of mine and pulled the weed and papers away. My eyes welled up with tears.

Rudy let me vent. He let me cry. It was the first time I'd talked to a friend. He said nothing the entire time I sobbed; he let me get it out, keeping his hand on my shoulder as I sat leaning over with my elbows on my knees and my hands holding my head. I begged him to not do anything or say anything to anyone, but I didn't need to. He wasn't going to. He was more of a brother to me in those moments of that afternoon than my own brother had ever been.

I left Rudy's house to head home around five thirty. I lit a joint on the walk home and stopped by the gift shop. When the shopkeeper saw me walk in, the shock and disbelief were unmistakable on his face. "Get the fuck out of here and never come back," he told me. He was alone.

"Why? You started this, and now I want my dick sucked, motherfucker. All these years I've come here because you made me, but now I'm here on my own and I want my dick sucked. And you're gonna suck it. So come on. Let's go to the back."

"I have no clue what you're talking about. I don't ever want you coming into this store again. I don't know you."

For a moment I stood there, shocked and confused by what he'd said. "Oh, your punk ass thinks I'm setting you up." I laughed. "Nah, man."

Then his expression turned to anger and he said in a low voice, "If you ever come around here again or say anything, you little motherfucker—" He paused. "Remember, I know where you live, and I'll kill your fat fuckin mom."

Out of nowhere, I yelled, "Fuck you, you sick mother-fucker! You ain't touching my mom or nobody, and if you know what's good for you, you'll fuckin kill yourself or dis-appear before I make it happen to you first."

"Get the fuck out. I don't ever want to see you again," he said calmly.

I turned around to walk out. As I went to open the door, I said, "You'll get what's coming to you."

Feeling good, I rolled another joint and walked home.

△▽△

From that day forward, Rudy did everything he could to make sure I was safe. He wouldn't leave my side at school. He'd offer to walk me home after school, too, which often made me laugh. He treated me the way I'd wanted my brother to treat me. He took care of me.

Shortly after the day when I told Rudy my secret, the guy who molested me and forced me to sleep with other men for years of my childhood disappeared. I never saw him nor his friend at the store again. It shut down soon after.

△▽△

The heavyset white female psychotherapist who was as-signed to me by the victim witness program did little to help me work through my issues of distrust, rage, and victimization. Even though I was in therapy, I spiraled downward fast.

My first appointment required my mother to be there, so she came without knowing what to expect. But she was willing to try anything to make sure I got the help I needed. The therapist's office was in a small cottage in a complex of eight Victorian cottages in downtown San Diego, near Little Italy. As we walked in, Amá and I looked around at the handsome furnishings—a long, dark green velvet chesterfield couch with a lamp on top of the end tables on either side, and a large black leather office chair tucked under a wooden desk in front of a window that looked out onto a garden in the courtyard of the complex. Amá made me introduce myself formally: "Jesse Leon para servirle." A customary phrase in my socioeconomic class—*Jesse Leon at your service.* Amá did the same.

The therapist shook each of our hands with indifference, directing us to sit down. Amá and I sat awkwardly on the velvet couch. The therapist sat in the black leather chair. She lacked the good grace often found in Latino culture to help others with smiles on our faces. She wouldn't even make eye contact with Amá when speaking to her. Instead she fumbled through papers, handing some to me for Amá to sign without explaining what they said.

"Do we have to fill this section out?" I asked, pointing to a document.

"Just fill it out for her as best you can and tell her to sign it," she responded, not looking at me, either.

Once the paperwork was out of the way, she told Amá

(as I translated), "Jesus will need to come see me once per week after school. You have no need to come back. If I have any documents that you need to sign, I will send them with Jesus and he can bring them back to our next appointment. Do you have any questions?" I hated that she was calling me Jesus when I'd already introduced myself as Jesse.

"Yes, I do. How do we make sure he gets better? How can we help him? Will we have a family therapy session? How will you give me updates on how he is doing if you don't have an interpreter?" Amá asked with tears in her eyes as I interpreted and her hand held mine.

"If I need to see you, I will let you know. I don't need an interpreter. Jesus here seems to be doing a good job at it. My meetings with Jesus will be confidential. I will not be discussing the things we talk about with you unless he decides he wants to hurt himself or someone else. As I said, I will let you know when we need to meet again," she told my mom, now looking directly into her eyes as though trying to intimidate her.

I could sense Amá tensing, wanting to lash back. "So we will not have family therapy sessions?" Amá asked coldly, wiping the quickly drying tears from her eyes.

"No, we will not. I need to get to know Jesus first. If I have any questions, I will ask them through Jesus."

"But he's been lying and keeping things from me for years. I see you're getting paid $125 per hour according to the documents I just signed. I'm sure you can afford an interpreter."

"The state does not pay for interpreters, and unfortunately, *you* can't afford it," she told Amá. Looking at me, the therapist said, "We are out of time, as we have gone over our forty-five minutes. I will see you here every Monday after school for our sessions. Now goodbye and have a good day." She stood up, walked to the door, and opened it, letting us know it was time for us to go.

Amá got up, frustrated, and went to shake hands and say thank you. But the therapist dismissed her gesture, which made Amá grab the woman's hand with both her own as she stood crying in the doorway. "Please, please help my son. He's a good, intelligent boy. I don't want him to get lost and turn to a life of gangs and drugs like so many other kids. Please help him."

Amá was now sobbing, and she went to hug the therapist, who quickly released her hand from Amá's grip and put her arms up while stepping back. This hurt my feelings, and I sadly started to translate what Amá was saying when the therapist cut me off. "No need to interpret, Jesus. It's clear to me that you come from an extremely emotional family. It's no wonder—" She stopped herself and then went on. "I'll see you on Monday. Now you have to go so I can prepare for my next appointment."

Amá and I left.

It was 1988, and my mom was making California's minimum wage at the time: $4.25 per hour. "Can you imagine how many days I'd have to work to pay for just one hour with her. Shit, forty-five minutes! It's not even a full hour. She must be rich. I just hope she helps you, mijo," Amá said, kissing the top of my head as we sat at the bus stop waiting to go home.

CHAPTER 8

One evening at around six o'clock, my mom was in the kitchen making dinner while I sat in the living room watching TV. My dad walked in without so much as a hello and looked into the kitchen to see what my mom was cooking.

"It's almost six thirty and I've been out all day trying to make money for the family and dinner isn't fuckin ready yet?" he said. "I don't know why the fuck I married you. Is it too much to ask to have dinner ready when I walk in?"

Amá ignored him and kept cooking. "Jesse, go grab your brother and set up the folding tables. Dinner is almost ready." My dad was about to sit next to me as I got up to do what she asked.

"No! You set up the tables. It's not his job. It's your job, you good-for-nothing whale!" He grabbed me by the arm and yanked me back down onto the couch.

The yelling commenced. I stormed out as my parents' voices faded into the background, frustrated that it was the same shit over and over again. It seemed like every minute my father was home, he was in a mood, angry. It felt as though we were constant reminders of everything he hated about his life. As I walked away from the house, I found myself walking back toward the store where I had been molested as if it were routine. When it occurred to me, I became more enraged. I could have walked to my friend Ariyel's house, which had become a common occurrence over the previous weeks and months, but a part of me wanted to be alone. I didn't want to be a burden to Ariyel, who came from an entirely different kind of family. There was rarely yelling where she lived.

I walked down Sixth Avenue, toward downtown, to Balboa Park. It was getting dark but I could still make out the park equipment. I went into the playground by the swings and the jungle gym, remembering the days I'd played innocently as a child in this exact spot. I lay down on the bright fire engine–red roundabout with the different-colored handrails, feeling the realness of the cold metal against my body. I stared up into the sky through the trees, wondering where the hell my life was going and if it was even worth staying alive as I lit and smoked a joint.

I was having suicidal thoughts—wondering if everyone, especially my mom, would be better off if I just ended my life—and they were becoming more and more frequent. As I lay on the roundabout, staring up at the sky, I felt small and insignificant.

When the cold metal became unbearable against my spine, I sat up and saw two guys leaning against a cream-yellow Cadillac. I sat there smoking my joint when one of the guys shouted out, "Hey, holmes, you got a light?" I shouted back that I did. Both guys started walking toward me. One of them was Latino and the other Black. The Black guy had long dreads pulled back. Both were dressed like gangsters. I gave the Latino guy the lighter. He lit up a joint and asked if I wanted to take a hit. I showed him mine as if to say, *Nah, I'm good, holmes.*

"Yeah, but this is Lovely, holmes," said the Latino as he took another hit. I loved smoking Lovely, marijuana dipped in PCP (or embalming fluid or horse tranquilizer or cat tranquilizer depending on who you ask, also known as Dip, Wack, Sherm, and Love Boat). Cigarettes dipped in PCP were called Kools since most of the time Kool brand cigarettes were used.

"Nah, I'm good, ese—I ain't tryin to get too fucked up tonight," I said.

"You should try it. The paper is made from hashish, not regular rolling paper. And the weed is Chocolate Thai—it tastes just like a chocolate bar, lil man," said the dude with dreads as he pulled a forty-ounce of Olde English 800 from the back pocket of his jeans and took a swig.

"Nah, I'm good, holmes, but I'll take a drink of that, ey—this weed gave me dry mouth."

I chilled with them for about an hour. They were funny as hell, and for a little while I forgot about the drama at home, my thoughts of suicide, and all else. I was guarded. Some people I knew would party with strangers just to get them fucked up and rob them. The junior high and high school gangster girls, the cholas, were experts in doing that, especially when setting up guys from rival gangs, so I didn't let myself get too comfortable with these two guys.

They asked what I was doing at the park so late. I told them my family was fighting so I'd come out to clear my mind and that was it. They looked at each other and smiled in a weird way.

"You wanna roll wit us and chill da rest of da night?" asked the Black dude.

I felt a little funny about the smirks on their faces, so I told them, "Nah, I'm good, I gotta go home. It's getting late. I got school tomorrow."

I shook their hands goodbye and walked back home. When I got there, my mom was awake waiting for me. "Where did you go? I was worried. Please don't storm out like that again."

"I'm sorry, Mom. I just don't like how my dad is constantly talking shit and picking fights. It's too much."

"I know, mijo. My heart's been hurting, too. I need to go to the doctor tomorrow. They are going to run some tests. I think the constant fighting is bringing up my blood pressure."

"Blood pressure? Since when do you have high blood pressure?"

"Ay, mijo. It runs in the family. I don't know how much more I can take. I don't know where I went wrong. If it wasn't for you kids, I would run away, far, far away from here where no one knows me and just disappear."

△▽△

The next day I went to the first two periods of school and then ditched. Roosevelt Junior High is conveniently located right next to the San Diego Zoo. My friends and I liked to cut the fence that separates the zoo from the school's playground with wire cutters and sneak in while we ditched class and smoked weed. I walked past the playground, climbed through the torn fence, and walked the zoo for hours. Afterward I went down into the canyon that lay at the other end behind the zoo and lit up a joint. I arrived at a section of the bridge that crossed over Highway 163. It felt freeing to just stand on that tiny bridge watching all the cars speed by. But that freeing feeling led me to wonder if I should end it all by jumping onto the highway below. I felt lonely and misunderstood. I held on to the rails at the edge of the bridge.

As I stood there listening to the cars go by below, I told myself that I should jump. The voice in my head became louder. I felt like I was the only one who had suffered what I did. And I so desperately didn't want to be different. Why couldn't I be like everybody else? Why couldn't I just make out with girls without feeling pressured into it? Why couldn't I just go back to reading books and coloring and playing chess with my dad when things had seemed familiarly chaotic but innocent? I hated that I had secrets.

I felt my thoughts shift, and a calming voice of reason took over. *You're not a coward, Jesse. Everything you've done, you have done to protect your family from that monster. Don't do this. Don't put your mom through more hurt than you already have.* Tears started to flow down my face. I regretted being mean to my mom. I didn't hate her. I just couldn't bear the love she had for me. How could she love a weirdo like me? The outcast. Although I didn't feel I deserved to be loved, there was a comfort in knowing that she loved me. I told myself to step down from the ledge. So I did.

I walked the dirt trails of the canyon as the smell of eucalyptus penetrated my senses. White people jogged by, paying me no mind. I envied white people their sense of freedom and privilege. They could do all these things like jogging, surfing, Rollerblading, flying kites, playing tennis or volleyball without a care about how goofy they looked. I couldn't do that in the hood. I had to always be on guard, hyperaware of how I appeared to the outside world.

As I walked closer to the Balboa Park side of the canyon, I noticed men walking the park in suits and military uniforms. I stared at them as they passed me, wondering what they were doing there. Then I saw two guys messing around in the bushes. One guy was going down on the other in broad daylight. I was intrigued. I kept walking and noticed guys checking me out as I passed by, and that irritated me.

What the fuck are they looking at? Can they tell I might be gay? Can they tell I've hooked up with men? Is it obvious—is that why they're looking at me? I didn't like feeling objectified out in the open.

I reached the top of the trails and sat on a bench in the open area of the park. It was a warm, sunny, clear-sky day in one of America's finest cities. It was a different world up here away from the trails. People walked their dogs, older Italians played boccie, and people strolled by lazily— blissfully unaware that here I was cutting school, having already smoked a joint and contemplated suicide that day. I felt as if no one could see what was happening—both in my own life and just a few steps behind me in the bushes. It felt bizarre, like I'd entered a different dimension.

I heard someone approach me from behind and say, "Hi. How are you?" I quickly turned around, and I didn't recognize the guy—a clean-cut, average-built white guy with salt-and-pepper hair on the sides and back of his head, though he was bald on top. He was dressed casually in blue jeans and a polo shirt. *I like his shirt. Another overly friendly white man making conversation.*

I started to turn back around, as I was unaccustomed to engaging in conversation with just anyone, but he continued, "I'm surprised to see you here. I was told you decided not to do this anymore."

"I have no clue what you're talking about. You don't know me."

He pulled some dollar bills from his pocket. "I met you at the store a few months ago and paid your friend a hundred fifty dollars. I can pay you seventy-five dollars if you let me suck it now."

I didn't know how to respond. I felt my heart speed up and my hands clench into fists as if I wanted to punch him. At the same time, I was taken aback by his audacity and intrigued at the thought of making that kind of money. I had never done sex work on my own before. He looked around and then back at me nervously and said, "So? Are you ready?"

Stuttering, I responded, "Nah, man, I don't know what you're talking about. I don't do that. And I definitely don't know who you are."

"Okay, okay. I get it. You want more money," he said.

"What if I give you a hundred dollars? Now you can cut out the middleman. How about it? One hundred dollars is my final offer."

This was still the eighties. And *that* was good money, more money than a kid my age would normally make. The most I'd made washing cars for legal money was forty dollars during an entire weekend.

The light bulb went off. I no longer had to wash so many cars to make money—or be trafficked at the store, where pretty much all the money was taken from me. Fuck being poor. When I was eleven years old, I asked my dad for five dollars to buy some coloring books and colored pencils. He said no. He told me that I needed to learn how to be a man and work for my own money. He told me I should get a paper route like my older brother. I decided that I would never ask my father for shit again. That weekend I grabbed a bucket from the garage and threw into it a bottle of my mom's dishwashing soap, a sponge, and some torn-up towels. Over my shoulder I carried the hose and up the hill I walked to the white-people neighborhood. I went knocking door to door asking people if I could wash their car for two dollars. Sometimes I would get a dollar in tips and if I was super lucky someone would give me a five-dollar bill. Assuming I didn't get any tips, in order to make forty dollars I would have to wash twenty cars on Saturday and Sunday for two dollars a car. That was a lot of fuckin work back then for a skinny eleven-year-old kid. When I did make thirty or forty dollars, I would give my mom ten or twenty and I'd keep the rest. I had never had a hundred dollars at one time.

The white guy showed me five twenty-dollar bills. My eyes widened. For a moment, I turned the idea over in my mind. Then, hesitantly, I said, "Yah, aight."

We went off the path, and he found a secluded place in the trees and told me to lean up against a tree. I checked to see if the tree had any ants first, then pulled off my creased white shirt, leaving only the tank top from underneath. The man squatted down, and I leaned the back of my head against the tree, shutting my eyes. I disconnected from myself again. It was all over within about a minute. He pulled himself back up and said, "Here, take your money, and let me give you some advice, kid. Next time, make sure you get the money in your hands first. I could have run off without paying you. And if the cops would have stopped us, all I'd have to say is that you tried to rob me. I'm white and you look like a gangster. Who do you think the cops would believe?"

As I stood there stunned, he handed me the money and walked away. I folded the bills and put them in my pocket. I didn't know what to say in return. *Thank you for the business advice? Come again soon?*

I'd made one hundred dollars in less than five minutes. Fuck being poor. After the business transaction with the white guy, I cased out the place, and it finally dawned on me that I was in the sex workers' section of the park. I noticed how the male sex workers postured themselves for better advertising. I noticed how they moved in and out of cars, unsuspected by the unfamiliar eye. I couldn't believe what I was seeing, and I was intrigued. I had come to this park throughout my childhood and had never noticed sex work-ers before. Why would I have? Now my eyes were open.

There were lots of boys who looked like they were be-tween fifteen and seventeen years old, which shocked me. For a minute I wondered who they were and what their lives were like. Why were they here? I also felt a sense of hope.

I thought to myself, *I can make some good money out here. My life's already fucked up. It's just a job. I just made more in a few minutes of work than my mom makes in a week with her shitty minimum-wage job as a school cafeteria worker. And just think—I was about to kill myself!*

While I was still coming to understand my own sexual-ity, I now knew one thing for sure: I was gay for pay.

As I watched the sex-work dynamics around me, I heard a voice say, "Sup, little homey?"

I turned around, and it was the Latino guy from the night before leaning against a tree. He'd seen me come out of the bushes with the white man. "So you're working the park? It's cool, holmes. We all do what we gotta do to get that feria, holmes. My name's Tito," he said as he walked toward me.

"Nah, it ain't like that," I said, getting into posture to fight.

He gestured, telling me to relax, and put his hand out to shake mine. "Look, it don't matter to me what you do, just don't take my clients and we good. But let me teach you a few things about how it works. It's rare to see Latinos like us out here, so you're going to get a lot of attention. I'll teach you how to make good money. But, most importantly, we gotta stick together out here because it can get ugly and dangerous. So what's your name?"

"I'm Tony," I lied.

"Follow me. I'll introduce you to some people, Tony."

"So you're gay? Or . . . ?" I asked him.

"Or . . ." He paused and laughed. "I'm gay, homeboy. It's not easy being gay and from the hood, but I'm not hiding who I am. I didn't hide when I was locked up in juvie, and I'm not hiding it out here. I've suffered too much to try to be anyone but me. If people don't like it, then fuck em. Why? Are you—"

"Nah, I ain't gay, holmes," I interrupted.

"Do you, homeboy. Ain't none of my business how you identify. We got all kinds of types out here in the park."

We walked up to a bench where two young white guys and one trans youth between the ages of thirteen and seventeen were talking.

"Hey, Tito—you got a port?" asked a skinny Black trans youth with severe acne. She had braided hair pulled up in a ponytail and couldn't have been more than sixteen.

"Yeah I do." Tito pulled out a pack of Newports and tossed it to her. "Y'all meet Tony. He's new here. We might be seeing more of him."

"Dayum, he fine," said one of the guys, making me feel uncomfortable. The Black girl joined in and said, "Hell yeah he is. By the way, I'm Jade," she said as she put her hand out for me to shake.

When I shook her hand, she leaned in and gave me a kiss on the cheek. I liked her friendliness. "This is Billy and Jimmy," she said, introducing me to the guys, who smiled.

"Yeah—he's cute," said Tito, smiling as he lit a cigarette.

"So how old are you?" asked Jade.

"I'm almost fourteen," I said, looking around awkwardly. All of a sudden I was self-conscious that someone might see me hanging out with this group. I reached into my pocket, pulled out a baggie of weed and some papers, and started to roll a joint.

"May I?" asked Jade, motioning for me to give her the stash and papers so she could roll.

"Go for it. Let's see if you got skills. Hopefully you won't tear the papers with your fake press-on nails." I laughed, talking shit. The group joined in on the laughter.

"Shiiiit, this queen got rolling skills, boo. Don't be hating on my nails just 'cause your little closet-case queen self ain't got the courage to wear em." Everyone laughed. So did I. She rolled a large joint that we all passed around.

As I took a hit, Jade pulled two cans of Olde English 800 from her backpack, opened one, and handed it to me with a smile. I took a swig and passed it to Tito. Jade opened the other can, took a swig, and passed it also. The sharing and camaraderie eased my discomfort. I'd never had a conversation with a group of gay people—let alone young gay people—outside of the storage room in the store. These people didn't look like me. They didn't act like me, except for Tito. The guys were white and flamboyant, and Jade was the first trans person I'd ever met. Also, Tito was the first gangster-looking homeboy and openly gay person I'd encountered. That above everything else was the most surreal—to meet someone who dressed like me, talked like me, but openly gay. I'd catch myself constantly looking over at him, up and down. *Damn, he's cute,* I thought to myself, and then I looked away, not believing that I had just met him the night before and couldn't even tell he was gay. I wondered if the Black guy with the dreads was gay, too. Was that why they'd been friendly with me the night before?

When we finished smoking the joint, Tito told the group, "I'm gonna show him around. I'll get up wit y'all later."

"Thanks for the weed and nice to meet you," said Jade, kissing me on the cheek goodbye as the others reiterated the appreciation.

While we walked through the park, Tito told me their stories. They were homeless kids whose parents threw them out when they found out they were gay and trans. They had nowhere to go. "There is one house that takes in gay youth, but it's always full. If the cops catch them on the streets, they get taken into the system, so they live in the park and do what they can to survive."

All this went way over my head. Changing the topic, I asked, "So when did you know and how old are you?"

"I'm nineteen. I always knew. But growing up around gangs in the hood, I couldn't show it or talk about it. So I hid it. Until I got locked up in juvie at twelve. I did two years and got out at fourteen. My cellie and I hooked up when we were alone until he got out. I got comfortable with my sexuality while incarcerated, but I had to fight a lot. And when I got out, I had nowhere to go. My mom was strung out on heroin and my dad in and out of jail, so I turned to the streets and eventually ended up here, living in the park, until I met my dude, who you met last night."

"Your dude? Like dude dude? Like boyfriend?"

He laughed, "Kinda. Not really. Well, it's complicated. Let's just say we take care of each other. Cool?"

I didn't dig any further. The rest of the afternoon we walked around and smoked more weed. He showed me all the ins and outs of the park that were invisible to those unfamiliar. He showed me places where I could take potential clients and paths to run if I need to escape from police raids.

My new career began. I learned that I could capitalize on a niche market, fulfilling the masculine male Latino sexual fantasy of white men. "No one else out here looks like us. It was just me until you came along," Tito said. "But it's cool."

Finally, I felt understood. Accompanied. I was not alone. Not broken. I smiled.

△▽△

When I got home, it didn't occur to me that it was weird no one was around. I was thinking about my time in the park when I noticed a note taped to the TV screen.

Nerd—Amá is in the hospital. She had a heart attack. They rushed her to the ER from work. Stay home until we call you.

No fuckin way. Here I am getting high, being a fuckin ho in the park, and my mom had a heart attack. Fuck!

The note didn't say which hospital she was at. I called Ariyel crying, scared. I didn't know what to do.

"Calm down, Nerd. I'm sure she's okay. Just be patient

and wait. Hang up the phone in case they try calling you. Do you want me to ask my mom to take me over there to wait with you?"

"Nah, it's okay. I'll just wait here. Maybe I should start calling the different hospitals?"

"Just wait, Nerd. Just wait."

They never called. I waited anxiously for hours, begging God to please take care of my mom, overwhelmed with guilt for how my sex abuse had stressed her heart. When my dad, brother, and little sister finally walked in, I asked, crying, "Where's Mom? Is she okay?"

"Sí, está bien," said my dad. *She stayed sleeping. Now you go to sleep.*

I went to lie down in my bed, and I couldn't stop thinking about my mom and about death and about what would happen to me if she died. *She is all I have in this world that loves me. What will I do?*

I cried into my pillow until I eventually drifted off from exhaustion.

△▽△

The next morning, I begged my dad to take me with him to see my mom at the hospital. I started crying as I stood at the entrance of her room. Seeing her connected to wires and machines scared me. My gasps woke her. I ran to her bedside and tried to wrap my arms around her in a hug. She kissed the top of my head as I cried into her hospital gown.

"Amá, I'm so sorry. I'm sorry I made you sick. I'm sorry you're in here because of me. I make you worry so much that you had a heart attack. Perdóname, Amá."

My dad stared coldly at me from the doorway. The doctor walked in as I cried.

"And you must be Jesse, the studious one," said the doctor to me.

I tried to smile in between the tears and said, "I am. Who told you?"

"Your amá told me. She's so proud of you. I need to do a few more tests before she can go home."

"So what happened? Did she really have a heart attack?"

"She did. And she'll need to make some serious changes. Her weight, high blood pressure, high cholesterol, and stress will only exacerbate the problem."

"Sí, eso es lo que le pasa por ser una pinche ballena gorda," joked my dad. *Yup, that's what she gets for being a fat fuckin whale.*

"Do you want me to tell him to leave?" the doctor asked Amá in broken Spanish.

"Ignore him, Doc," said Amá.

"This is how it is at home all the time," I said quietly to the doctor.

"I'll wait for you outside. I have a lot of things to do today. So hurry up and say goodbye to your mom," my dad said to me, then walked out of the room.

Amá came home in a taxi the next day. Apá never went to pick her up.

Angry, I vowed to make enough money to buy a car so we wouldn't have to depend on my dad anymore. Within months, I bought my first car, a brown two-door 1971 Buick LeSabre for five hundred dollars cash. I was fourteen years old and in the ninth grade. My brother registered it in his name because I wasn't old enough to even have a learner's permit. I had handed him the cash, and he never asked me how I got the money. The deal was that I'd put up the cash and my brother could drive wherever he wanted as long as I could drive once in a while without our parents knowing.

The car helped a lot with groceries, and it helped us bring my mom to her doctor's appointments as her health kept deteriorating. Going to the doctor became routine. She was diagnosed with high blood pressure, diabetes, heart problems, and rheumatoid arthritis throughout her body, which explained why her hands had started locking up every once in a while when dicing vegetables or washing dishes.

△▽△

Midway through my ninth-grade year, my mom filed for a divorce. All the fighting had pushed my brother to move out. He'd found an apartment that he shared with friends. Luckily for me, he left the car for emergencies.

My father's womanizing took on new forms of disrespect. Women started calling the house at various hours of the day and night. Over the phone, they called my mom a bitch and an idiot and threatened to steal her husband. My mom would simply hang up.

"Please have some dignity and don't give out our home

number to these random women you're sleeping with. This is the home of your children. Have some respect. If not for me, then at least for them," my mom pleaded with him.

"Don't tell me what the fuck to do. If you were half the woman they are and knew how to please a man, then I wouldn't do what I do."

My brother's leaving was the last straw for Amá. One day I came home to find my dad was gone, and I learned the papers had been filed. His departure left a void—I was familiar with his chaos and toxic masculinity. The house became quieter without him. Financially it made little difference, since Amá carried the family and I chipped in as often as I could now, with my brother gone.

Then one evening, at around six thirty, halfway through my second semester of ninth grade, after I'd left school and turned tricks at the park for a few hours, I came home to find my mom sitting on the bathroom floor with blood all around her legs. She looked defeated with a blank, confused, almost scared expression on her face. It looked like she had slipped on her own blood trying to get up. I was terrified.

"Amá!" I screamed. I went to help her up, ignoring the blood, but she wouldn't move.

"Me duele, mijo. No me quiero mover." *It hurts, my son. I don't want to move.*

No longer crying, I said in a stern voice, "You have no fuckin choice. Either I call 911 and the ambulance is going to come and make a big scene or you're getting in the fuckin car now to go to the emergency room. You fuckin decide."

I helped her sit on the toilet and dampened a towel to wipe the blood from her legs. Still she tried to help me.

"Ya, ya, mijo. Yo puedo." *There, there, my son. I can do it.*

I called Ariyel, and then I helped my mom wrap a folded bedsheet around her waist in case she started bleeding more. We helped her into the Buick and I drove her to the ER, afraid I'd get pulled over for being underage. As I drove, I looked at Amá and noticed how pale she was. I was too scared and determined to get us to the hospital safely to even cry.

Once we arrived at the ER, Amá seemed too weak to walk, so I ran in first and begged for a wheelchair. A nurse came out to help me, and they took Amá in while I went to park the car. In the ER they ran a bunch of tests and found she had sixteen large fibroids that were causing blood clots and bleeding. They rushed her into surgery to do a dilation and curettage, an extremely painful procedure where the insides of the uterine walls are scraped to clear everything out.

A little over one year later, she was hemorrhaging again. This time it was the summer between tenth and eleventh grades. I was fifteen years old. "Mijo," my mom said, "let's go to Tijuana. I heard there's a doctor there, a gynecologist, who might be able to run some tests to find out what's going on. I saved some money, so let's go."

I drove Amá to Tijuana to a tiny doctor's clinic. It was nothing fancy. It was in a commercial space on the ground floor of a two-story building with apartments upstairs. Inside, a small waiting room with a desk, a phone, and a door separated the doctor's quarters from the entrance. A woman welcomed us and took our payment. The doctor came and escorted us to the back. He asked me to leave and I refused. "It's my mom. I don't mind seeing her naked. With her permission, I'm not leaving her alone after what we've been through." After my mom undressed from the waist down and put her legs in stirrups with a sheet covering her, more to keep her warm than for privacy, she explained to the doctor what had happened. "Forgive my son. We are just very scared that I'm bleeding again and afraid those gringo doctors are misdiagnosing me on purpose."

He told her he was concerned and wanted her to get some X-rays and other tests. When the images came back, he told her she had cancer in her uterus and cysts throughout her fallopian tubes.

"All of this could have been avoided. Had you come here years ago, we could have solved this problem. Them gringo doctors aren't helping you any. I'll write a report, and you will take that with the images and demand the doctors do something. But unfortunately, you will need a full hysterectomy at this point. Don't let them tell you otherwise. It's the only solution to stop the cancer from spreading. Demand to get a second opinion.

"Don't let him tell you no—that's what I hate about the gringo system, it refuses to offer healing treatment to avoid spending money, which keeps people sick. As a matter of fact, don't make an appointment with your doctor. Go to the emergency room because of your blood clotting and show the ER doctor these images and this letter."

On the drive home across the border and to the ER, I was upset at her diagnosis and at the fact that my mom hadn't received the care she needed and deserved from the hospitals in San Diego. Amá, however, tried to look at the positive.

"We can't avoid the past, mijo. And if surgery is the best solution, so be it. May God keep watching over us."

"God? Where the fuck has God been all this time?" I yelled.

Now she seemed deflated. "Thank you, mijo, for helping me. It's not for me to question a doctor, especially when I only went to fifth grade in Mexico, mijo. I wish I was smart and knew how to communicate to them in English. But I don't, mijo. This is my fault."

"It's not your fault, Mom." But the care she'd been getting was all we could afford. Other healthcare options were too expensive.

Amá was deferential to the doctor because we were poor and uneducated. In Amá's eyes, it wasn't proper to challenge a doctor. There were no patient advocates at hospitals focused on helping Latinos. When we got back to San Diego, Amá was rushed into another surgery, only this time—they performed the full hysterectomy.

△▽△

The nightmares I'd had since my molestation at the shop started coming back with a vengeance and turned into violent night terrors. Amá's declining health and the nights I spent in the park, as well as the collapse of my parents' marriage, all haunted me as I slept. The nightmares always started with me walking into a bright, colorful, bustling hallway at school. Then I would find myself in a long, dirty, and abandoned hospital corridor where the lights were flickering on and off. I'd look into rooms, and as I passed them, I'd see people I knew, like Ariyel, in the beds, with Kaposi's lesions on their bodies. I'd end up in the last room, which was brightly lit. There I'd see myself, skinny, with Kaposi's sarcoma, gasping for air, eyes wide open, looking up at myself standing by the bed in fear. I couldn't scream and was alone, looking at myself dying in agony. That was when I always awoke, screaming.

I had yet to see my first AIDS-related death, which made the nightmares even scarier, as if they were premonitions of what was to come. There were no movies about HIV at the time, and the diagnosis was still a death sentence, common in my line of work and in the gay community in general.

A few months later, Billy, one of the white boys I'd met at the park, got small dark purple marks across his face, neck, and arms. He didn't know what they were. I told him to go to the hospital. I heard he ended up at the AIDS hospice, where he later died.

CHAPTER 9

From tenth to twelfth grade, I was living many different lives. At school, I was a straight, inner-city, wannabe-gangster kid who dated girls. I had friends. I was high all the time. Occasionally I stole cars and shoplifted. I broke into abandoned warehouses and lofts downtown, and threw crazy nitrous- and candy-flipping (a mix of Ecstasy and acid) parties. I partied across the border in Tijuana. All this I hid from Amá.

I also worked at the park more as my drug habits developed. I made twenty to fifty dollars per person, which helped pay for whatever I was into at the time: smoking weed, using PCP, sniffing paint thinner or spray paint, or doing crystal meth.

I was also the lonely teenager who took refuge at Ariyel's house when I was not at home. She lived a happy, sheltered life. Her house was decorated in nice matching furniture. There were real crystal candleholders, ones she actually used, with scented candles on her coffee table. We'd play gin rummy for hours while listening to 45s on her pink-and-white record player and talking about anything and everything under the sun. Her bedding was pink, purple, and white, and her bedroom furniture matched. Her home was calming and serene and provided an escape from the tensions at mine.

One night I convinced Ariyel to sneak out and go with me to a house party at another friend's deep in the barrio. She had never sneaked out before. We were both nervous. We turned the doorknob on the back kitchen door slowly, trying not to make a sound.

Our friend's house was awkwardly positioned between industrial warehouses, which was convenient for a house party with a DJ and loud music. The streets were poorly lit and had cracked pavement. The house was a large Craftsman with a long dirt driveway that led to a large dirt-and-cement backyard with big lemon and orange trees. The backyard was surrounded by a tall wooden fence, which opened up to a back alley. Our friend's dad fixed low-riders back there, so there were two beat-up oldies, a '57 Chevy and a '63 Impala, parked in the yard among the partygoers. It was our friend's older sister's birthday party.

As we approached, we saw a group of older gangsters on the front porch. They ignored us as we walked down the drive toward the red-and-blue party lights. Cholos and cholas were sitting and standing around the back fence drinking and laughing among themselves. Other friends of ours were dancing to Debbie Deb's "When I Hear Music." It was feeling like a fun family environment when all of a sudden gunshots rang out. We all hit the ground except for Ariyel. She didn't know what to do and froze in place until I grabbed her and yanked her down with everyone else. We crawled behind the DJ booth between the house and the yard, from where we heard the tires of cars speeding away. The gangsters at the party ran toward the front and got into their cars to chase the cars that sped away. As soon as I thought it was clear, I grabbed Ariyel.

"Follow me and run to the car," I yelled toward her. Not looking back, we bolted to my Buick and sped home. The adrenaline was a huge rush for me. Ariyel was panicking out of shock, but I laughed the entire way home. I dropped her off and waited for her to sneak back into her house. On my way home I took a detour to the park to see if I could make some money. It was around 1:00 a.m. As I approached the park, police lights lit up behind me. The moment I saw them in my rearview mirror, I knew I was in deep shit. My heart pumped in my chest, pulsing in my ears as I gripped the steering wheel. My whole car lit up red and blue from the flashing lights.

I wasn't more than a few miles from one of the wildest parties I'd been to in a while. And with wild parties always come wild drugs. I knew I had a vial of PCP on me, probably worth a thousand dollars, and an eight ball of crystal meth. I'd gotten them from some homey at the party who I couldn't even remember now. I hadn't given it a thought at the time, but I could feel the weight of those vials in my pocket as the lights came closer behind me.

I had a decision to make. I was either going to attempt a high-speed getaway and risk getting killed, or let the cop pull me over and also risk getting killed, but if not, pray that the cop didn't search the car. The 1971 Buick LeSabre had long front seats like a couch. I had torn the stitching along the leather for just this situation, thinking I could stash any drugs inside the cushion. I quickly stuffed the vial of PCP and the bag of crystal under the foam padding of the seat beneath me.

The cop walked to the driver's side window holding his gun in one hand and a flashlight in the other, pointed right at my face. He asked for my driver's license and registration and said something about a busted taillight. I murmured back that I didn't have a driver's license, but I showed him the vehicle registration, trying to play as cool as I could. He asked me how old I was and if I had any form of identification.

"Um, I've got a school ID on me. I just turned fifteen years old." I fumbled with my words, trying to think of any way to get out from under his glare. "I, uh, just left a house party, so I didn't think to bring no ID. My cousin got drunk and left me stranded with the car keys while he went off with his girlfriend. I understand it's past my curfew, Officer, and I am sorry, but I had to get myself home. No one would drive me because everyone was drunk." I pleaded for him to understand.

Clearly he knew I was lying. I thanked God I wasn't high.

He looked at my ID and then asked me to step out of the car with his gun pointed at me. I was scared but figured it best I cooperate. It was dark and no one seemed to be around. Then came the famous words, "Assume the position." Before I could assume the position, he put his gun away and slammed me hard on the trunk of my car. The impact of the cold metal against my face made my head rock backward. As the top of my body lay flat against the car trunk, he kicked my legs open and managed to get handcuffs on me. My face and head were throbbing as my cheek lay on the cold surface of the car when he squeezed the handcuffs tight. I screamed, "Ow, that hurts!"

He laughed, pulled me up, and then slammed me hard on the trunk a few more times. I felt like a rag doll being tossed around as the metal handcuffs burned and tore my wrists. He dragged me toward the back door of his car, pulling on the handcuffs. With his free hand he opened the door and threw me in. My wrists, face, chest, and head were pulsing. It felt like blood was pouring from my wrists onto my hands. I was out of breath, and I didn't know what to do.

He walked back to my car and searched it. I wondered why no other cop car had shown up for backup. The cop searched for ten or fifteen minutes, opening compartments and checking under the seats, while I sat there praying he wouldn't find my stash. When he finished, he walked toward me. Every step he took pounded through my body. He opened the back door of the cruiser and laughed at me, his mouth open wide. The vial of PCP and the bag of crystal were in his hand.

"So it looks like I have a tough decision to make here." He laughed. "Do you know how much time this vial will get you? Or even this bag of crystal?" He paused for dramatic effect, slipping both into his shirt pocket, and said, "But I'm sure this will come in handy some other time."

What he meant, I don't know. Maybe he was going to use it, sell it, or plant it on someone. All these thoughts raced through my mind even as he walked back to my car, turned off my headlights, grabbed my keys, closed my doors, and called someone on his radio. Next thing I knew, I was headed downtown.

I was not booked but placed in a room with a desk and a chair by myself. No picture of me was taken. I found this odd but didn't know what to expect. It was my first time at a police station. I sat there anxiously waiting, nervous as hell about my mom finding out. Within thirty minutes the cop pulled me out of the room and walked me outside to where my mom and brother were waiting for me. It was around 3:00 a.m. My mom, wearing her pajamas, looked cold and angry, shaking her head in disapproval. My brother, in a sweatsuit and slippers, squinted his eyes at me.

The cop looked at me with a sly smirk and told my mom in front of me, "Please keep an eye on him and make sure he doesn't get into trouble. He shouldn't be driving a car at his age. And he should not be out past his ten p.m. curfew. I am letting him go this time. Others won't be as nice as I am."

The cop handed my mom a copy of a citation for me to appear in court and the car keys. My mom, crying, told my brother to tell the cop that she'd thought I was sleeping at Ariyel's house, the car parked outside her house. My brother told the cop what she said, but the cop ignored her and told my brother where the car was parked now. My brother didn't say anything else.

I sighed in relief that I wasn't arrested, figuring the cop didn't want to run the risk of me ratting him out for taking my stash of drugs. I felt lucky.

We walked to the car in silence, the gravel crunching loudly under our shoes, until my mom said, crying, "¿Ay, Jesse, qué voy a hacer contigo?"

My brother drove us home in his own car, a dark blue 1984 Buick Regal he'd just bought. He was eighteen years old. On the way, he had me show them where the car was. He looked at me through the rearview mirror, shook his head, and started a yelling session that would last the entire way home. "If you're going to be a badass, at least don't get caught, you fuckin dumbass."

When we got home, my brother rode his bike to where the car was. Then he threw his bike in the back seat and brought the car home. My mom didn't say a word other than "You're sitting there and not going to bed until your brother gets home." The silence was enough to stress her disappointment in me. We sat in the dark with the candle to the Virgencita dimly lighting the room. I couldn't tell if Amá silently cried. She showed no reaction or movement.

△▽△

My brother forbid me to drive the car from then on, so I had to resort to riding the bus to school once again. He had moved home after getting his girlfriend pregnant with his first child. A few days later, I told him what happened and how the cop took all the drugs I had been planning on selling. "You need to quit fucking around and get your shit together. Look at what you're doing to Amá."

My brother knew I smoked weed and drank and occasionally smoked PCP, but he didn't know about the crystal meth. He assumed I'd bought the car with money from selling drugs, not sex work. Amá, I assumed, had an idea of the pot smoking; I'm sure she'd smelled it on me. But she didn't know about the rest. How would an immigrant mom know about crystal meth and PCP? These weren't things she was exposed or accustomed to.

I'd wake up, open my drawer, pull out my hidden stash of crystal and do a line, hop in the shower, and get ready for school. On the walk to the bus stop I would light a joint and smoke it until the bus arrived. Every morning the driver was the same: an older Chicano man. I'd show him my bus pass, and he'd always just smile at me and say, "One day at a time." I'd nod with a *What's up?* and think to myself that the dude was weird.

My addiction took off hard-core when I started mixing crystal meth with heroin. I was at a hotel party when some guys told me about this crystal called peanut butter. They told me I had to smoke it in foil because it was too chunky and creamy to sniff. I decided to eat a little bit instead. It tasted nasty going down my throat. I got a rush, but I preferred regular crystal. Peanut butter felt different, but according to them I hadn't done enough. When they told me it was crystal meth mixed with heroin and that I would get the full effect by smoking it, I told them they were crazy. I wasn't about to freebase. I vowed never to do it again, but a few months later, out of curiosity and self-hatred, I melted some heroin in a spoon, poured it over some crystal on aluminum foil, mixed it to a chunky consistency, and smoked it alone. The effects were similar to those of a speedball, with the euphoric, orgasmic feeling of heroin and the elevated rush of crystal meth balancing each other out. It was a heavenly feeling, and I came back to it again and again. I no longer wanted to see anyone who didn't get high, not even Ariyel.

△▽△

Before I was sixteen, I was a full-on sex worker in various San Diego neighborhoods. I would tell my mom I'd be at Ariyel's and stay out all night. My clients were mostly "straight" married businessmen, military men, and less often gay-"identified" men. Many of the married men preferred anonymous sex with someone they could pay because they didn't want the risk of someone falling in love with them. Discretion was a must, especially if I wanted repeat business. Rarely would anyone ask my age. And when they asked, they didn't care.

I played the roles I needed to play. I was Carlos, Jose, Tony, Xavier, Adrian, Robbie, Miguel, or any other name that would come to mind. The sadness of the reality I was living eventually caught up with me, and the pain became unbearable. To lose my name was to lose myself. I lived a constant masquerade. I was one person at home, irritable and difficult to talk to. I was a different person at school—fun, in with the cool crowd. At the park and in the streets, I was a sex worker—used to being objectified with no human value other than sex.

My encounters were all business transactions, yet I felt less and less human each time. I wanted to have a regular family life where I wasn't an irritable asshole and was a good student, a good son, and a good friend. They were all parts of me that never came together. I felt pulled in different directions. And I was great at convincing myself that I had no other choice. Each time I got into a car with a stranger and each time I walked into a bush with someone, I told myself that this was my reality so I just had to make the best of it.

I believed that my value came from sex, and my therapist did nothing to work with me through these issues. How I kept prostituting myself as a child with her knowing yet not doing anything about it baffled me. Therapy was an obligation that I had to fulfill as part of the victim witness program. I kept going, hoping that one day it would help, that it would work and make me well.

I rarely spoke with other sex workers anymore. The people from that original group were all gone. AIDS was rampant and people died young. As my drug use escalated, I stopped trusting others. Faces changed often and didn't stay around long. Only me and the Black dude with dreads were constants. But he wasn't a sex worker; he was a drug dealer. Sometimes I would see other groups of sex workers laughing, bonding, or joking around, and I'd feel a sense of loneliness and isolation come over me. Sometimes one of them would walk up to me and start a conversation, but short antisocial responses would usually give them the hint that they should leave me alone. A part of me didn't want to get to know anyone out there—for what?—they'd just disappear soon. Besides, none of them even knew my real name.

One night I met a guy in the park who drove a small red truck that looked like it was used for construction work. He was a tall, skinny, very pale blond white guy who claimed to be straight and married. He wore faded blue jeans with construction boots and a white T-shirt. He walked toward me, smiled, and said hello as he grabbed his crotch.

It was around 8:30 p.m., and customers and workers strolled casually in the dark. The man asked my name; I gave him a fake one without even thinking about it.

He asked me what I was doing. I said, "Nothing. Seeing what I could get into."

"What are you into?"

"Depends," I said.

He laughed nervously. "Depends on what? Are you a cop?"

"No. Are you?"

He said no and then asked how much for him to blow me.

I told him a hundred and he laughed. "I'll give you twenty," he said.

It was the same routine over and over again, only the

faces changed. I laughed again with a cute, sexy smile and said, "Oh hell nah, man. Find yourself someone else. I can do ninety dollars."

"How about fifty? It's my best offer, bro. I'm married and can't spend too much money. I need some cash for the kid's diapers. You know how it is? But I'm horny."

"Really, fifty dollars? Give me seventy-five and it's a wrap," I told him. We landed on seventy dollars.

"You seem too young to be out here," he said.

I laughed and said, "Nah, man. I'm old enough."

We took off in his truck. I took him behind the San Diego Zoo to a dead-end street above Highway 163, along the bridge I'd wanted to jump off a couple years before. It was a great place to take clients who were exhibitionists as it provided the rush of potentially being seen by the highway traffic below. I opened the door after we parked, but he grabbed my arm and said, "Nah, man. I'm too nervous to get out. Let's just hook up here in the truck."

"Come on, man. Let loose and experience life," I said as I shook free of his arm, walked to the front of the truck, and hopped on the hood.

He turned off the headlights, walked out, and asked, "Now what?"

I leaned back on the windshield. He jumped on the hood and went to work. Within seconds bright lights were shining on us. I pushed him off and he rolled off the hood, hitting the ground hard.

I quickly jumped off the hood and adjusted my pants. We hadn't heard the cop car pull up because of the sounds of cars on the highway below. Over the police megaphone, we heard the unmistakable voice of a cop: "Step away from the vehicle with your hands in the air."

The guy was standing up, dusting himself off. "Oh shit, oh shit. What now?" he kept murmuring.

"Just shut the fuck up," I spit, "and let me do the talking. Just go along with me. Trust me."

My eyes were still adjusting to the bright lights, but it was clear that the cop walking toward us had his hand on his gun. I spoke up first and said, "Good evening, Officer? Is there a problem here?"

The cop, a tall, Black, and handsome man with a football player's build, could not believe my audacity. He stood directly in front of me and said, "'Is there a problem here?' Are you seriously asking me if there is a problem here? You tell me, smart-ass. What do you think the problem is? Both of you show me your IDs now. I can take you both to jail for what you're doing out here in public."

I laughed and with a smart-ass voice responded, "You didn't even pay a fee for the peep show, homeboy. Did you enjoy it, Officer?"

The cop said, "Man, shut up and give me your ID."

The white guy was pulling his ID out of his wallet when I said, "Hold up, man. I don't have an ID. I'm fifteen years old and only have my high school ID."

They both quickly turned their heads toward me.

As the white guy held a hand out with his ID, he told the cop, "I had no idea, Officer. Please. I had no idea."

I jumped in to defend the white guy and said, "Yeah,

man, he had no idea. I met him at a coffee shop and hit on him. I told him I was eighteen and he believed me. Let him go. He had nothing to do with this."

The white guy turned his head to look at me in disbelief and said, "You told me you were eighteen. Why did you lie to me, man? I have a family. Don't you realize you could destroy my life?"

The cop jumped in and said, "You both shut the fuck up!" He looked over at the white guy and said, "He is still a minor. Give me your ID." The cop grabbed the ID out of the white guy's hand and asked, "So you have kids?"

"Yes. A nine-month-old daughter."

"You make me sick, man. So your wife is at home with your daughter while you're out here sucking this kid's dick? I should take you in and lock you up right now. You know what they'll do to you in prison?"

I quickly told the cop, "Nah, man. Let him go, Officer. He seriously had no clue. This shit would devastate his family, so please let him go."

The cop looked at me, then looked at him, and then looked back at me. He handed the guy his driver's license and said, "Go on, get in your car and get the fuck out of here before I change my mind."

The white guy looked at me with disgust, shook his head as he got into his truck, and drove off. The cop stood there staring at me in disbelief. He then grabbed me by the back of my T-shirt and pulled me toward his car. He slammed me hard against the side of the cop car, pulling one hand behind my back and then the other, handcuffing me. He put the cuffs on so tight that I knew my wrists would be bruised the next day. He opened the back door of the cruiser and pushed my head down with one hand while his other hand was on my arm, directing me into the back seat. He slammed the door shut, got into the front seat, and just sat there. The cop turned off all the car's lights and looked at me through the mirror.

"So now what do I do with you?"

"Why don't you and I continue the show? I haven't gotten down with a cop in uniform yet. I'll keep the handcuffs on while you suck my dick on the hood of the police car." I heard myself say this as I stared back at him through the mirror. I couldn't believe what was coming out of my mouth. But I didn't care.

"Hell nah, little man. That ain't gonna happen. I'm married with kids. My son is your age. I would kill him if I found him out here doin what you doin," he said. His tone had started as one of disgust but quickly turned to empathy and sadness when he brought up his son.

"Yeah, I bet he's a good kid, too. Prolly plays sports and gets good grades in school with his daddy being a cop, right? You make sure he got good friends, too?"

He stared at me through the mirror and shook his head. "Wow. Where do your parents think you are?"

I pictured his son playing sports with other kids. I was jealous of this kid who had a father who cared. "They think I'm spending the night at my best friend's house," I said, then added, "But why do you care, anyway? You're just a sellout pig arresting your own kind, you fuckin sellout motherfucker."

"Is that what you think I am? A sellout pig?" he said with a sneer. "I could have taken you both to jail. Now I'm stuck here with you and need to figure out what to do next. Kid, there is a god watching over you. You"—he paused—"remind me of my son."

"Well, I ain't your son. If I was, I am sure my life would be totally different, but it's not. Just take me to my best friend's house, where my mom thinks I am, and we can both pretend nothing happened. You won't ever see me again."

"Just be quiet a minute and let me think. I can't arrest you, because I let the other guy go," he added. "I have to drive you home and tell your parents what I caught you doing and hope they are willing to get you some help. You're too young to be putting your life in danger like this. Don't you love yourself, lil man? Don't you think your parents love you? You need help."

His compassion made me want to be held by him. Hugged by him. I wanted to feel protected by him. But I knew that could never happen. So I became angry over the confusing emotions.

"Look, you punk-ass motherfucker, you ain't a fuckin psychologist, so just let me fuckin go." I jerked against the already tight cuffs, feeling them dig deeper into my skin, but I didn't care. I kicked the back of his seat.

What poured out of me next shocked me to my core: "I am confused about my sexuality. I might be gay, but I don't fuckin know." Still I screamed; still I struggled, even as I had this revelation. "I have girlfriends, but I keep hooking up with guys for money."

I sat there, handcuffed, with my forehead pressed against

the metal screen between the front and back seats. Tears flowed down my face. I cried loudly near his ear as he cranked the engine and started to drive. He ignored me and asked for my address. I began to bang my head on the metal screen, screaming, "You motherfucker, you can't do this. You can't tell my parents. You can't."

He continued ignoring me until I gave him my address in between sobs. Then I became quiet with my head pressed against the metal screen. Every few blocks I'd scream at him, "Please! Please don't!" but my fight was petering out.

"You said you have a son my age. Imagine if a cop brought him home late one night and knocked on your door to tell you he caught your son getting a blow job from an older man in a public park. What would you do? How would you feel? Please don't mess up my life more than it already is." The whole way home, he was quiet, while I sobbed in defeat. I didn't want to disappoint my amá more than I already had, and I was terrified of what would happen if my dad found out.

When we pulled up, the cop opened the back door. I sat there very still, crying with my head down. He said, "Come on out."

I said no in a very low voice.

"Come on. I don't want to have to drag you out."

"You're going to go home after work and walk into a nice home where you'll be greeted by your wife and your son full of joy and go live your happy life while I'm stuck here in this fucked-up ghetto-ass apartment with a brother who hates me, a father I always disappoint, and a mother who doesn't know what to do with me. You're fucking up my life more than you know," I told him.

"Come on. Get out of the car. You're not such a badass now, are you? Get out. Now." His voice was firm and unwavering.

I did as he said. He grabbed the handcuffs and led me forward. My wrists were numb by this point. He knocked hard on the screen door. No answer. When he knocked again, harder, a light came on in the bedroom. We heard a voice from the other side ask in broken English, "Who is it?" but it sounded like "Who eeess seeet?"

My mom looked out the curtain and saw the cop standing there as he said, "It's the police. Open the door."

The neighbor's porch light went on and their door opened as Amá opened our door. The neighbor popped his head out, shook it in disgust, and went back in. My mother looked at the cop and then back at me and, with tears in her eyes, asked, "¡Ay, Jesse! ¿Qué pasó? ¿Qué hiciste?"

The cop asked if she spoke English as my brother's head appeared behind her.

"Yes. A little," my mom said.

My brother spoke up. "I speak English. What did my dumbass brother do this time?"

The cop looked over at me, sighed, and slowly turned me around to take off my handcuffs. He told my mom, "I caught Jesse hanging out with some friends at a park. Everyone was over eighteen except him. They were not causing any problems other than being loud. There were no alcohol or drugs involved. I'm bringing your son home because it's past curfew and I don't want to take him to Juvenile Hall for you to pick up or for him to get a record. He is a very nice young man. Please talk to him. He needs someone to listen to him." He looked at me with a stern face and said, "I hope I don't ever see you again. Be good to yourself."

I stared at him with disbelief in my teary eyes. He walked away, down the stairs and out to the front of the apartment complex, not looking back.

"Gracias, Officer, for bringing my son," my mom said as he kept walking. He didn't say another word to me.

This could have been the moment that changed a person's life, but not for me. Instead, I went on a rampage.

CHAPTER 10

One summer night before my senior year, I met a guy named George at a loft party. I was sixteen years old. George was thirty-six. He was with a bald, white, skinhead-looking guy named Micky who was covered in tattoos, into urban art and graffiti, and loved dating Chicanos. We got high together and then they talked about the urban art movement and reminisced about living together in Spain. They talked about their love of foreign and independent films. I just listened.

That night they invited me to go to Los Angeles. It was to be a short visit, and George promised to bring me back to San Diego the next day. Since it was a Friday and I was out of school, I decided to go. That overnight trip turned into almost two weeks of straight partying. I called my mom to tell her I was staying at Ariyel's house for the weekend, but when Monday came, I called and told her the truth; that I was in LA with some friends. My mom begged me to come home. I hung up on her.

George got me a fake ID from one of his friends in East LA, which got me into all the trendy Hollywood clubs, like my favorite, named Does Your Mama Know? Afterward we'd end up at someone's mansion party in Beverly Hills or Bel Air. I hardly slept the first few days. The glamorous after-parties at the mansions were out of this world, with top DJs, endless supplies of drugs, and sex everywhere. I never thought I'd experience this kind of nightlife being a poor Mexican kid from the ghetto.

After a few days of partying, doing drugs, and sleeping with each other, George grew tired of driving me to the pay phone to call my mom. He knew how old I was. One night after taking me to the pay phone, he drove me to East LA instead of his house in Hollywood. We pulled up to an abandoned house and got out of the car. A few homeboys were hanging out on the front porch. They nodded to him. I followed him through the house, which was full of people shooting dope—it was a shooting gallery. We walked to a trailer in the backyard and he knocked on the door. Someone pulled the curtain and looked out and then his white skinhead-looking friend, Micky, opened the door. We walked in. He had a crystal meth lab going.

"I need you to watch over him for a few days," George said to Micky, *him* meaning me. "I have a lot of shit to do and can't take care of him."

"Yeah, I guess. He can stay here, but you know nothing's for free. He'll have to help me out with the cooking to earn his keep," said Micky.

They talked about me like I was a dog that needed a pet sitter.

"Here," George said, "take this money to buy whatever

you need," as he handed me a wad of bills. Then he reached into his backpack and pulled out a brick of weed and an eight ball of crystal and said, "The crystal's for you, but sell the weed to make some pocket money until I come back to get you."

Then he motioned for Micky to talk to him outside. There I was, alone in a trailer in the backyard of some shooting gallery in East LA, wondering how I ended up there. Micky walked back in, went to the fridge, and pulled out beers for the both of us.

"Don't get too comfortable. Cooking lessons start now," he said.

After a few hours of teaching me how to cook crystal meth, he took me to my first gay Latino bar. We walked in behind a cholo and a chola who were holding hands like they were a couple. But as soon as they got in, the cholo and chola separated hands and each walked to their own section. The chola started making out with some other chola and the homeboy started hugging a bunch of homeboys who looked like straight gangsters, only gay. These guys could not be out publicly and would not go to West Hollywood as they felt they had nothing in common with gay white people.

My jaw must have dropped, because Micky said, "Dude, don't stare so much. Mostly everyone here just can't be out in the real world or they'll get killed. Bars like this provide a safe space for people to meet and socialize. But don't piss anyone off. People will think you're mad dogging them if you stare too much. Come on and I'll introduce you to some homeboys so you don't feel alone when you come out by yourself."

"Come out by myself? Fuck you, dude! I ain't gay," I said.

Micky laughed. He knew I was in denial. "Pleeeeze! C'mon, holmes. It's only a couple years before you decide to come out. Just chill out."

I changed the subject. "So what are you doing here if you're not Mexican?" I asked him. "And why do you live in a trailer in East LA? What's up? You trying to be Mexican?"

Micky laughed and said, "These people are my clients. I sell crystal. Where does all my money go? Why do I live in an almost abandoned trailer in East LA? Well, I don't pay rent, and most of my money goes to my medication. I have AIDS, little homey. Not just HIV but AIDS. I maybe got it from shooting up or from fucking without condoms, or maybe both. Who knows? But I can't change it."

"Does George have AIDS, too? Am I one of the booty calls for one or two weeks?" I asked.

"George likes you. He brought you to my place because he is caught up in some crazy shit and doesn't want you to get hurt or caught in the middle. As to whether or not he has AIDS, that's a question you'll have to ask him," said Micky.

I had been having protected sex with George the entire time I was in LA. I dropped the subject. Micky took me around and introduced me to the bartenders and a bunch of his friends. They all took a liking to me. A few muscular cholos asked me to dance. I said no every time—even though deep inside I was curious and wanted to. I had never danced with a dude before. Besides, I was in denial about being gay. I told myself I only hooked up with guys for drugs and money. But seeing all them homeboys and homegirls who spoke, walked, dressed, and danced like I did made me feel in some weird way I actually belonged. I could be me. This was a space for cis men who were Latino and gay; at least here, within these club walls, they could be themselves without fearing reprisal or having to fight to defend their masculinity. *Wow! Maybe I am gay?* I thought to myself. *Nah. I think I'm still bisexual. Why is this so difficult, with all these labels? Why can't I just be attracted to whomever I'm attracted to, like the guys in this bar?*

When we got back to the trailer, I asked Micky again if George had AIDS.

"I don't know, man. You should actually ask all the dudes you hook up with," he said. "He's in his late thirties, and I don't think he's trying to get someone your age infected. How old are you, anyway?" Micky asked.

"Sixteen," I said.

Micky didn't respond. He just sighed deeply, shook his head, turned on the TV, hit PLAY on his VCR, grabbed some Lovely, took a few hits, and told me to relax and just watch the movie. It was called *Women on the Verge of a Nervous Breakdown*. He passed out as I laughed my ass off watching the crazy Spanish film.

The next day when we were cooking crystal, Micky said, "I'll take you tonight to a Latino club on Santa Monica called Circus. You'll see a bunch of cholos and vaqueros there."

"But it's Tuesday," I said.

"Tuesday is the best night at Circus," he said and laughed.

There was a club in the front part of the block called

Arena. Circus was in the back. It was the perfect location for people on the down-low because they didn't have to worry about being seen going into the bar. Circus was a megaclub with a large dance floor on one side, a hip-hop room upstairs, and a banda music room toward the back with a huge patio area. They even sold tacos. The club was packed. It wasn't as gangster as the other club, but it was still mixed as he'd said, full of cholos and vaqueros, or Mexican cowboys. It was the first time I had seen vaquero men with sombreros, huge belt buckles, and boots dancing together to banda and quebradita music. It tripped me out. It made me rethink all my own stereotypes of gay men.

During last call we left and saw some of the same homeboys who'd been acting fem inside the club turn gangster outside. As we were walking out, one of the cholos, a small skinny guy, was in a shouting match with a bigger guy in another group. I had seen the smaller cholo earlier, voguing, having a good time, laughing, dancing, spinning, and doing death drops. His joyful dancing had made me smile. I remembered seeing the bigger guy mad dogging him with a disgusted look on his face. Now it was all coming to a head.

It was the first time I'd seen a gay dude throw down, boxing. It made me think of how in Latino culture we equate being feminine with not knowing how to fight. It reminded me of times as a kid when I would tie my shirt in a knot and spin around the living room after watching an episode of *Wonder Woman*, twirling and twirling, pretending I was Lynda Carter—and of how scared I was about getting caught. I admired the little guy for being who he was and for being able to defend himself. I wished I had been able to do the same growing up.

Micky grabbed me and walked me to the 7-Eleven on the corner of Santa Monica Boulevard, away from the commotion.

At the store, Micky introduced me to some of the older queens that had been working the streets for years. I didn't know if they were trans women or drag queens as I was too afraid to ask, so I just went along, soaking it all in. Micky also knew a lot of the older gay guys, who looked like they were once good looking but had just used a few too many drugs or stayed up too many nights, and now they were on the decline. I wondered if that would be me one day.

Micky called over a tall Black trans woman wearing knee-high black boots, a tight pleather bodysuit, and a Diana Ross Afro wig. "Momma, please make sure you keep an eye on him and teach him the ropes when you see him out here."

"I'll keep an eye on him, boo," she said to Micky while looking at me. "And you can call me Momma," she said directly to me, bending down to give me two kisses, one on each cheek. We crossed the street with her and were sitting at a bus stop when she said, "So school is now in session. This is my spot. If you look up and down the street you're going to see some guys from the club walking back and forth with their shirts off or sitting on the top of bus stop benches. Remember, the top of the bench means you're working."

"Where do they go from here?" I asked her and Micky.

"Alleys. Backstreets. Hotels. Just don't let them take you

too far or you're really fucked. You don't want to end up way out in San Bernardino or Pomona. And also, don't be stupid enough to drink anything a trick gives you or you'll end up chopped up in some back-alley dumpster."

We watched and listened for about fifteen minutes until a car stopped and Momma said, "Bye, boo, and don't worry, by the time you get here tomorrow, the word will be out that you're my child and under my watch, so no one will fuck with you." Then she hopped in the car and off she went into the night in the City of Angels.

The next day I rode the bus to Santa Monica Boulevard. I hung out with Momma when she was in between clients. It was different walking here than being in Balboa Park. In Balboa Park the sex trade was fairly hidden along a side street, and it was quiet. In Los Angeles, it was out in the open, with the constant sound of cars, trucks, and buses honking at each other and loud music of all kinds blaring out of loudspeakers from cars driving by. Guys had their shirts off, grabbed their crotches constantly, even made catcalls to people driving by. I didn't like loudly calling attention to myself. I preferred drawing people in with my silence and my postures. Here, cars would block traffic as sex workers hopped in and out not giving a shit who was watching.

For a little while, I became one of the many streetwalkers in Hollywood. And it ate away at my spirit.

A few days later, George showed up. I had made enough money on Santa Monica Boulevard to leave LA and was planning on catching the Amtrak home that day. He walked into the trailer and woke me up loudly.

"Hurry up. Get ready. We have to go," he said.

He rushed me into his truck and sped to San Diego. As we approached Carlsbad, he started accusing me of threatening to rat him out to the cops for me being a minor as he tightly gripped the steering wheel. "I had no idea you were only sixteen. You fuckin lied to me. I thought you were over eighteen. You better not even think about calling the cops on me." He rambled incessantly, as if he was tweaking on crystal. I had no idea what he was talking about or where he got this idea. I could only assume that Micky had told him how old I really was. I had no intention of telling on him or ratting anyone out. I was actually grateful, especially to Micky, for introducing me to so much—but crystal has a way of making people paranoid.

I didn't want to argue and only wanted to get home as quick as possible, so I ignored him, which only pissed him off.

"Fuckin say something! You trying to rat me out to make me look like a pedophile, you little manipulative motherfucker?"

I looked over at him. How could he think I would do that to him? He shoved my shoulder hard, making me hit my head on the passenger side's window. He turned the wheel fast and lost control of the truck. I didn't have my seat belt on; my body jolted and I hit my head again on the window. We spun out and ended up facing oncoming traffic. For an instant I saw the oncoming traffic swerving around us, their honking echoing in the distance. It was a miracle we lived.

CHAPTER 11

It was the early '90s and the peak years of gang violence and drive-by shootings in Southern California. It was the era of gangsta rap and the war on drugs. San Diego, America's finest city, with the most amazing weather and the prettiest beaches, was also a city that housed extreme poverty, drugs, and crime. On our side of town, crossing neighborhood boundaries often meant crossing gang boundaries and risking getting shot. Death was a reality. Gang fights of between twenty-five and fifty people in front of our school were a common occurrence. Sometimes cars would pull up slowly in front of the school and just start shooting. Race riots at the high school were also common given the increase in tensions between Blacks and Mexicans.

Before I turned seventeen, over twenty of my friends and acquaintances had died of gang violence, overdoses, or accidents from drinking and driving. At one point it seemed like I was going with Ariyel and her mother, Joy, to one funeral a month for San Diego High School students who'd been caught in the crossfire. Even at funerals you had to be careful, because you never knew if a drive-by was going to happen at the cemetery.

Growing up, I couldn't wear blue in some neighborhoods, couldn't wear red in others, and couldn't wear green either. Neutral colors like gray, black, beige, brown, and white were the safest options. Being Latino was reason enough to get hurt. Driving while Mexican was evidently a crime. It was routine to get pulled over, even if we weren't breaking any laws. It was those times when I most felt like I was waiting to explode. My powerlessness in the face of brutal force enraged me even more. The fighting, the violence, the helicopters, the screaming, the cops, the sirens, the bullets, and the constant fear of being a target at someone else's whim made the reprieve that drugs provided all that much more addictive.

That anyone could inflict violence on me or kill me at their pleasure made me feel insignificant. I would go down the list of my friends who had died before they were eighteen and be unable to comprehend how I'd survived. Living an insignificant life overwhelmed me. Why was I alive? What purpose did I serve on this earth? I didn't care about anything anymore. I was consumed by anger, hatred, self-pity, and the obsession to get high. All I knew was that I hated everyone.

My anger toward the world was out of control, and so was my drug use. My daily routine was like clockwork. Wake up. Open drawer. Find secret stash of crystal. Do a line. Take a shower. Get ready for school. Smoke a joint on the way to the bus. Get to school. Go to the bleachers.

Smoke another joint. Go to first period high and smelling like weed. By lunchtime, do another line or drink with friends. After school I'd hang out a bit with friends, do another line, then go to the park to turn a few tricks before going home.

I was still going to therapy once a week as part of the victim witness program, but it wasn't helping. I tried to open up to the white woman therapist about the sadness I felt inside, but she would shut me down by changing the topic to bullshit at school or surface family issues, like my dad leaving, instead of addressing the realities I was living in. I told her over and over that I didn't want to live like this no more, and she still did nothing. She never engaged my parents. She never engaged authorities. Nothing. She knew about the places I would go to for sex—public parks, adult movie theaters, bookstores—as a minor, and still she did nothing. During the three-plus years that I saw her, no matter how many times my mom asked to see her, she refused. For her, I was a steady paycheck.

In my senior year, I finally told her I no longer wanted to see her. The next week I requested a transfer to another therapist. I did try to find help. I searched for solutions. I tried churches of different denominations. A good friend, a former chola, took me to a famous church for reformed gangsters, and they prayed over me, for the drug use and for the "gay behavior" to be excised from me.

I met her one night at the church. Service was over, but her pastor and a group of people were waiting, apparently for me. When I walked in, she ran up to me and walked me to the group. "This is him. This is my friend I told you about who is confused and needs the devil taken out of him. He's a very good person and I know we all can help him."

I felt embarrassed. They'd been told I was sleeping with men and that I needed the devil taken out of me. I wanted to leave but also wanted some type of salvation. What if they were right? What if I had been possessed by the devil the very instant I opened that card with the naked guy in it in the gift shop?

I believed I was a freak of nature. An anomaly who shouldn't exist. Maybe all this was the devil's doing. The pastor welcomed me and asked me to be open to receiving Jesus Christ as my lord and savior while they prayed over me.

"Kneel here," he said, pointing to the floor in front of him as the group surrounded me in a circle. He put his hand, which shook the entire time the group was praying, on my forehead. Some women were speaking in tongues while others prayed for my soul to be saved and for my sinful desires to be expelled from me forever. This went on for about thirty minutes. I'd occasionally open my eyes to look around without moving my head, the pastor still holding his hand on my forehead. I saw only people with eyes closed, deeply focused in strenuous prayer to save me. I cried a little bit but mostly out of embarrassment and shame, not only because I was a drug addict but because, worse, I was confused about being gay.

The small hope I held that God would change me quickly passed. I felt no chills and no empowering sense of hope. In

the end, the pastor pushed on my forehead so hard that I
fell backward. I am not sure if they were expecting something from me, that I would speak in tongues or convulse,
but I just lay there on the floor, looking around at them all,
confused.

"There, my son. You are saved. You will never desire to
be with men again. Your life of living in sin is over."

I left the church, went to the park, lit a joint laced with
PCP, and did a line of crystal with a trick who offered me
some before I went down into the bushes to have sex with
him.

△▽△

Ariyel tried to help me and to understand my desperation.
But the deeper I got into my drug use, the more I pushed
her away, too. Our relationship changed. I became the biggest asshole to those who loved me the most, including Ariyel. When I came home one day to find her sitting on the
couch holding my mom as she cried, I went off in anger,
"What the fuck are you doing here? And why the fuck is she
crying?"

"You can't hide it from her anymore. Your mom's not stupid. She knows you get high. She's known for a long time
but is too afraid to confront you or to say anything out of
fear that your yelling at her will escalate and you will hit her.
Your anger is out of control. Don't you get it? She feels like
she's failed you. We all feel like we've failed you."

For an instant, I wanted to run to my mom and console her.

But instead, I yelled. "Man, fuck you both," I clapped back. "You don't know what the fuck I've put up with to take care of her, her health, against my dad. You got no motherfuckin clue 'cause your mom gave you everything. A nice house. Nice furniture. You can have nice things and your mom did it alone. We had a dad and he was fucked up. What the fuck do you know? I'm tired of being made to feel bad for the fucked-up life they gave me." And I stormed out.

I surrounded myself with others who used drugs as I did. I stopped calling Ariyel after that day. When she'd call me, I'd ignore her. I wouldn't go over to her house like I used to. I was bored around people who didn't get high. My life revolved entirely around getting high and having sex. I couldn't find a sense of meaning or purpose for my life. I was too afraid to kill myself, but I didn't want to live anymore, either.

The deeper I got into my drug use, the more violent my outbursts became. I physically fought with my teachers, other students, and school security. I'd ditch class and go to the boys' restroom, then stand on the sink and hold a lighter flame under the sprinkler until the school fire alarms went off. I did this every day in different bathrooms for about two weeks.

Ariyel's mom, Joy, was the school's registrar, so I would hear about how badly the principal wanted to catch the fire-bug. The last time I did it, I decided to put a piece of rolled-up paper in the sprinkler and set the paper on fire. While the students were all rushing to get out to the field, I ran through the crowd. But the music teacher grabbed me tight by the shoulder. Normally I would have fought back. That time, I didn't. Maybe because I knew the music teacher and liked him. Maybe because I didn't want to fight anymore. Maybe what Ariyel had said to me when she was holding my mom had sunk in and I was reaching out for help in the most destructive way possible. Either way, I allowed him to lead me to the principal's office.

News spread quickly that I was behind the fire alarms, Joy stormed into the principal's office as he was going off on me: "You know, I could expel you from the entire school district and you could be charged with arson. Setting off fire alarms is an offense, and it costs the fire department money each time they come out to investigate. Don't you ever think? What is going on in that thick head of yours?"

Joy lobbied for me and pleaded for me. She made me promise to stop pulling these pranks. When the principal walked out of the office to deal with the police and the fire department, Joy turned to me and asked, "What were you thinking?"

"I don't know. I was bored I guess," I told her.

"Bored? Are you serious? Don't you want to graduate?" She was angry.

I just sat there listening with my head bowed.

The principal strode back into the office, and the first words out of his mouth were "I have to suspend him for a week. If I expel him, he will most likely get expelled from the entire school district. And the other school districts in the county won't take him. So we're not pressing charges. I convinced the police and the fire department to let it go."

That entire afternoon, I sat next to Joy's desk. After a few hours, she handed me some papers and said, "Here, come with me. These papers are going to go into these filing cabinets in alphabetical order. I need you to punch holes in them and put them into the correct folders. When you're done, come back to see me. I'll have another stack for you." The filing office was right next to her desk, so I was only about ten feet away from her.

After about thirty minutes, I went back to her and said, "Okay. I'm done."

She handed me another stack of documents, and I did the same thing. I was proud of my organizational skills. I felt useful. Before I knew it, I was back at her desk, ready for the next pile. I actually enjoyed the work. And Joy thanked me as I executed her tasks. It was satisfying to be helpful and appreciated. I felt like I was a kid again, cutting up vegetables in the kitchen with my mom or hanging clothes with her on the clotheslines.

CHAPTER 12

When I returned to school the following week, the first thing I had to do was check in with the principal. I promised again that there would be no more fire alarms. During third period, a security guard walked into my class, whispered something in the teacher's ear, and handed her a paper.

The teacher looked at me and said, "Jesse, they want you in the counseling office. Security will walk you down."

In unison, the class started in on me: "Ooooooh, you're in trouuuble."

In the counseling office, Joy wasn't at her desk. Security walked me toward the very back of the office—a familiar walk for me now. I thought, *Oh fuck! What now?*

The guard handed the paper to a guy sitting in the back corner office, which was just big enough for two chairs and his desk. He had an open backpack on the floor and a stack of books; two were open, as if he'd been studying. I'd never seen him before. He closed the open books, walked out of the office, and said, "Jesse? Come into my office and have a seat please." Security told him he'd be waiting outside. The man had a friendly demeanor. He wore a flannel long-sleeve shirt, like a Pendleton, with a white T-shirt underneath, creased jeans, and a pair of black-and-white Converse. His hair was cut in a high fade, longer on top.

I plopped down on the chair he indicated, leaning way back. I pulled my beanie out of my back pocket, put it on my head, and rolled it down to just below my eyebrows, crossing my arms and resting my chin on my chest to give off my typical I-don't-give-a-fuck attitude.

"I'm Izmael, but you can call me Z. I go to San Diego State University and work in a program to recruit Latinos to go to college. Have you thought about what you want to do after high school?" he asked.

"Nope."

"Have you considered going to college after high school?"

"Nope," I responded with the same I-don't-give-a-fuck attitude.

"Has anyone in your family ever gone to college?"

"Nope."

"If you could be anything in this world, what would you want to be? Have you given that some thought?"

"Nope."

"So what have you thought about? What are you think-ing about right now?" Z asked. His demeanor was changing from friendly to annoyed.

"Nothing," I responded as I moved my head up slightly, enough for him to see my eyes from under my beanie. "Why you asking me all these questions, and who the fuck are you, anyway? You don't fuckin know me. So quit actin like you give a fuck."

He slowly got up from his desk. He walked toward his

office door, told the security guard still standing outside, "I got this. It's all good," and shut the door.

Z walked slowly back to his desk and reached for his stack of books with both hands. He took a deep breath and let out a heavy sigh as he lifted the books and slammed them hard onto his desk. I jumped back, moving my gaze up toward him. He bent over right in front of my face, so close I could feel his breath, and I stared right back at him, directly into his eyes, in defiance.

"It's motherfuckers like you who make my fuckin job hell. Motherfuckers like you who give Chicanos like me a bad fuckin name," he said with a sneer. "Motherfuckers like you who act like badasses while your moms cry and pray to God that you live another day. Motherfuckers like you who make your parents' sacrifices and journeys into this country not seem worth it. I should just fuckin quit my job because it's a waste of my time trying to help out knucklehead motherfuckers like you who don't give a fuck to stay in school, to think of your futures, and to help you find what motivates you."

He pulled away, breathing heavily. The man looked like he wanted to punch me right in the face. "What? You think I can't fuckin relate to you. You think I don't come from the barrio? You little shit, you don't know anything about me, so don't assume. I care enough to give back and help others, just like others helped me. That's why I'm asking you these questions: because I care. Because someone cared enough to ask me."

I sat there, motionless. Amused. Shocked. But also curious about who he was that he should call me out on my shit without even knowing me.

He paused again and returned to his chair. In a lower, softer voice, he said, "And here you are, acting like a fuckin asshole, like you don't give a fuck, but I know you do. Inside, you do give a fuck. So quit acting like you don't, Jesse. And I apologize for blowing up like that. I shouldn't have snapped at you and disrespected you like that—so I'm sorry, home-boy. I apologize."

I was shocked that he apologized. After that, he was quiet, and his small office was uncomfortably silent. Something stirred within my spirit. He had seen and recognized me as a person, a human being. I crossed my arms even tighter, moved my gaze away from his, and put my head down. Tears gathered in my eyes. I pulled the beanie farther down my face, trying to cover my eyes so he wouldn't see me cry. But it was no use.

He too was quiet. He moved toward me and put his hand on my shoulder. I don't know why I didn't pull away like I normally would have. But I didn't move. He didn't say anything for a few minutes. He didn't give me a Kleenex. He didn't ask anything. He just let my tears flow down my face in silence. His silence made me feel understood. Supported.

After a few minutes, I said, in a very low, deep voice, almost a whisper, "Man, fuck you. I do give a fuck, but I just don't know what to do anymore."

"I know," he said. "Trust me, I know."

He took his hand off my shoulder, pulled a piece of paper from a notepad, wrote something on it, and handed it to me. "Here. This is my phone number and my beeper number. You can call me anytime. I don't care what time it is, day or night. If you want to talk, hang out, talk shit, have someone listen to you, or just hang out and not talk about anything, you can always call me. Sometimes it's nice to just chill with someone and not have to say shit. I don't want anything from you other than for you to think about your future, homeboy."

He touched my spirit. And then, in a flash, I stopped my crying and started laughing at myself. I pulled the beanie off my head, wiped the tears from my face with it, laughed some more, and said, "Damn, I really am fucked up, ain't I?"

I looked up at him, and he gave me a soft, genuine smile and said, "It's cool, homeboy. Don't trip. We all need a good cry every once in a while. No need to be embarrassed around me. And no, you're not fucked up—you're just a young man of color, raised in the hood, dealing with life. No judgment from me."

I laughed at myself some more. We talked for an hour. He told me about his life and his family. He told me about his time in college. He told me about crazy college parties. He talked about being a Chicano in college and how he learned from his Chicano mentors that it was okay to be smart, study, and have fun. He got my attention.

I called Z that weekend, and he invited me to a Latino college event—interestingly enough it was being held at the Balboa Park Club Ballroom, only a few hundred feet away from where I turned tricks. When I showed up, I nervously looked around, hoping no sex workers would catch me walking into the event, come talk to me, and expose me for what I was. I wasn't high yet, but I wished to hell that I was. I wanted to go back to the car to smoke when Z saw me and called me over. I walked to him fidgeting, nervous. I didn't know what to expect.

There was no drama. There were no fights. And I was surprised at the number of good-looking Latinos and Latinas who were students and actually knew how to dance. I had expected to find myself among a bunch of nerdy, dorky guys and girls, but I was wrong. This was a whole world of Latinos I had not been exposed to. As we talked, an extremely good-looking guy with a preppy model look walked over to us. Everyone seemed to know him. Z introduced him to me and said, "This is my homeboy slash boss, Frank. He heads up the recruitment program for Latino students at SDSU."

"Nice to meet you, Jesse. How you like Z? Is he doing his job?" he asked.

I laughed and said, "Yeah, he's cool. He's good people."

"Well, enjoy yourself, man," said Frank. "All these people go to SDSU; even the ones who look like gangsters are students. We know when to work hard and when to have fun. The secret is to not fuck up in school, man. Learn how to play the game. But first get in the game," he said.

I nodded my head as if I understood. What could I say? He was talking about a world I knew nothing about. A world I thought belonged to white people. But he helped water the seed that had been planted by my mom when she hammered home the importance of an education. I felt something shift inside me. Seeing these Latino students gave me hope that it could be possible for me, too. Maybe I could also go to college one day. I wanted so much to grab one of these students and ask, *How did you do it? Do you think I can do it, too?* But it felt pointless—they'd probably never had to deal with my reality. I'd probably only remind them of that fucked-up cousin, brother, or nephew who we all had in our families—only in mine, it was me. Still, the party gave me hope and exposed me to a world that I didn't know existed. One that maybe, somehow, might one day open up for me, too.

I wish I could say that this was all it took for me to change my life and that I immediately got off the dope and all the crazy partying. But it wasn't. Every day I fell deeper into the grip of addiction. I did more lines of crystal, smoked more PCP, smoked more heroin, popped more Ecstasy capsules, dropped more acid, chewed more mushrooms or peyote, popped more pills, and smoked more weed. I was always high, stoned, blazed, baked, toked, or fucked up, and I was still turning tricks.

△▽△

One evening when I came home, Ariyel and Joy were on the couch talking to my mom. I knew something was up immediately. Joy only ever came over for birthday parties or celebrations where my mom made sopes, tostadas, or her famous pozole. Joy and my mom got along well, and Joy never blamed my mom for my troubles. The language barrier, however, meant she never stayed for very long.

When I walked in, Joy told me to sit down. "I have no choice but to put you into the high school diploma program," also known as the Block Program, she said. "The program will help you get the necessary credits at an accelerated pace to be able to graduate with your class. But I need you to commit to us that you will make that happen. Your school schedule will change from the standard hours to noon to seven p.m. Your mom and I both think it's the best thing for you to make sure you get your high school diploma."

Since I hated getting up early and always showed up late, I knew this was the best schedule for me. Then she added, "I also think it's best that you don't hang out with Ariyel for a while. You're doing too many drugs, and I don't want you to put her life in danger."

I looked at Ariyel as she started crying. "I'm sorry, Nerd."

When they got up to leave, my eyes filled with tears. But I shut down and said, "All right, it's cool."

The hurt in Ariyel's eyes was unbearable, so I walked out while she hugged my mom and cried. Before they left, Ariyel tried to hug me, but I wouldn't hug her back.

"Don't do this, Nerd. You know I love you," she said.

"I know. I just gotta do me," I replied, hardly looking her in the eyes. When I walked back into the house, my mom looked at me and just shook her head. "¿Qué puedo hacer para ayudarte? ¿Qué puedo hacer, mijo?" *What can I do to help you? What can I do, my son?*

"I'll be fine, Amá," I told her.

Amá's only hope was that Joy would be right. Amá trusted Joy. And in truth, the Block Program helped me. I finished assignments faster than most other students, and I helped tutor others with my remaining time. And although I stayed high, at least the program refocused my energy to get the credits I needed to graduate. I tried to finish as quickly as I could to get passing grades, gain the credits I needed, and move on to the next subject. Graduating became an attainable reality again. School had normally been a reason to get out of the house, a way to eat free lunch, and an opportunity to hang out with friends, but now I was motivated once more. I wanted to graduate.

The Block Program was diverse, and interestingly, no one had beef with anyone since we were all focused on completing our credits as fast as possible. The teachers were strict. We couldn't be one minute late to class or the door would be locked and we'd lose credit hours.

I created a very strong bond with a white girl named Tina who was short and rocked a rockabilly style, with an A-line black bob and Bettie Page bangs. We sat next to each other in our classes. Each time I'd walk in after a break reeking of skunk weed, she would do things to make me bust up laughing. One night after classes she said to me, "Rather than go party with your homeboys, why don't you walk me home? And on the way I'll take you to a different type of party. You down to try something new?"

"Hell yeah, I'm down, but where you takin me? I hate surprises."

"Don't trip. You'll like it. I'll get you some of my good weed from Humboldt County. It will make your skunk weed taste like nasty leftover shake."

I laughed and said, "Aight, let's do this."

Tina lived in the heart of the gay neighborhood, Hillcrest, only a few blocks away from the store where I was molested. On the way to her house we stopped at a lesbian bar called the Flame to meet one of her DJ friends. We weren't carded, just allowed to go right in. Everyone knew her. People were dressed like taggers with baggy jeans shredded at the bottom, baggy shirts, and colorful beanie hats or truck-driver caps. Some girls had their own style, which later became known as "raver." The DJ was playing some amazing deep, soulful house music. The beats were sick. People were busting dance moves that incorporated footwork, popping, breaking, and two-stepping. It was on point. The vibe was like nothing I had experienced before. I was enjoying myself, rocking my cholo style, standing out like a sore thumb, slowly bobbing my head to the music while holding up the wall.

A blond girl walked up and offered me a glow stick. I said, "For what?"

"For what?" she asked. "Are you serious?"

She then bent one to light it up and started dancing in front of me with a glow stick in each hand. She moved her hands fast as she danced to the beat. I had never seen anyone dance like that, with rapid hand movements that made the glow sticks move to the rhythm of the music. I was captivated. She offered me the glow stick again and told me to come dance with her and her group of friends. I declined. These people were part of a national underground house music movement I'd never even heard of before.

"We throw parties throughout San Diego and LA all the time," Tina told me over the music. "Sometimes we throw parties at clubs, but most of the time we break into abandoned warehouses, where we bring the sound system, the DJs, the lights and the laser systems, and of course all the nitrous, Ecstasy, and acid you can imagine. You should go with me sometime."

"I'm down," I called back to her over the music, still bopping my head to the beat.

As we smoked some bud, she asked me, "You wanna roll? I got some good E."

"Nah, I'm good. Not tonight. Besides, I can't stay out late, and I'm not trying to roll at my house with only my family around."

Tina and I started to hang out all the time. She invited me to parties at empty lofts downtown with groups of people rolling on Ecstasy, candy flipping, or inhaling nitrous. If I wasn't chilling with Tina, I'd be at some hotel, smoking crystal with heroin and drinking all night. Each night, I'd get home late. My poor amá didn't know what to do. She'd be awake waiting for me every night, even though she had to be up at 4:30 a.m. to catch the five-thirty bus to get to work. She'd be sitting in the living room with only the light of the candle on her Virgen de Guadalupe altar illuminating the darkness. When she'd see me come in and as I'd walk past her, she'd thank God and the Virgencita for bringing me home safe. Then she'd blow out the candle and go to bed. I'd wake up the next day, go to school, and do the same thing all over again.

Some nights I would wake up from nightmares, sweating, only to find my mom praying over me. One night I dreamed about the family laughing as we collected aluminum cans at the beach. The dream was full of joy. Then it shifted into a nightmare. I was walking in Balboa Park at night, and all around I heard screaming. It echoed through the skies. The man who molested me was behind every tree, leaning on every parked car, sitting on every bench, and driving every car that went by. I woke up yelling.

I woke up to my mom watching me, praying, begging God to save me, again.

"Ay, Amá, una pesadilla," I told her. *Geez, Mom, it's a nightmare.* She sat next to me on the bed, made the sign of the cross on my forehead, and said Our Fathers and Hail Marys until I went back to sleep.

△▽△

I graduated with the class of 1992 from San Diego High School, thanks to the high school diploma program. Everyone, including Joy and Ariyel, was there. I wouldn't have been able to graduate without them.

As I crossed the stage, I noticed Amá, Joy, Ariyel, and my brother waving and cheering loudly. I smiled, yet I felt an emptiness and disappointment inside. I felt like a fraud. I was only graduating because Joy had maneuvered the pieces for me. All I'd done was suit up and do the work, but I reminded myself that that was what it was all about. Still, I doubted myself. I wished I was high. I had refrained, as I wanted to enjoy this day in its purest form without it being altered by a substance. Their cheers made me smile again, and the self-deprecating feeling passed. It was nice to not be high.

When the principal handed me my diploma, he said, "Promise me, no more fires."

I smiled. "No more fires, I promise." I leaned in and hugged him.

As I went back to my seat, I danced an exaggerated, happy cabbage patch, just to be the class clown. The crowd cheered and laughed.

After the ceremony, we all went to Amá's house to eat. I was happy high school was over. And then, right there in the middle of the living room as we all ate, I was hit hard by the thought that I had no clue what I was going to do next. I looked down at my plate of enchiladas and my mind went blank.

I blurted out in a somber voice, "Now what? What am I going to do?" When I looked up, I saw everyone staring at me.

Joy smiled and quickly filled the silence. "We are very proud of you, honey. It was amazing to see you get your diploma." She lifted her plastic cup of soda, made a gesture to toast, and said, "To Jesse! For graduating high school! Congratulations!"

Everyone raised their cups and said, "Congratulations!"

My mom, in her broken English, toasted, "Kongrachu-layshons!" We all laughed. My mom got up and gave Joy a hug. "¡Gracias! ¡Por todo!" They hugged each other tight.

Then Joy said, "Tomorrow you go to City College and sign up for their summer immersion program for incoming students. I called David, a counselor at the EOPS office,

and he'll be waiting for you to walk you through the enroll-
ment process. Ariyel will go with you." Then she gave me a
pointed look. "Don't let me down, Jesse."

The next day when I woke up, Ariyel was helping my
mom in the kitchen. They were making chilaquiles rojos
con carne deshebrada—my favorite. It was nice having Ariyel at the house again and seeing her happily helping my
mom. I knew her mom had only let her stay the night as a
reward for my graduating high school. I felt bad for having
pushed Ariyel away, but it was easy to get along, as if no
time had lapsed between us at all.

"Go take a shower and get ready," she said, "so we can
eat and then head out to City." City is what we all called
the college—it's short for San Diego City College, the local
community college.

We drove to the college. We walked into the EOPS (Ex-
tended Opportunity Programs and Services) office and
asked for David. I was reserved, distrusting, and quiet.
I walked slowly with my head down and wore my beanie
down to my nose to cover my eyes.

"What's up, Jesse? I heard you just graduated. Congratulations, man," said David as he walked out to greet us. He
had on slacks with a guayabera shirt and dress shoes. He
had a bald head and a goatee and carried himself with
the confidence of a veterano from the barrio. I hadn't expected that; I'd expected some white man who was going
to tell me what to do. David put his hand out to shake mine.
When I shook it, he quickly changed it up to give me the
homeboy handshake and, with a smile, said, "It's all good,
brother."

As soon as we sat down, *the* conversation began. It started very much like the conversation I had with Z about what I planned to do next. David asked me, "Are you interested in going to college? Because if you are, we can get you enrolled today to be an official college student."

I quickly looked at Ariyel with a huge smile on my face and said, "Really? Just like that?"

"Really. Just like that," he said. "We will sign you up for testing to gauge where you are in English, reading, and math. If you score high enough, we can bypass remedial classes," he said.

"That's cool. Then what?" I asked.

"I recommend you do our EOPS summer program for incoming students. It helps prepare new students for college life. It will give you the opportunity to meet other EOPS students, make new friends, and do some cool projects. You will get college credits for the courses also. I think the spaces are all taken, but I will see what I can do to get you in. Hold up, I'll be right back," he said, leaving me with Ariyel.

Ariyel turned to me and said, "Man, if you can get into that summer program, that would be the best thing for you to do. I hope he can get you in. I'll ask him if he can get you a work-study position, too, so you can work on campus in between classes and get paid. My mom says it's worth it."

When David walked back into the office, he said, "It's done. I can get you a space if you fill out the paperwork and commit today. So come on, let's do it."

Without my having a chance to think it over, we stood up. His energy was so catching, I just followed him and did what he said.

"Before we walk out of this office, I need you to look into that mirror on the wall and read aloud what it says," said David. "Don't be embarrassed. Just read it. That is the commitment you are making to yourself and to me. Loyalty is key, and our word is gold."

Embarrassed, I read in a low voice the sticker that was placed on the top of the mirror on his office door: YOU ARE LOOKING AT THE FACE OF THE PERSON WHO IS RESPONSIBLE FOR YOUR HEALTH, ATTITUDE, WEALTH, AND HAPPINESS.

"Thank you, Jesse. Your new journey starts today. We are making you a college student," said David as he gave me a solid gripped handshake. I was glowing with pride, and my embarrassment at reading that affirmation faded away.

David walked Ariyel and me over to the financial aid office and introduced us to a group of Latina women. "This is Jesse. We are going to make sure he is a successful college student and graduates to go to a four-year," he said to them. Their energy was welcoming. They hugged me and told me not to worry, that they would help me through the entire process. They told me that my job was to let them help me. Their job was to not let me get overwhelmed about the process.

All these people around me who were helping me and providing support felt good—overwhelming, too, but, most important, good. It made me reflect on my life and think about new possibilities. *Maybe I can get an associate degree. Who knows? Maybe I can even get a bachelor's degree one day. People like me don't make it. But hey, you never know. Today is a new start.* The next chapter of my life began—the world of community college.

PART
3

Grandma Lola recounted the tales of bandits, including gringo bandits, who tried to steal from the family mines or set up camps near rivers shimmering with gold. She would say, "Those bandidos and gringos had no respect for the land or for people. They would pollute the rivers and take what they could and then scram like cowards—if the bastards were lucky enough that we didn't kill them first."

She would send Ricardo, as a child, to the river with a metal bucket to grab mud to patch up holes or cracks in the walls of the house. In the mornings she would watch the sunrise as she walked back to the house from milking the cows. She marveled at how the light made the house glimmer from the gold flecks that dotted the mud. "Mi casita de oro," she would say. My little house of gold.

Sometime around 1921, Ricardo's father, my grandfather Roberto, died as the result of a bullet wound he received while fighting in the Mexican Revolution. A few days after my grandfather's funeral, once the novenario (the nine days of prayer) was over, his cousins tried to seize the land and the gold mines that Roberto had left to my grandmother. They threatened to kill her and her kids if she stood in their way. The dispute over the ranch tore the family apart forever.

Lola hired some workers to protect the ranch and the land, but Roberto's cousins kidnapped my dad's older sister, Victoria, and held her for a ransom in exchange for the property. But Victoria stole a horse and escaped. She succeeded in reaching her uncle, General Domingo Arrieta León, and told him what happened to her. This story became so famous that a Mexican ballad, or corrido, about my aunt's kidnapping and escape was written. To this day it is sung in the region.

The general, with a few of his men, returned Victoria to my grandma's ranch. He ordered soldiers to bring Roberto's cousins to the ranch. They talked throughout the night. My grandma never said what was discussed that night. But the next day, Lola's family left the Sierras with whatever portable wealth could be amassed on short notice. She gathered some horses to pull the wagon, one each for my father and his sister, and several more to sell and trade along their journey. She freed all the other animals. Then she grabbed dynamite, made her way to the entrance of each of the family's gold mines along the mountainside, and blew them up. She never looked back.

△▽△

I never found out who kept the land or the gold mines. My grandma Lola, eleven-year-old Ricardo, and my fourteen-year-old aunt Victoria left the mountains and made their way north. Along with the horses, they brought a few fam-

ily belongings and bags of gold nuggets in a wagon. Even the family's deer followed them until one day it disappeared. As children we were told never to return to the lost land—we would be killed because of our last name and our ties to the land. The people who kept the gold mines would think we'd returned to take back what was once ours.

Up north, the family settled in Mexicali, near Yaqui territory. During those times there were many Yaqui and Apache raids on towns in and around Mexicali. A few days after arriving, my grandmother went into Mexicali to sell some gold, trade horses for supplies, and hire workers to build their new home. She had Victoria with her but left Ricardo with neighbors. When she returned, the neighbors informed her that my dad had been kidnapped. They said a Yaqui warrior woman had spotted Ricardo hiding behind a tree, grabbed him, and taken him away.

My grandmother Lola grabbed her rifle, climbed back onto her horse, and, with a few men, went to track down her son. She had no luck. Later that day, my grandmother returned to Mexicali to round up soldiers. She offered them gold and her remaining horses to help get Ricardo back. They were no match for the Yaqui, either. Eventually the government stepped in to negotiate with the tribe and convinced the Yaqui woman to give my dad back to Lola. It took six months of negotiations to reclaim my dad. The Yaqui woman had taken my father because he looked like her son who had been killed. She'd felt justified. An eye for an eye. My grandmother built her house during those negotiations, but most of her gold and possessions went to paying the soldiers and the government.

For three months after he was returned, Ricardo refused

*to speak Spanish with anyone other than his mom and sis-
ter. With everyone else, he spoke Yaqui. My father said he'd
attempted to escape but stopped trying the day the Yaqui
woman told him that his mother and sister had been killed by
the same men who'd killed her son. The Yaqui told him they
would help him avenge their deaths. Many years later, prior
to his death and while beset by Alzheimer's, my dad would
mix his Spanish with Yaqui.*

△▽△

I started the summer EOPS program right away. College
courses were very different from high school. I didn't feel
forced to be there, which made it easier to go. Most students
had full-time jobs, some had kids, others had been working
for years and felt they needed to go back to school. I felt I
belonged. The teachers seemed to care and asked engaging
questions. They would even call on me and other quiet students to encourage us to speak up. They showed an interest and seemed happy when we contributed. These teachers
made an effort to make sure no one felt left out.

Introduction to Psychology was one of my favorite
classes because the teacher would give us assignments to
observe people outside of class to better understand the
human psyche. The assignments felt fun and engaging, like
getting into an elevator and, once the doors closed, turning around to face the other people and say hello. It was
interesting to see how people would react so nervously or

respond to me in kind. It made me think about the world around me.

I was fascinated by the psychology of space and gender and enjoyed observing interactions between men, between men and women, and particularly between genders of different races. Men always take up more space, sitting with legs wide open, while women are taught to take up less space. And people from different cultures have different definitions of what is a safe distance. In the United States, people's safe space tends to be arm's length. I observed how different my safe space was when I was talking to other Latinos versus white people. I would start a conversation with white people from a safe arm's length distance, and slowly I would take small, almost unnoticeable steps closer to them. I would laugh inside at how they always moved slightly backward. I'd move in and they'd move out. I'd sit with my legs wide open next to other big guys and play battle of the armrest in packed movie theaters. It was hilarious because guys who go to movies together almost always sit with an empty seat between them.

I enjoyed the courses that involved topics of race, class, gender, and sexuality. Chicano Studies, African American Studies, and Ethnic Studies took my knowledge to new heights. I learned the political meanings behind the terms *Chicano*, *cholo*, *pachuco*, *Latino*, and *Hispanic*, their social connotations, and why those terms meant different things to different generations. I was intrigued by the history of my community's clothing styles, dating all the way back to my Indigenous roots. I learned about the Caló dialect, which is an argot of Mexican Spanish that was spoken among many of us in the barrio, and its origins dating back to Romani culture.

My desire to learn was reinvigorated by my professors, who encouraged me to research and pursue new interests. I enjoyed being back in a library, like when I was a kid, and looking at books to help me with assigned topics. I loved being encouraged to come up with my own conclusions or interpretations of historic and current events when professors would ask me, *So what do you think about that, Jesse?* I was slowly beginning to feel empowered. My professors urged me to write and talk about the many things going on in the world that I was questioning. For example, I started to question why, as a person of Mexican descent, I always said "Mande" or "Mándeme usted" instead of "¿Qué?" as most other Spanish-speaking cultures do. Where did this subservient, oppressive language come from? Why is it specific to Mexican culture? It made me angry to realize how deeply servitude and subservience have been engrained in my people by colonization, demonstrated just by the shift of a simple word, from *What?* (*¿Qué?*) to *Order me* (*Mande*).

For the first time I watched documentaries like *Eyes on the Prize* and learned about Emmett Till. I learned that the Civil Rights Movement was successful partly due to the support of the Jewish American community and other cross-cultural alliances. I especially loved learning about the history of neighborhoods in the United States and how bad policies like urban renewal had placed highways smack-dab in the middle of communities of people of color, disrupting economic and political power. I learned about the racist history of housing policies and how the creation of suburbs, coupled with the help of the GI Bill, created concentrations of economic poverty in the urban core, leading to decay in many of America's cities. My mind was absorbing information like a sponge.

It was in community college that I first read excerpts from amazing books like *The Underdogs* by Mariano Azuela, *Their Eyes Were Watching God* by Zora Neale Hurston, *The Fire Next Time* by James Baldwin, and *I Know Why the Caged Bird Sings* by Maya Angelou. These are only a few that come to mind, but each author had a gift for storytelling that changed my life. For the first time since my sexual abuse began, I was transported to other worlds through books. It was an intoxicating feeling.

Before the end of the summer program, I was assigned an EOPS counselor. I was hesitant to work with her at first because she was a white woman with blond hair, reminding me of my victim witness therapist. I walked into my first counseling appointment with my usual posturing and defensive attitude. She turned out to be a blessing in my life.

Ruth had a welcoming energy about her. And she asked me the same question everyone else had been asking, but she did it differently. Instead of saying, "What do you want to do with your life?" Ruth asked, "So, Jesse, if you could travel anywhere in the world, where would it be?"

The question caught me off guard. "Um, I don't know. Maybe Omaha."

"Omaha?" she asked, puzzled. "Why Omaha?"

Irritated, I responded, "Well, duh—to go see all the animals from the documentaries."

Smiling and trying hard to hold back a laugh, she asked, "What kind of animals do you want to see in Omaha?"

"The kind you see in the Mutual of Omaha's *Wild Kingdom*. They keep all the animals from Africa there."

Her smile grew big, and I couldn't help but smile back. "Well, let's work on getting you to graduate from here and then we'll get you to transfer to a four-year college where they have a study-abroad program, and we can map out your future travels together. Whether it's Omaha or Africa or anywhere else in the world, we can make it happen. We can talk about zoology and marine biology courses, too. Cool?"

"Cool!" I said with skeptical enthusiasm.

When I found out there were no such animals in Omaha and that the show's title was based on the sponsorship of the insurance company Mutual of Omaha, I laughed hysterically and thought that it was cool that she hadn't tried to correct me.

"You tested very well, and I want to make sure I put you in a transfer program to go directly into a four-year college of your choice. But before we talk about majors, let's talk about what you like to do and what you don't like to do. Talk to me about the things you dreamed about becoming when you were a child," she said.

The question triggered me into a manic answer that went on forever and ran the gamut, from how poor my family was to how I wanted to be a good swimmer or a marine biologist and clean the tanks at SeaWorld, even though, I told her, I'd never seen a Mexican clean the tanks there before.

After about five minutes of my rambling, she put her

hand on mine and said, "Don't worry about it. I'm here to help. There is no immediate rush to find you a major. We will start with general education requirements, and then move from there. I also suggest you start to research four-year colleges and universities you might want to transfer to."

"But why so soon? I am just starting my first semester," I said.

"Because it's never too early to start and I don't want certain opportunities to pass you by, so I need you to focus with me," she said.

"Órale," I said as I got up and started to walk out the door. But then I quickly turned around and asked her, "So what do I do about learning a trade, because I may have to drop out of school to help the family. I think I could be a good hairstylist and meet cool people that way. What do you think?" I asked her.

"Well, the cosmetology program has a one-semester waiting list, so I am sure I can get you in next semester, but you have to do very well this semester."

"Okay."

"Also, give me your word that you will not stop school if you take a full-time job."

"Yeah, you have my word. I will finish cosmetology school, get a job, and take classes at night. Is that cool with you?" I realized that I really did want it to be cool with her.

"That's good. It will keep you busy and focused. Is that a deal?" She reached out her hand to shake mine, solidifying the agreement.

"Yes, it's a deal."

I felt an unexplainable consciousness that there was a

better way to live. But I was still an addict, and as time went on, I needed more and more crystal and heroin to function. At some point, I'd crossed an invisible line. There was no way to go back. Physically, I was deteriorating. I was like a skeleton, even though I thought I looked amazing. I had been doing so much crystal meth that I'd gone from 185 or 190 pounds to 150 pounds. My cheeks and eyes were sunken. And I was still tricking at the park.

I finished my first semester and was accepted into the cosmetology program. I was hesitant because I was concerned that others would think I was gay for choosing cosmetology, but I moved forward because I had committed to my EOPS counselor.

During beauty school, I went downhill fast. I met a new group of friends, and we hung in between classes and got high at almost every break. I'd snort until my nose bled.

The worst part was always coming down, so I tried my hardest to stay high as long as I could. But after being up for three to five days straight, the drugs took a toll. I wore sunglasses all the time because bright light hurt my eyes, and when coming down, I drank water and milk. The flu-like symptoms, muscle aches, and stomach cramping coupled with constipation and then diarrhea were horrible. Then came the depression and the paranoia—I felt like the entire world was out to get me.

I'd became one of "those" druggies that I'd seen a few years before on Santa Monica Boulevard with their shirts off, looking skinny, used, and tired, and I was doing everything I could to get noticed by some sexually desperate men to get paid. As soon as I got out of some trick's car, I'd hop right into another's. When I'd scraped up enough cash, I would meet with meth heads to get my hands on some crystal. School was the only thing in my life that kept me engaged and grounded.

One night a new friend invited me to a rave at an abandoned warehouse along the Tijuana border in an area called Otay. The warehouse was surrounded by junkyards. News about the rave had traveled throughout Southern California. The map point was a record store in Chula Vista right next to a taco shop. When we arrived, we saw dozens of cars in the parking lot. Other *Mario Bros.*–looking ravers sat around waiting for the map point to open. Because the parties were illegal, the map point was where you'd get a first set of directions to a second map point; from there you'd receive the final directions to the rave. If the people at the map point thought you were a cop, they would give you fake directions. At the first map point, my friend and I sat next to two girls and one guy who were smoking weed. The girls quickly offered us the bowl to smoke with them.

"Hell yeah. Don't hide it, divide it," I said.

"We've seen you before at other raves. You're so cute together," said one of the girls. She had a short bob haircut like Velma's from *Scooby-Doo*.

"Are you guys boyfriends? Like, a couple?" asked the other girl, pointing to me and my friend. The girl had long wavy brown hair and big blue-gray eyes. She sported a natural look.

My friend laughed as he took a hit and passed her the pipe, responding, "No. We're not boyfriends. But it's not the first time people have asked. I wonder why?"

Their guy friend said, "I think it's 'cause y'all dance amazing and flow off each other well. I love watching you both dance. I wish I had a boyfriend just to dance with like you both do."

"Aw, that's wassup. But nah, we ain't gay. Why ain't you got a boyfriend? You're totally cute with a gorgeous smile. You look like an Italian model," I told him, shocking myself with how I was complimenting him. He was tall and skinny, with dark brown spiky hair and very chiseled features but in an androgynous-model-like way, big lips, and a smile with pretty white teeth.

"Thank you. That's super sweet of you."

"Dayum, this is some good weed," I said while I took a hit. "Are y'all rollin tonight? Our friends are over there copping some E for us. It better be good, 'cause I wanna candy flip tonight like a muthafucka," I said as I pulled out a ziplock bag with ten LSD sugar cubes wrapped in foil. "Y'all want some? They're sugar cubes with acid."

"Nah, we're good. We brought our own, but thank you," said Blue. I'd forgotten her name, which is why I kept calling her Blue Eyes that night, or Blue for short.

We hit it off. As Blue and I exchanged numbers, a guy walked up and handed us directions to the next map point. We compared papers to make sure they were the same and hopped in our cars. The next map point was a drive-through taco shop, where we had to order a half Sprite, half hibiscus tea and pay the cashier the entrance fee in exchange for fluorescent green wristbands.

At the rave, I popped three hits of Ecstasy and two hits of acid and inhaled large balloons of nitrous. At sunup, the

DJ played one of my favorite songs by Zoë called "Sunshine on a Rainy Day." I was in a state of bliss, dancing, when the police arrived. The music cut off immediately and we heard someone screaming in a megaphone: "Evacuate the premises and go home. No one will be arrested as long as you cooperate."

"Hurry up. Hurry up," people were telling one another all around us as we walked to the car. It was daylight now, and police cars were everywhere, with officers standing around. I was scared I would get called over because I was *fuuuucked up* on both Ecstasy and acid and felt like I was still peaking. My friends guided me to the car as I giggled my ass off.

"Hey!" a cop yelled in our direction. I froze, scared I'd get arrested. "Make sure he goes straight home and doesn't drive." They were talking about me.

I was way too high to go home, and since my buddy was awake on crystal, he suggested we go to Balboa Park together and hang with some other ravers who had started a weekly rave on Sunday mornings where the DJs would set up using generators to power their sound systems.

I eventually came down at eleven o'clock that morning and asked my buddy to take me home. When I got home, the front door was open. I walked into the house, passed through the living room, and went directly into my bedroom as I had done a million times before. Only this time, I didn't notice all the family members who were sitting in the living room, visiting from Mexico. There were about ten of them, eating. They stared at me as I walked straight to my room like a zombie.

My aunt stormed into my bedroom to yell at me. "I can't believe how fucked up you are. You need some help. You're killing yourself."

"Shuuuuuut up . . . You don't have to yell," I slurred as I got off the bed and walked past her into the living room. I said hello to everyone. After that I went into the kitchen, pulled out a gallon of milk, and took a huge swig. I looked at my mom and said, "What? Yeah, I partied last night—so what? What are you going to do? Nothing! All you ever do is cry."

That night I was awakened by my mom sitting in a chair next to my bed, praying over me with a rosary in her hands.

I exhaled in frustration and thought to myself, *Oh God, here she goes with her damn prayers again,* but I didn't say that. I said, "Mom, I'll be fine. I promise. You'll see."

She ignored me and kept calmly praying. I felt her thumb do the sign of the cross on my forehead as I fell into a deep sleep.

△▽△

Two days later I called the girl from the rave who'd given me her number. I wanted to smoke some of that good weed she had.

"Ummm, hello. Ummm, this is Jesse from the rave the other night. Is the girl with the big blue eyes there?"

I could hear laughter on the other end of the line. "Blue eyes? Well, they're more green-blue-hazel with a hint of gray. But yes, it's me. And of course I remember you, Jesse. My name's Hope."

She gave me her address and told me to come over. I arrived at her place, a nice condo on the second floor of an upscale two-story condo subdivision near San Diego State. She had coordinated furniture with a beige-colored sectional sofa, a matching lounge chair, a large wooden coffee table, and a wooden TV stand with a large TV, a VCR, and a stereo system. She had a nice dining room table next to two doors that opened onto a large balcony. There was art on the walls. Her kitchen was large and spotless, with marble countertops. There was a tall red bong and a small sandwich bag of bright-colored weed—exactly what I'd come to smoke.

I sat on one of two tall chairs lining the countertop, grabbed her bong, and said, "Wow, this is nice, and so is this." I picked up the sandwich bag of weed, opened it, and sniffed. "Wow. Really good."

"You want some?" she offered with a huge smile on her face.

"If you insist," I said, laughing as she got ice cubes from the freezer. She put them in the bong with fresh water, then she handed the bong back to me with a lighter.

"Go for it."

I packed the bong and took a nice long hit, enjoying the flavor and the immediate feeling of relaxation. Her weed was top quality. No stems or seeds. Bright green, sticky buds. I passed her the bong.

"Come on. Let's go sit outside on the balcony," she said as she walked toward the balcony doors, motioning for me to follow her. She had three dark brown chairs with cream-colored pillows, a patio table, and a few plants lining the balcony. We talked about our lives. We came from two very different worlds. I was from the barrio, and she came from a stable upper-middle-class white family. I would have felt awkward sitting there with her, but she was very welcoming and friendly. Our conversation flowed. A part of me felt bad, as she seemed like a good person, and I was really only there to get high.

I stayed, and we kept talking. Later on, as we were about to eat sandwiches in her kitchen, I saw her open a drawer and pull out a small machine, a needle, and a tiny bottle.

"What's that for?" I asked.

"I'm diabetic. I check my blood three times a day and take insulin," she told me. She used the machine to prick her finger to check her blood. It was the first time I'd ever seen a diabetic use a machine to check their blood.

I stared in silence as she read the machine, put it aside, filled the syringe, lifted her shirt, and injected herself with insulin. I had seen hundreds of people shoot up heroin, cocaine, and crystal before, but for some reason this was different. I felt sad inside. I took a bite from the sandwich she'd prepared for me and asked her, "So how long have you been diabetic?"

"Since I was five," she said. She showed me her fingertips. They were calloused from years of checking her blood.

"Dude, that sucks," I said as I took another bite of the sandwich. She started to educate me on the different types of diabetes. For a quick second the thought of kissing her crossed my mind. But I didn't. Her eyes were big, with very long, curly eyelashes. They seemed to penetrate me as she talked.

When I left a few hours later, I gave Hope a soft kiss on the cheek and said goodbye. We made plans to hang out the next day.

The next day, Hope came over to pick me up in blue jeans, black Docs, and a white T-shirt. Amá was washing dishes; she looked through the screen door at Hope as she approached the apartment. "¿Y ella quién chingados es?" she asked as I opened the door. I introduced Hope.

"Hola, señora. Mi nombre es Hope," she said in stilted Spanish with a huge friendly smile as she put out her hand to shake my mom's. My mom dried her hands on her apron and shook Hope's hand as they both stood in the doorway. Amá took to Hope instantly, given her attempt to speak Spanish.

"Where'd you learn Spanish?"

"En la universidad. Pero no lo hablo muy bien." *At the university. But I don't speak it very well.*

Amá smiled. Hope's upbeat, positive, and optimistic attitude was contagious. "You speak it perfectly. ¿Cuál universidad?"

"San Diego State," said Hope, at which my mom smiled even bigger.

"¡Guau! Es una universidad muy buena. Allí quiero que vaya mijo." Amá was talking about me, telling Hope that she wanted me to go there someday.

My mom gave us her blessing and we left, hopping into a nice two-door black Acura that looked and smelled new. Hope drove me to her favorite sandwich shop and asked what I wanted. Standing in front of the deli's glass counter, I responded, "I don't know. Whatever you get."

"I'm getting a turkey-and-provolone sandwich with avocado, mayo, lettuce, and tomatoes. Do you like provolone?" she asked.

I had no clue what provolone was and just stared at her with a blank face. Then I looked at the guy behind the counter, who was looking at me with impatience. I felt stupid. She caught on quickly and told the guy to make us two of the same sandwich. I watched him make it. When he added the provolone, she pulled me close and whispered in my ear, "That's provolone. It's a type of cheese."

I smiled at her. I pulled her close and kissed her again on the cheek. She smiled. I didn't feel judged. I didn't feel stupid, either. We grabbed the sandwiches, and she drove us to a lake in the mountains outside San Diego, near a small town called Julian. We parked alongside the road and pulled a blanket from the trunk of her car. We laid it under a tree with a perfect view of the lake and the mountains.

"Have you been up here before? It's my favorite spot to clear my head," she said.

"We drove by this place a lot when I was a kid because my mom's cousin works at an egg farm, separating single-yolk from double-yolk eggs, in a small town called Ramona near here," I said, pointing in that direction.

"My dad was a software engineer. He has a house in Florida on the water with a big boat, his new wife, and a dog. After the divorce my mom had to make a living, so she became a flight attendant. And here I am at college, living in a nice condo," she said.

I pulled her close and kissed her. Her lips were soft. Our lips parted and our tongues touched. As she traced my lips with her tongue softly, I opened my eyes and she opened hers. Her gaze was penetrating. I closed my eyes again, allowing myself to go with it. My mind went silent, lost in our kiss. It felt right. It felt innocent. It felt natural, unforced. We stopped kissing and hugged each other tight. Smiling. Laughing there under the tree as we looked toward the lake and mountains.

"Thank you," she said.

"For what?"

"Just, thank you."

I understood.

Love sees no gender, I thought to myself, and then said in a whisper, "I wish everything else felt this right."

When we got to her place, she asked, "Do you want to watch movies and spend the night?"

"That's cool," I responded with a smile.

"Okay. Here," she said as she handed me the phone. "Call your mom to let her know so she doesn't worry about you."

No one had ever told me to call my mother, let alone cared whether I did. When I hung up the phone, Hope smiled and kissed me. We went to her room and made love for the first time. It flowed so naturally. There was no pressure. Our bodies molded to each other, moving rhythmically, as if we were embracing while floating in water. We savored each other's touch and scent in bliss.

I slept like a baby.

CHAPTER 14

I spent a few days turning tricks at the park before going back to Hope's condo for a visit. I was still in community college, but it was oh so easy for that to take a back seat when I went down the drugging-and-tricking rabbit hole. That evening, while watching the computer-animated film *The Mind's Eye* and jamming to house music, I placed two tabs of acid on my tongue, let them dissolve, and then swallowed a capsule of Ecstasy. "You want one?" I asked Hope. She declined, so I swallowed a second.

The next morning when I woke, she was not next to me. I looked around and saw the light on in her bathroom. I peeked in through the crack and saw her bending over a mirror on the counter with a cut straw in her hand, snorting a line of crystal. I opened the door as she straightened back up and wiped her nose. She snorted, making that sound that only tweakers make after doing a line of crystal, and said, "Hey, what's up?" in her bubbly, friendly voice.

"Nothing," I said. "I'm tired. And still sort of tripping. What's up with you? Are you gonna share?" I asked.

"Of course. I wanted to let you sleep," she said as she

poured some crystal onto the mirror, crushed it with her driver's license, and made a line for me to snort. The crystal had a purple hue. I felt the burning sensation in the back of my nose and down my throat from all the god-knows-what chemicals that were in it. "Where did you get this from? I thought you told me you didn't have any."

"I always keep a secret stash. This is from a friend who specializes in purple crystal and Hawaiian Ice. He's bringing some Ice next week, because I have finals coming up and need to stay up to study."

"Shit, I gotta get to school. I can't miss class or my ass ain't ever gonna graduate."

The crystal was strong. It gave me a shitload of energy. I pulled her into the shower and we showered together, laughing and making out.

"We gotta stop if you're going to make it to class in time," she said, trying to push me out of the shower.

We toweled each other off. As I was getting dressed, I caught her staring at me through the mirror. She was smiling. I smiled back.

As she drove me to school, she asked, "Don't you get scared? Do you think you're an addict? You're using a lot."

"Nah, I'm good. Why? Do you think you're an addict?" I asked in return.

"Ha ha ha. This isn't about me. I'm talking about you. What do you think you're running from? And where do you go when you disappear for hours or days without calling?"

I looked at her with confusion. *Is that what she was smiling about when she looked at me in the mirror while I was getting dressed? Is she falling in love with me?* I said, "Dude, you must be tweaking hard, 'cause you're talkin nonsense. I ain't no addict. Just like you aren't. We're just having fun. And I ain't running from shit. You know why? Because I don't give a fuck. About anything," I said, trying to laugh it off.

She didn't answer. That was the beginning of the end.

I became restless in the car. For the first time, everything about her annoyed me. The way she breathed annoyed me. The way she drove annoyed me. The feeling of her hand on my leg annoyed me. Was it because I cared about her and she'd started to ask me questions I didn't want to answer? Was I afraid that she was starting to see through me? Would she think differently of me if she knew I had sex with men? If she knew the real me, she would reject me—I was sure of it. I wanted to push her away first, before she found out the truth about me and pushed me away.

After she dropped me off, I watched her car pull away. I took her secret stash out of my pocket—I had stolen it while she was getting dressed. I didn't go to class. Instead I finished her stash in the bathroom and walked to Balboa Park. I sought the comfort of the familiar. And the only thing that was familiar, that gave me a sense of validation, was what I was good at—nameless, empty, transactional sex with men.

That night I found a large bush hidden among the trees in the park. I cleaned the leaves out of the way and laid my head down on the dirt. The feeling of soil against my face grounded me and gave me comfort. I lay on my back and looked up at the sky through an opening in the canopy. Tears flowed down my face as I stared at the night sky. I asked God, *Why? What did I do to deserve this?*

I slept in the park over the weekend. I had a home to go to, but I didn't want my family, especially my mom, to see me in the state I was in. Why was I living such a disgusting, deplorable, despicable life? I degraded myself to an animalistic level for drugs and stole from someone who cared about me. Was this really all life had to offer? Was this really all that I was ever going to be good for? And the secrets I had been living all these years started to eat me up inside in a way I hadn't felt before. I didn't want to see my family. I didn't want them to see me. I didn't want to be seen. I wanted to disappear. I wanted to get high as much as I could, to the point of feeling nonexistent.

I hid away from the world under that bush, and the only comfort I felt was the soil beneath me as its scent blended with the smell of eucalyptus leaves.

I didn't call Hope. I didn't call Ariyel. I didn't call my mom. It was easier to be alone than to face those who cared for me. A few days later I called Hope. I wondered if she'd found out that I had stolen her secret stash of crystal. I had crossed a line. The realization set in—*I'm a drug addict*. She was right.

I asked her to pick me up and was relieved when she said she would. As we drove to her house, we spoke as if nothing had happened. She was her usual nice, cordial, upbeat self. I took off my clothes, put them in her washing machine, and hopped in the shower. When I got out, she was in the kitchen getting ready to make coffee. I tried to hold her from behind and attempted to kiss her neck as she busied herself with her espresso machine. She was distant and cold. I kept my arms around her waist.

"So why did you call me?" she asked. "Did you figure you would come over and steal some more of my shit? I trusted you," she said as she maneuvered herself out of my embrace and turned around to look at me with tears in her eyes. I recognized those tears. They were tears of disappointment, betrayal, hurt, and sadness.

I used the first self-defense mechanism I knew, which was anger, and responded with "Well, what the fuck you expect? I was coming down. You had more than enough. Besides, you got money. Why the fuck you tripping?" I walked away and plopped on the couch. I knew I was being an asshole.

"That's not the point. I trusted you, and you betrayed that trust. It's not okay to steal from me just because you think I have money," she shouted as she followed me into the living room and sat directly across from me.

"I'll get you some more. Shit, how many times have you and your roommates gotten high on my stuff, and you don't hear me complaining about it. I'll go get you some right now," I yelled at her.

I got up and stomped toward the door, only to feel her grab my hand in a very loving, caring manner. "When people borrow something, they normally ask. You didn't ask; you took. You're an addict, Jesse. And you need help. You use way more drugs than anyone I know, but for some reason you seem to function just fine in school. You disappear for days at a time and no one knows where you go or what you do. And look at you. You're wasting away. You're pale and you have bags under your eyes. Let me get you some help," she pleaded.

I laughed right in her face. "You're calling me an addict, but you get high with me. Aren't you the one with a problem?"

"I'm not saying this because I want to fight with you. I care about you and want you to get help. I'm serious." In her eyes I saw genuine love, concern, and a desire to help me— similar to the looks I used to get from Amá and Ariyel but now saw less and less often.

Lying, I said, "I know you're serious, baby. I love you. I'll cut down. I promise. I'll just smoke weed and that's it. I promise I'll change." I held her close and kissed her forehead, knowing I wasn't being authentic. "Baby, I love you."

As I held her with her head resting on my shoulder, I couldn't hold it in any longer and started laughing loudly, taunting her.

"Damn, I'm good. Check me out. I had you believing every single word. Fuck, I guess you're right. I must be a dope fiend." I started laughing even harder. "I promise you, *baybeee*," I said again in a Chicano accent, slurring my words like I was Cheech in a Cheech & Chong movie. "I won't do it again, homegirl. I promise, ey." I fell backward onto the couch, hysterical.

Hope looked at me with disgust and went into the kitchen. When she came back, she dropped the yellow pages on the table in front of me. "Here. Look up 'drug addiction' or something. You need to do something to help you stop. If you don't do something about it, then I need you to stop coming around here or calling me."

I did what I was told, laughing as I flipped through the pages. I don't remember exactly what section I looked under, but I remember calling a number for Narcotics Anonymous (NA). I laughed the entire time, playing it off like it was some joke, even though deep down inside I knew there was truth to what she was saying.

Someone picked up and said, "Narcotics Anonymous hotline. This is Boozer and I'm an addict, how can I help you?"

"Um. Yeah. Um. My girlfriend here thinks I have a problem with drugs, holmes. She told me to call, so I'm calling," I said, laughing nervously.

The guy with the deep voice was friendly and told me he understood all about that. He suggested I check out an NA meeting that night. He told me the time and address of a meeting not too far from Hope's house, which was starting in less than an hour. I didn't think Hope was serious, but she demanded I get in the car with her, and so I went.

It was dark outside when we pulled into the poorly lit parking lot of an old church. We watched people milling about outside the church, smoking cigarettes. Then they went into what looked like a basement along the side of the building. We waited about ten minutes and then I asked Hope, "So now what? It looks like the meeting thing must be starting. Do you want to go in or not?"

"Okay, let's go in. Come on. You ready?"

"Hell nah, I ain't ready, but fuck it. Let's check this shit out," I said as I exhaled with nervous energy.

It was dark outside as we walked toward the light coming from the open basement doors. *What the fuck am I getting myself into?* I thought. As we looked inside, I pulled my black beanie down almost to my nose. I was wearing khaki Dickies with a white tank top. Slowly we walked in, not knowing what to do.

Inside people were sitting around in a circle listening to some white dude with a thick goatee speak. I didn't really make out what he was saying as I worried about my appearance and who was looking at us. We must have seemed like two lost rabbits sniffing our way around. A woman with flaming red hair and rockabilly bangs, covered in tattoos, waved to us to sit next to her. We walked toward her and grabbed two chairs. Everyone else was silent, listening to the guy speaking. I looked around and then slouched backward into my metal folding chair, crossed my arms, buried my chin deep in my chest, and stared at the floor with a mean, hard look on my face. Every so often I would slowly look around from under the edge of my beanie.

I tried to focus on the guy sharing his story. I heard him say that anyone was welcomed in a meeting and it didn't matter how old they were, if they were gay or straight or bi, or whatever race or religion the person belonged to. He was looking directly at me. Immediately, I thought he was lying and had only said it because I was the only young Chicano in the room. I put my head back down but kept listening. He started to tell crazy stories about his past. When he talked about his deeply painful experiences, the people in the room were laughing. I began to smile, too (while hiding a laugh), because I too could relate. Obviously though, I was too cool to let any of them see me smile or chuckle.

After he shared about his using, he began to explain how he got clean and what it was like to live without drugs. He talked about feeling hope. As I listened I felt comfort come over me. As if a tiny glimmer of light from an almost-snuffed-out candle started to slowly brighten. Something came over me. I began to cry. I didn't just let a few tears come out; I started to sob and slouched forward in my chair. I ducked my head between my knees and held my face in my hands and just cried. Tears formed a small puddle on the floor. Hope had her hand on my back. No one got up to grab me or tried to hold me. The guy didn't stop talking. No one told me to shut up. No one gave me a tissue. They just let me cry. And so I cried.

Something magical happened at that meeting. I felt like I was in the right place for the first time in a very long time. I felt like I identified with everything he was saying and that others identified, too. I mean, only those of us who have gone through the same crazy insane shit that he was talking about would find humor in the identification.

When the meeting was over, everyone got up to form a circle with arms around one another. Two people had their arms around me on each side as I stood there with tears crusted on my face and my arms limp by my sides. They recited a prayer in unison that I had not heard before. They called it the Serenity Prayer.

God, grant me the serenity to accept the things I cannot change, the courage to change the things I can, and the wisdom to know the difference.

It was beautiful yet simple. Afterward, the red-haired woman introduced herself and gave us a meeting schedule, on which she wrote her phone number. She called over two

guys who were already walking toward us. When she introduced us, I put my hand out to shake their hands and one
of them grabbed me into a bear hug. "We hug around here."
The guy who'd been speaking came up and introduced himself. I didn't pay attention to his name, still being shocked
about having been hugged by this strange dude in a non-
sexual, welcoming way. He was shorter than me at around
five feet, ten inches, looked like he was in his late thirties,
and was of average build. He appeared Italian, with his dark
hair and thick goatee. "Welcome," he said, and wrote his
name and phone number on the meeting schedule that the
red-haired woman had handed to me. I would learn later
that he wasn't a special paid speaker but a regular guy telling his story, just like everyone else. I don't remember much
else from that night except that they were very welcoming
and hugged seemingly incessantly. They suggested I go to
ninety meetings in ninety days and not use drugs or drink
in between meetings.

"So what are these steps you were talking about, and
what is a sponsor?" I asked him. "Will someone pay me and
sponsor me to go through this process? If so, how do I find
the person who pays me? Is that how it works?"

He laughed and said, "For right now, just go to ninety
meetings in ninety days and don't use in between meetings. A sponsor is someone who will guide you through the
twelve steps. And no, you don't get paid to do this. And you
don't have to pay anything, either. Just keep coming back
and it will all start to make sense." He pulled the schedule
from my hand and circled the meetings he went to.

He said, "Here, these are the meetings I like to go to.

Come see me there. I'll introduce you to some people. Even some who look like you."

"But . . . I'm too young. Look at me. I'm an eighteen-year-old Latino. And you're an old white guy. There ain't any young people here who look like me," I said.

He laughed again like he'd heard it all before and told me to hold on as he walked over to a table and grabbed a pamphlet. He handed it to me and said, "Here, read this." The pamphlet had information about being young and in recovery. He then grabbed a thick blue book from the same table, handed it to me, and said, "Here, read this, too. You will like it. But don't start at the front. Start with the stories in the back of the book. Those stories are written by addicts for addicts."

"But I'm not an addict," I said. "At least, I don't know if I am yet."

He smiled and said, "Just check it out. I'm buying the book for you—as long as you promise to one day buy a book for someone else. I'll see you at the meeting tomorrow."

On the way home I felt like a huge weight had been lifted off me. I felt light. I didn't feel alive and free, but I felt different. There weren't any bluebirds circling my head and chirping, but something did feel right. I asked Hope if she would take me to the meeting the next day. She said, "Yes."

CHAPTER 15

I went to a meeting every day and didn't use any drugs during the next eleven days. I was sick, exhausted, and detoxing hard. Going cold turkey was brutal. The cold sweats, shivers, flu-like symptoms, headaches, muscle aches, stomach cramping, irritability, and trouble sleeping were horrible. At least I was able to avoid some of the sadness and depression by staying busy with school and going to meetings to listen. Still, I stayed clean for eleven days.

It was February 1993. I didn't necessarily feel like I was a part of the group, but I enjoyed listening to people's stories even though they were a lot older than me and most were white. Then, on a Friday, some friends invited me to go clubbing in LA.

I never made it to LA. I stayed in my friend's bedroom with the blinds and curtains closed, playing music, smoking crystal nonstop out of a crystal bong, and sniffing lines. Yet I couldn't stay awake. I sniffed about seventeen lines of crystal, each the size of a brand-new number-two pencil. I would do a line, then I would become tired again and do another line. I figured I had built up a tolerance, but I hadn't been high in almost two weeks. I didn't understand. And although I didn't feel the full rush effect that often accompanies methamphetamines, I did feel the regret of getting high. I don't remember how I got home, but I woke up there on Sunday feeling horrible. My entire body ached once again, and I felt shame and guilt for having used.

I'd had eleven days clean. That was a long time for me. It was the longest I had been clean in years, and I'd thrown it all away. Now that I had experienced eleven days off drugs, I knew that getting off drugs was possible. I called Hope and told her I'd gotten high. She told me that she still loved me and that she was still clean and had gone to meetings the two days I was gone. She offered to pick me up that same day to go to a meeting. That was the evening I shared for the first time.

"I'm tired of getting high," I said. Then I told the group that I felt out of place and different because I was young and there weren't other young people who looked like me in the meetings I had been going to. It didn't occur to me that I was doing what almost every newcomer to recovery does. I was looking for what made me different rather than what made us the same. Over the next twelve days, I went to one meeting a day and made it a point to find a sponsor to help me with the so-called twelve steps. People recommended I check out a meeting in the barrio, where there would be a lot of people who looked like me. Hope and I went to check it out. The barrio meeting, as it was called, was on a Saturday night in a big pink church near Chicano Park in southeast San Diego's Logan Heights neighborhood.

The meeting was packed. There was a bunch of hard-core, tatted-down-looking cholos, dressed in their starched, ironed clothes, chilling outside the church smoking. They looked like they had done some serious time in prison. There was also a bunch of Black guys dressed in their starched, ironed clothes but with the Black Cali gangster swag, also smoking. And there were three or four white guys standing by their Harleys smoking, which also tripped me out because I never saw white dudes on Harleys in the barrio. They looked like white biker gang members. I had never seen all these three groups together in the same place without some drama breaking off. I was nervous as we walked up. My fists were clenched, and I kept looking over my shoulder.

All of a sudden I heard one of the Chicano gangsters call my name. "Hey, Jesse! What's up, ese?" I'd seen the guy at a different meeting but didn't think he knew my name. He waved me and Hope over and introduced me to the other guys. They hugged me enthusiastically; that definitely felt weird coming from gangstered-out cholos. I still wasn't used to all the hugging people did in NA meetings. "Welcome, little homeboy," they said.

Before the meeting started, a woman we had met at other meetings asked how we were doing, and I told her that I needed a sponsor to start working the steps that everyone kept talking about. Hope said, "Well, I have someone in mind who I am going to ask the next time I see her, but Jesse still hasn't found someone he likes who he can relate to. Maybe he will at this meeting."

"Well, what are you waiting for, little homeboy?" said the

woman. "There are a lot of old-timers in this meeting, so it shouldn't be hard for you to find someone here."

The meeting started with birthday celebrations. There was a buff gangster-looking Black man with clothes impeccably creased out who celebrated six years clean. He had a very strong message about being raised in the hood, being a former gang member, going in and out of prison, and dealing with race issues and had been able to stay clean all these years. He came across as tough and hypermasculine. His demeanor and exterior reminded me of myself. It was my armor to keep people from getting to know me.

After him, a Latino man with strong Indigenous features and wearing dress slacks and a neatly ironed guayabera celebrated thirteen years clean. He had a Chicano accent and a calmness that I liked. His smile and his laughter when he shared made me think of an uncle I'd never had. He felt wise in his calm. Like an elder. "That's him," I said to Hope and the friend we were sitting with. "That Latino dude is who I'm going to ask to be my sponsor."

During the meeting, I didn't listen to anything. I spent the entire time rehearsing in my mind how I was going to ask the Chicano guy to be my sponsor. I had never done anything like this before. I'm not one to ask for help and was worried he would say no. I also didn't like going up to people to introduce myself. It was not something that came naturally.

As the meeting closed, I was gathering the courage to go up to the Chicano guy when the woman who'd sat next to us stopped me and said, "Why don't you ask that Black guy who celebrated six years to sponsor you?"

"Say what? Oh hell nah! What's that Black dude going to help me with? I'm a Chicano and from the barrio," I said.

"I think you should ask the Black guy," she said, and went on, "You already know how to hang with Chicanos. I think you don't want to ask the Black dude because he reminds you of yourself. It's up to you." She took Hope with her, leaving me standing in the middle of the room.

"Dammit," I said in a low voice. I was now more confused, frustrated, and nervous than before. Who was I going to ask?

Then I heard someone next to me say, "Hey, what's up, lil man?"

It was the Black dude who'd celebrated six years clean.

Without really thinking, and with my head down and my arms at my sides, I let out a deep breath and said, "Fuck . . . Ey, holmes, my homegirl over there says I should ask you to be my sponsor, but if you don't want to, it's cool. I won't trip."

He pulled a schedule and a pen from the table in front of him and said, "Here, write down my beeper number and home number. If you really want me to be your sponsor, you have to call me every day for thirty days. This will help you get in the habit of calling me. If I don't answer, then go ahead and page me and I'll return your call within the hour as I'm probably in a meeting at work. So call me tomorrow and we'll start you on step one. Sound good, lil man?"

I was irritated, but I agreed. "Yeah, it's cool."

He gave me a hug and asked me my name. He introduced me to the other people standing there and said, "Hey, everybody, this is lil man Jesse. He just asked me to be his sponsor, so if you see him at a meeting, make sure you ask him if he's called me that day." They all laughed and hugged me. I was so caught up in my own head that I forgot to congratulate him on being six years clean.

I called. I called. And I called some more for the next couple days. I would page his beeper and if he didn't call back in ten minutes, I would call his home phone. Sometimes his wife would pick up, and if not, I would leave a message. If I didn't hear from him within an hour, I would beep him again and call his house again and leave another message. I was persistent. They told me to chase my recovery like I chased my dope, and I did. He gave me some writing assignments as part of beginning the first step. So when I'd call him, our conversations would go like this:

"Hello," he'd say.

"Hey, holmes, can you believe this shit . . ." and blah blah blah, I would go down a list of things that went wrong that day, and he'd jump in and cut me off midsentence, saying, "Hold up, hold up, Jess. You should start off by saying, 'Hey, sponsor, how are you?' before you go into talking about yourself. It's called being courteous. Have you done any of your writing assignment today?"

"Nah, I didn't because . . ." and I would start rambling again, and he would quickly cut me off and say, "Stop. Stop. Stop. First, I want you to do some writing on your assignment for about fifteen minutes and see what comes out from that writing, and then call me back. Before and after you write, I want you to say the Serenity Prayer." And then he'd hang up on me.

I'd think to myself, *Why the fuck did I ask this mother-fucker to be my sponsor? Fuck him for hanging up on me.*

Then I would breathe, say the Serenity Prayer, and, while still angry, huffing and puffing, I would pull out my note-book and start writing. After about an hour of writing I would call him back, and he'd say, "So did you do your writing?"

"Yes. I did," I'd say with an attitude.

"Do you feel better? Did you get some clarity?"

"Yes," I'd say.

"Okay, so how are you doing today? Still clean?"

"Yup! Still clean."

"So that makes it a great day," he'd say, and then we'd get into a conversation. This went on for the next twelve days. I called him every day. I went to meetings with Hope every day. I was writing every day. I started to feel better physically. But no matter how many meetings I went to or how many people in recovery I hung out with, I didn't feel understood. Mostly I felt different because I was still going to the park to turn tricks in between school and meetings.

Sex work was the only thing that felt familiar to me. It was the only thing I felt good at. And I made money from it. Even though people told me not to beat myself up for the relapse I'd had, I still judged myself and felt that I wasn't even good at staying clean. Deep inside, I felt that sobriety was possible for everyone else, but not for me. I was too broken.

At school I had told my friends that I was going to meet-ings and was going to try this recovery thing, which they all supported. They agreed to not offer or sell me any drugs, even if I demanded they do.

Amá was elated that, after the meetings, Hope would drive me home on days when I didn't spend the night with her. I'd sit on the couch journaling while she watched her Mexican soap operas. Having me around was a comfort for her, but I didn't know what to talk about with her so the silences were uncomfortable between us. But I finally got the courage to tell Amá I was going to meetings even though I felt it would be another disappointment. I was disappointed in myself—the son, the sexually abused drug addict who had to go to these meetings because I was no good at living life.

I didn't reach out to others to ask if all these ideas running through my head were normal. I didn't realize that depression, anxiety, and being overwhelmed are also by-products of detoxing; this is why a lot of people go through structured drug and alcohol treatment. The meetings started to get boring, and I kept asking myself, *Is this all I have to look forward to for the rest of my life? Meetings, coffee, cigarettes, and hanging out with a bunch of people older than me at the same coffee shops after each meeting, doing the same boring shit every day? There aren't any young people like me to hang out with other than Hope. I'm eighteen.*

Also there were a few assholes in the meetings who'd say some fucked-up shit to me, like "Man, you're way too young to be an addict. Go out and use some more until you get a real habit." Others would say, "I've spilled more dope than you've used," and then laugh at me. The reality was that not everyone in recovery was welcoming. These comments would make me angry. As if now I had to prove that I was a bad-enough dope fiend to be allowed there with them.

Even though I was calling my sponsor, it was a struggle every day to not get high. I would pray for my obsession to be lifted, but the desire to use remained. I wanted to get high every day. I had to literally sit on my hands at school to prevent myself from going out and getting high with my buddies.

Each day I grew angrier and more anxious. I was frustrated that I had to stop before most "normal" people had their first drink. I believed my life was going to be boring without alcohol and drugs. I would ask myself, *Will I ever be able to smoke weed again?*

Sometimes people would tell me, "You are so lucky to get this at your age. I wish I got clean at eighteen." But that would make me feel like I was being talked down to, and I'd respond with "Well shit, you're lucky your old ass got clean when you did because the way I used, I could never have used for that long."

My sponsor would tell me, "It's just for today, man. Just don't get high today. You can get high tomorrow." That kept me pushing forward into the next day, day by day.

On March 11, 1993, during an evening meeting, I looked at every single person in the room and ran down an entire list of reasons why I didn't belong there. At the end, time was set aside for a burning desire, when anyone could share about wanting to get high, or hurting themselves or anyone else. I didn't raise my hand to tell the group that I wanted to get high. I didn't tell the group that I was struggling with letting go of the lifestyle. I didn't tell the group that I was looking for the smallest excuse to use again.

I stayed for the Serenity Prayer and stood around after the meeting to see if anyone would approach me to invite me anywhere. Hope wasn't there because she had gone to a women's meeting with her sponsor. Hope was establishing a network of women to support her in recovery, and I was jealous—I still had no "buddies" to hang out with. I made it about race and told myself it was easier for her because she was white and pretty. No one offered me a ride home, and no one invited me to coffee. It didn't matter that I was giving off a don't-fuck-with-me-and-don't-approach-me attitude. I still wanted them to approach me.

Fuck them! I don't need these people or these meetings, I told myself that night, and walked away.

I felt empty inside. I felt alone. It was around 8:00 p.m., and on my walk home a car drove by, slowed down, and made a U-turn. The car, a red Trans Am with a primed fender, stopped right in front of me with its windows rolled down. Inside was a man in his forties with long dreadlocks and a goatee. He asked if I wanted to go with him to smoke some weed. I didn't know him but knew immediately that the dude was looking for sex. I thought about it for a quick second. Then, on autopilot, I reached for the door handle, opened the door, and hopped in the front seat.

He handed me a joint, and I waved it off and said, "Nah, I ain't seen you roll it. Give me the weed and some Zig-Zags and I'll roll my own." He gave me a sack of weed and some rolling papers. I rolled a fat joint and began to smoke it. As soon as I took the first hit, I knew I was off to the races again. I leaned farther back in the seat and let light-headedness sink in. He laughed. I had smoked two joints by the time we got to his apartment. He told me he worked as a mailman and that he had recently gone through a divorce. He seemed cool and cracked jokes to make me feel comfortable. The entire way to his place, I kept thinking that I didn't need to do this, that I had a choice, that I should just get out of the car and catch the bus home, but I didn't. I figured I'd already gotten high, so I may as well just get high the rest of the night.

He lived in a neighborhood called Golden Hills, right next to the Golden Hills Recreation Center and across the street from a baseball field, in a town house with brown stairs leading up to his apartment on the second floor. He asked me if I would take a shower first. I left the door open and searched the bathroom for hidden cameras before I took my clothes off and hopped in the shower. When I got out of the shower, he was standing in the doorway with only his boxers on.

He handed me a towel and said, "Here, use this to dry off."

He had a lit joint in his hand, so I figured he had already taken a hit. He handed it to me. I took a hit from the joint and quickly felt its potency. I grabbed my clothes and sneakers from the floor and followed him into the living room, where rolling papers and a sack of open weed lay on the coffee table with two more joints rolled. He asked if I wanted a drink. I said, "Nah, I'm good. But listen, I can't take too long, man. I got to get up early for school. So can we get on with it?"

"Chill out, homeboy. Let me smoke a bit more and get my drink on first. Relax," he said as he took his boxers off and sat back down on the couch completely naked. "Come over here and let me hold you while we smoke," he said.

"Aren't you forgetting something?" I asked. I made the international sign for money by rubbing my thumb against my index and middle fingers.

"Oh damn. Homeboy's a businessman. Even though my weed you smoking is alone worth more than the fifty bucks I was thinking about giving you. Keep being persistent and I'll drop it to twenty-five dollars," he said.

"Come on, holmes. Don't be about games. Just give me the fifty dollars," I told him.

"*Óraleeeee*, I got you, holmes," he said, laughing while mocking my Chicano accent. He got up, walked into a bedroom, and came out a few seconds later with a twenty-dollar bill. "When we're done I'll give you the other thirty dollars," he said as he sat back down on the couch.

I finished my joint and walked over to where he was sitting. I laid my head in his lap as he put one arm around me, using his other hand to smoke his blunt. I felt safe for an instant. Then he put his hand on the back of my head and motioned me to go down on him. As I moved into position, a different type of light-headedness came over me. It felt like the room was spinning. I ignored it.

With each minute that passed I grew more and more light-headed. Until, all of a sudden, I felt a pair of hands grab me from behind, pulling me backward. As quick as I could, I jumped up. I saw a man who hadn't been there before. "What the fuck?!" I shouted with my fists in fighting position.

"Chill the fuck out, man, these are just my homeboys. Since I'm giving you fifty on top of all the weed you been smoking, I figure it's only fair you take care of my homeboys, too," he said. I noticed there was another man standing near the stereo. He turned up the music.

I looked at him and the other two guys. I tried to figure out how to get away. There I was, naked. My clothes were on the other side of the couch. All three of them were bigger than me. The only other person naked was the guy on the couch, who said, "Just chill the fuck out and do what you're told and you'll be okay."

"Nah, man. Fuck you! Let me get the fuck out of here. Keep your money and let me go. Give me my clothes, ese," I said. I realized that I was feeling drugged as I moved toward my clothes.

The guy who'd been behind me was now standing where my clothes were on the floor. With his foot he kicked the clothes even farther away from me. The guy on the couch said in an eerily calm voice, "You little punk faggot. You ain't goin nowhere."

"Fuck you and your homeboys. Let me get outta here," I yelled at them. My mind was swirling, and my sight was blurred. The guy near the stereo rushed toward me and punched me in the head. I fell to the floor hard. A foot pressed my face into the carpet while a pair of hands held my back down. An extremely sharp pain made me try to move away as I screamed loudly and pointlessly into the carpet, which muffled my screams while tears rolled down my face. My screams became sobs. The pain from the tearing of my insides was horrible. I attempted to fight back, but it was futile. I shut down as I tried my hardest to separate my essential self from my body and to force my body to avoid tensing up from the pain.

The guy who'd picked me up rubbed one of his hands around my back as if trying to console me and said, "Just relax and don't fight. It's better if you don't."

My body tensed, and I tried to fight again when I felt a hard kick in my rib cage blowing the air out of my lungs while the guy's other foot pressed my face violently into the carpet. My skin felt like it was on fire from rug burn.

The three of them raped and beat me for what seemed like hours. I felt such hatred for God then. After a long time, I gave up. Defeated. Crying. Bleeding. My spirit felt dead. When they were finished with me, I couldn't control my bowels, and a mixture of blood and other fluids flowed out of me. When the guy from the car saw that, he beat me more. I was like a rag doll with no life left. I just lay there.

"Man, get this little bitch the fuck outta my apartment before I decide to kill the muthafucka for dirtyin my carpet," said the Trans Am guy to his friends.

The other guys grabbed me by my arms while I begged, "No. No. Wait. Let me put my clothes on." I kept trying to get up as they dragged me, but I only stumbled. They threw me down the stairs into the cold night, then tossed my clothes out behind me. The door slammed as I struggled to hold myself up and grab my pants. I found my tank top but had no clue where my shirt had gone. I stumbled around barefoot trying to find my shoes. They were toward the bottom of the stairs with my socks scattered a few feet away. I tried to run barefoot with my shoes in hand, leaving behind one sock and my boxers. I held my pants up with one hand and stumbled around in pain. My face, nose, and ass were bleeding. I reached the bleachers of the recreation center park across the street. It was cold, breezy, and foggy. I stayed there a few minutes, too afraid to look back but then looking back anyway out of fear that someone would come up behind me to shoot me or beat me to death. I told myself, *Hurry up. Hurry the fuck up and get the fuck out of here.*

I put on my shoes with only one sock. I walked along the main road because I was too afraid to cut through the park at night. Cars sped past me, and no one stopped to ask if I needed help, even though I am sure I looked like a bloodied wreck. As I walked, I kept telling myself over and over again, *See, you ain't worth shit. No one's even stopping to help you 'cause you a worthless piece-of-shit drug addict. Just like your dad said, you're a good-for-nothing. You deserve what the fuck happens to you for not getting your shit together. This is your fault 'cause you're a fuckup. And that's all you'll ever be—a fuckup.*

I got to downtown San Diego and found a pay phone on a well-lit corner. I begged someone for some change and called the only person that came to mind to ask for help, my sponsor. I prayed to God that he would answer the phone and not be angry with me for calling so late. Luckily he answered. He'd been asleep.

As soon as I heard his voice say hello, I felt safe again. There I was on Broadway on a pay phone, crying, with him on the other end of the line. I didn't tell him what had happened, but in between sobs I kept saying, "I don't want to live like this anymore. I don't know what to do. I'm tired of living this life. I'm tired. I don't want to live like this anymore."

He responded in a loving and caring voice, "You don't have to live like this anymore, Jesse. Let me guide you, lil man. Stop fighting. You lost the war. Not just the battle, but the war. Tell me where you are and I'm on my way to pick you up."

Relief swept over me. I finally understood the true meaning of powerlessness. I didn't have to fight anymore. I can't explain the feeling of that spiritual awakening, crying on a pay phone on Broadway in downtown San Diego, beaten up, raped, drugged, and bloody.

This man—who I hadn't wanted as my sponsor, who I did not think had anything to offer me—had, with his simple comment, summed up all my years of suffering. I felt his compassion and his empathy. And I felt understood.

"I don't want you to see me like this, so I'll call you tomorrow," I said and hung up the phone.

I walked into a McDonald's bathroom across from City College. I locked the door and looked into the mirror and couldn't believe the face that was looking back at me. My bloody face was swollen in various places. I looked like I had just lost a boxing match. I washed my face and used paper towels to clean the blood off my chest and shoulders. I pulled down my pants and wiped between my legs as best

I could. I left the bathroom, ignoring looks, and walked home.

When I got home, no one was awake. I opened the door as quietly as I could. As I walked to my bedroom, I heard my mom stir to get up. I whispered, "Amá, soy yo." *Mom, it's me.* I quickly took off my clothes in the dark and hid them under my bed. I wrapped a dark brown towel around my waist and hurried into the bathroom to shower. I didn't lock the door so I wouldn't raise Amá's suspicions.

I turned on the water and stood in the shower. My mom opened the door to take a pee. This was common in our house since it was a small apartment with only one bathroom; we never had any privacy. "¿De dónde vienes a estas horas? ¿Estás bien?" she asked while sitting on the toilet. *Where are you coming from at this hour? Are you okay?*

"I'm fine, Mom. Just tired. I was with friends after the meeting. I need to go to sleep to get up for class tomorrow. I walked home, so I'm sweaty, and you know I hate going to bed dirty. Go back to bed," I told her.

"Okay pues. Buenas noches y que Dios te bendiga."

"Igualmente," I responded. *Same to you.*

I put my head under the water and stood there with my hands against the tile, letting it wash away the horror. I cleaned myself with soap as best I could, but the pain along my ribs, face, and ass was nearly unbearable. I softly washed with only soap and no washcloth. I slouched down in pain, pulling my knees close to my chest, held myself with my head bowed, and cried, letting the water pour down my head and back. I stayed that way for a few minutes, then forced myself up against the tile. As I dried myself off, I again saw how bad my reflection looked in the mirror. Bruises were already showing on my ribs.

I got into bed, too afraid my mom would hear me cry, so I just let the tears come as I laid my head on the pillow and stared at the ceiling until I fell asleep. That was my last day getting high: March 11, 1993.

CHAPTER 16

If the drugs weren't going to kill me, the lifestyle would have. I wasn't just addicted to the drugs; I was also addicted to the life. I had to let go of old people, places, and things and try on new ways of thinking and doing. That meant I had to stop turning tricks at the park. I didn't tell my sponsor, but making all those changes at once wasn't easy. Still, I knew that if I kept doing what I'd always done, then I would continue to get what I always got.

My first year clean was my most difficult. I didn't go to a treatment center or a sober living facility or a detox. I went to meetings and kicked on my own. I started asking questions and talking to people who understood the withdrawal I was going through. It was helpful, especially because the obsession to get high didn't dissipate overnight. I made sure my time alone was as limited as possible, because an addict alone is in bad company. Going out of my comfort zone to ask for support was also hard for me. Yet I was willing to do anything to stay clean.

The first week, it was difficult to fall asleep. When I did

sleep, I'd sweat, and my morning breath stank no matter how much I brushed or rinsed with Listerine. I would go to sleep late and wake up early. When I did fall into a deep sleep, my dreams were intensified and I would often wake up in night terrors. My screaming woke my mom in the other room or Hope if she was sleeping next to me. I didn't sleep well my entire first year clean. My body didn't stop twitching for a year. It took months for me to feel normal again.

My sponsor had me start working on the concepts of powerlessness and unmanageability. Willpower alone was not enough for me to stop getting high. I surrendered to the facts that even one drink would set off craving for more and that I had no mental defense against using after the first drug or drink. I did as I was told and spent as much time with my sponsor as I could. He introduced me to other people in the program, which helped create a strong network of men and women in my life.

I started to see people at City College who were also going to meetings, so I'd meet them during lunch and in between classes just so I didn't have to be alone. I realized there were people in recovery all over the place. Finding the people turned out not to be too difficult. It was going out of my comfort zone and asking those people to spend time with me that was hard. Fortunately they didn't reject my efforts in reaching out.

My sponsor had me write about my life. When it was on paper, it hurt to look at the sick, demoralizing, and degrading behavior I had been forced to engage in as a child. And although I prayed all the time, I felt abandoned by God. My sponsor had me write about the positive aspects of my life. It was important for me to start to recognize my positive traits and those of my family and the people around me in order to rebuild my self-esteem and my relationships with others. I learned that in having been present in my life and in the life of my family I'd also been courageous in not giving up. I was able to start seeing that my family was more supportive than I gave them credit for and that they never gave up on me. They didn't hate me after all. I learned that I was generous. Even when using and turning tricks, I gave my mom money to help out with food and rent. And by suiting up and showing up to meetings, to school, to meet my sponsor, I was being disciplined and committed. All these little things helped me restore feelings of self-worth and feel good again. Most important, I was learning to forgive myself.

When we got to the second step of the twelve-step program, which is about coming to believe in a higher power, I went on shutdown. I could not separate the idea of a higher power from the God I'd been raised with, a punishing God. Every time I heard the word *God* in a meeting, I cringed. I felt betrayed, misunderstood, and forgotten by God.

My sponsor tried everything. He had me ask other addicts in the program how they came to believe in their higher power. He had me write down examples of times I'd been pulled over by police and removed from my car while other cops searched it, to understand that, in those moments, the police were a power greater than me. I wrote down examples of the times that I was held at gunpoint and could not escape. The other person had the power to determine whether I was going to live or die. The person with the gun was a power greater than me. I wrote about the times when I would hit the floor because someone was doing a drive-by. The shooters were a power greater than me. I wrote about the guy who molested me, beat me up, drugged me, showed up at my house, and manipulated me into a place of fear so I would be under his control. He was a power greater than my eleven-year-old self.

My sponsor invited me to a spiritual retreat in the mountains of Julian, California, where he would speak. He suggested I find a quiet place to write and gave me a new assignment. My assignment was to tear a page out of my notebook and fold it down the middle. He suggested that on one side of the page I list all the qualities of the God I was raised with and words describing the type of relationship I had with that God. On the other side of the page I was to write down all the qualities I would want my God to have and words I would use to describe that ideal relationship. He suggested I not hold back, not erase anything I wrote down, and most of all not feel stupid for what I was writing. "There is no right or wrong answer, Jesse," he said.

I went up a hill and found a large boulder to sit on. I took a deep breath and looked around me. I took in the expansive view from where I sat and said to myself, *Great Out Doors and Good Orderly Direction*. I said the Serenity Prayer as I looked out into the wilderness, then folded the page as I'd been told and drew a line down the middle. I wrote on the top of one side *The Higher Power I Was Raised With*, and on the other side I wrote *The Higher Power I Want*. On one side of the page I listed all the qualities of the higher power I was raised with.

- *Punishing*
- *Unforgiving*
- *A he*
- *He tested me*
- *He allows horrific things to happen to good people*

On the other side of the paper I listed all the qualities of the higher power I wanted:

- *Loving*
- *Forgiving*
- *Caring*
- *Understands me and will never abandon me*

The list went on and on. And it turned out I wanted a higher power that would not judge me, abandon me, or stop listening to me. I wrote:

I can speak any way I choose because he understands what I am feeling at that moment. I can find my higher power [HP] anywhere and without reservation. I can find my HP in the great outdoors, in my kitchen while cooking, or in a Jewish synagogue, a Muslim mosque, a Buddhist temple, a Catholic church, or any other place

of worship. I can find my HP in the spiritual practices
of inipi or temazcal ceremonies. Most importantly,
my higher power will never abandon me and even in my
darkest moments will provide me signs of hope. My HP
speaks to me through others. My HP doesn't care if I
am gay, straight, bi, trans, or two-spirit, and it will
allow me to remove that ugly feeling of insignificance
I carry.

When I went back to meet my sponsor, he was talking to a group of people. He saw me coming and walked toward me. He asked, "You ready?"

"Yeah," I said. "I'm ready."

He grabbed an aluminum coffee can, and we went back up the hill and found a different place to sit. He had me read to him everything I had written, and he confided in me, too. When I was done, he told me to tear the page in half. We burned the paper that listed the qualities of the higher power I was raised with in the aluminum coffee can and kept the one I wanted.

He told me, "Keep that paper. And over the years feel free to add to it. That is your new higher power if you choose it to be. I will never judge you for your higher power, and please don't ever judge me for mine or anyone else for theirs."

It was that simple for me. From that moment, everything changed. I learned to find my higher power wherever I was. That is one of the biggest blessings I gained from recovery. I became open to the endless possibilities in front of me simply by changing my state of mind. I reawakened old dreams. And I understood why people said, "I thank God for introducing me to recovery, and I thank recovery for introducing me to God." Now it was time to start building on that relationship.

I still had no notion of where my life was going. The only things I was certain about were that I didn't want to use anymore and I didn't want to go back to the life I had been living. I worked full-time at a hair salon during the day and attended school full-time at night. I went home to sleep every night. And although my mom didn't understand these meetings I went to, she supported me.

In school, I asked questions when I didn't understand. I sat in the front rows. I visited my professors during office hours and asked for guidance as if they were my sponsors. I would tell them flat, "I have no clue what I am doing. I don't know what I want to do." My professors consoled me. "Don't worry," they'd say. "Just stay in school. This is your time to figure it out. Don't pressure yourself."

It wasn't easy. But it was better than the alternative. Sitting still was the hardest thing for me. I needed to keep something in my hands, like a pencil, a pen, or a Styrofoam cup, to fidget with. Fidgeting helped me focus. I couldn't study in libraries because the silence drove me crazy and I would look at others to see what books they were reading. In silence, my mind would drift off. I learned it was best for me to study with noise in the background, so I often sat in the community college's cafeteria or the mall's food court during breaks at work and in coffee shops at night. I needed activity around me to focus.

I forced myself to journal every night before bed. Even when I didn't want to write, I would open my notebook and write down *I don't want to write today*, then put it away. Every morning I practiced letting go of my anxiety and fear of the unknown. I stayed busy and productive, which also helped me appreciate the time I spent at home with Amá.

I did, however, sometimes struggle with wanting to go back to the comfort of what was familiar. The life of addiction, living in the streets, sex work, and sleeping in parks was more comfortable to me. I knew what to expect in the streets. I knew what to expect when I got high. I didn't know what to expect now.

When I had these feelings, I'd call my sponsor or share about them in a meeting. I learned that when I stayed focused on the moment, I was okay. And I learned that feelings pass, as everything does.

Sober, my confusion about my sexual identity started eating me up inside. I found myself attracted to men more and more. My relationship with Hope changed, as I felt I could no longer talk with her honestly about what I was feeling or the changes I was experiencing. Even though we were both in recovery now, how could I tell her I found men attractive after all she had done for me? I believed it would destroy her. Instead, I recoiled every time Hope tried to sleep with me. I felt guilty. She'd sacrificed so much for me. She was the reason I got into the rooms of recovery in the first place. Yet having sex clean, without drugs, was an entirely different experience, and having it with her made me uncomfortable. But it wasn't about Hope. I needed time to get to know myself.

After almost a year clean, I wanted to give up again. No matter how much support I received, old feelings of confusion over my identity and about being misunderstood and different resurfaced. I was lonely, and I fell back into thinking that maybe I was too young to be clean. When I told my sponsor that I wasn't sure I belonged in the recovery community anymore, he reached into his glove compartment, pulled out a cassette tape, and handed it to me.

"Here, listen to this tape. Someone gave it to me a few years ago. I found it at home and thought of you. If you still feel hopeless and still want to get high after you listen to it, you let me know, and I'll take you to buy your first bag. Shit, I'll even buy it for you," he said.

Not knowing what to expect, I popped the cassette into my Walkman and listened to it that night. It was a recording of some kid from LA telling his story at a convention on the topic of youth in recovery a few years prior. The kid got clean at fourteen years old. His story wasn't like mine, but I related to him. He was four years clean when the tape was made. I thought to myself, *If he could do it, then so can I.* I had needed to hear someone else who was young tell their story, someone with some time clean behind him. I fell asleep with a smile on my face, hoping to one day meet this kid.

I listened to that tape every morning, as getting up was always the toughest part of the day for me. I used to pull out my secret stash of crystal and smoke a joint on the way to the bus stop every morning. That was my first cup of coffee. Now that I had this tape, I put it in my Walkman and listened to it on the way to school. That tape gave me the courage and the hope to stay clean for another day, day by day. It gave me hope.

△▽△

Every weekend a group of young people in recovery played volleyball at a place called Crown Point in Mission Bay, San Diego. Hope and I decided to check it out. As we parked, I saw that everyone was white and sporting a nice beach body. They were laughing and having a good time. I had a flashback to elementary school, when I was standing by the pool in my hand-me-down cut-off jeans and the white kids teased and bullied me. I'd learned to avoid situations exactly like this one as if they were the plague.

Then I looked at Hope, and I saw how pretty she was. She had on a white tank top with a bathing-suit top beneath it and some blue jean shorts. Her skin was silky smooth now that she was clean. Her eyes shimmered with life. She was letting her hair grow long. I smiled, admiring her.

Hope, who was halfway out of the car, said, "What's up? Are we going?"

"Nah. I wanna go home. This ain't my thing. You probably used to this white shit since you go to San Diego State and all that, but it ain't me."

She looked at me, then at the group playing volleyball, and then back at me. "Come on." She laughed. "We don't have to play or say anything to anyone. Let's just go watch people play. It's a beautiful day. We said we'd try new things, and this is definitely something new for me, too. Shit, normally I'd be over there on the sand smoking bowls, not playing volleyball." Her laughter made me smile. She was right.

She wasn't a bikini-wearing, volleyball-playing type. So I agreed.

"Aight, but I ain't gonna play no fuckin volleyball, and if they make me feel uncomfortable, then we out."

We walked to the volleyball courts but stood across from where people clustered on blankets and beach chairs. They had three or four games going at the same time. The court farthest away seemed to be the one with the serious volleyball players, two against two. But in the rest of the courts, people were just people having fun. It wasn't competitive. I put my head down and clenched Hope's hand tight. She looked over at me and put her hand on my shoulder. Suddenly I became full of anger. I was envious. I wanted the freedom they had to have fun. It seemed unobtainable to me. I'd longed my entire life just to be able to have fun and not feel judged. And the only way I knew how to be goofy and laugh—to let loose and be free—was by being high.

I was afraid I wouldn't be welcomed. I had on creased cutoff Dickies, long white knee-high socks, my black gangster corduroy slippers, an ironed and starched white T-shirt with a white tank top underneath, and my black beanie down to my nose. I definitely did not look like I belonged on a volleyball court.

Then a volleyball was thrown in our direction. It stopped at my feet. I picked up the ball and froze, unsure of what to do. A buff dark-haired guy with no shirt ran up to us. "Thank you! You both here for NA volleyball?" he asked.

"Yes we are!" said Hope in her bubbly voice.

"What's up? My name is Joey. Is this your first time out here?" He had a heavy New York accent.

"Yup, it feels awkward 'cause we don't know anyone here," said Hope. I was jealous of how easy it seemed for her to talk to other people. I stood there in my homeboy stance staring at them.

"So what's up, man? What's your name?" he asked me.

"Jesse," I said in a low voice with attitude.

"Nice to meet you. Come on, let's play, and I'll introduce you to people."

"Nah, I'm good right here, holmes."

"Man, c'mon, we all cool . . . ," he said as he put his hand on my shoulder, motioning for me to walk next to him. He led us to the group of people on blankets and in chairs.

"Yo, listen up," he said to the group in a loud voice. "It's their first time here, so introduce yourselves and make them feel at home." His accent made it sound more demanding. Then, looking at me, he said, "Take off your cholo slippers and socks, 'cause you gonna play, too."

He ran off, not giving me a chance to say no. The folks sitting on the sides got up and introduced themselves. The majority were our age. The older guys were at tables playing pinochle.

The pinochle players were all tatted-down biker dudes. I clammed up when I saw some had swastikas tatted on them, but, smiling, they all quickly got up, hugged me, and introduced themselves. It was as if I were in a *Twilight Zone* episode; this shit didn't make sense. Why the fuck would these big biker dudes, with goatees, long beards, and tatted sleeves and looking like they just got out of prison, hug me or welcome me?

A very heavyset one with a goatee and salt-and-pepper hair said to me, as if he was reading my mind, "You look uncomfortable, man. You probably feel like you don't belong. Trust me, we've all felt that way at some point. But a young Mexican from the barrio must really feel outta place with all us white Yosemite Sam–looking guys." He laughed. "Relax, man. No one here's gonna bother you. How long you been clean?" he asked as he sat back down.

I put my head down and said, "A few months." They all looked up at me, then got back up and hugged me again, each congratulating me. This shit was tripping me out.

"How old are you?" asked the big guy.

"Eighteen."

He laughed and said, "Eighteen with a bullet, huh?"

"How about you? How long you been clean, holmes?"

"Fourteen years," he replied.

"What? Fourteen years? Wow."

"After I got out serving a ten-year bid, I couldn't get clean until I hit bottom. Here I am."

"And he just got his PhD in psychology! He graduated a few months ago," said Joey as he walked back up.

"What? Are you serious? A PhD?" I asked, shocked.

"Simón, holmes, anything is possible, ese," he said, smiling.

"C'mon, man. Take off your gangster slippers and let's play volleyball," Joey said to me.

"Fuck it," I said as I took off my slippers and white socks

and left them next to Hope, who was sitting on the blankets talking to a few girls.

"Have fun!" she said.

People gave me high fives, cheering me on and saying shit like "Cool, dude. Right on. Let's do this. Awesome." I awkwardly responded to their high fives. We didn't really high-five in my neighborhood. After several minutes spent missing a bunch of balls, running into others, and having people pat me on the back and give me more high fives, I began to feel strangely comfortable. After about thirty minutes, I was having a good time. After forty-five minutes, I was having the time of my life, so much so that I opted to stay when Hope mentioned she needed to go. It was the first time in a very long time that I laughed from my core.

Joey offered to take me home. When he dropped me off later, he said, "I know it was awkward for you to go out there and play volleyball, bro. It was awkward for all of us at first. We're all drug addicts, man. I'm proud of you."

Then he offered to take me to a meeting where young people hung out every Thursday night in a beach area called the Zoo. I agreed, and a new world opened up for me. Life-long friendships bloomed.

For the next three years, Joey picked me up every Thursday evening to hit the Zoo meeting in Mission Beach. He got clean at fourteen years old, like the guy on the cassette tape, and had four years clean when I met him. He and his friends taught me that in the world of recovery, it was my duty to be there for the addict, regardless of their race, sexual identity, religious beliefs, or age. We were there to help one another. They counted on me, and I counted on them. When I was weak, they were strong, and I was strong when they were weak. And together we could accomplish anything.

At times I felt like I'd bought into a dogma and was brainwashed by a cult. But it didn't really matter. It was working, and I was staying clean. My family was still my family and life was still life. My perspective, however, was shifting.

△▽△

One night my sponsor recommended I begin my next assignment, which was to do a "searching and fearless moral inventory" of myself and my life, writing about all my resentments, fears, and relationships to identify patterns, where I'd done harm to others, and the parts I'd played.

Through my writing, I was able to come to terms with the fact that I no longer wanted to be with Hope.

I broke up with her. I went over to her house, and we talked.

I started gingerly. "I'm sorry for doing this. But as I'm writing, I'm reliving a lot of my old traumas, and I'm confused about my sexuality and don't know if I'm bi or gay or what. I know you've noticed. I hope you understand. I never meant to deceive you."

"Have you slept with men?"

"Yes. I have."

"But have you slept with men since you've met me?"

With tears in my eyes and feeling ashamed, I said, "Yes, I have," and put my head down.

"Get out. I don't want to see you. I wouldn't be so upset if you'd just told me you were gay or bi. But you lied. That's not okay, Jesse! You hurt me!"

I went to hug her, sad that I'd hurt her, but she shouted, "I said get the fuck out of my house," and started crying.

So I did, upset and feeling horrible that I had hurt her, the person I felt safest with.

△▽△

For another year, I worked on my personal inventory, a rite of passage known as the fourth step for people in recovery. It was one of the most freeing experiences I've gone through. In this painful journey of writing, I opened up to my sponsor about details of my sexual history, my resentments, and my fears. I would share here and there, feeling him out to see his reactions. Many nights I cried with him. He'd sometimes put his arm around me in a fatherly way, telling me it was okay.

One night I finally told him: "I don't know if I'm gay. I don't know if I'm bi. I don't know what I am. I am confused. I don't want my family, my friends, or you to love me any less." I cried. And he just let me cry. I was finally able to let him in.

"Nothing is wrong with you, Jess. If you're gay, bi, straight, or whatever, I don't give a fuck. I love you no matter what. I love you exactly for who you are. Remember, Jess, people who judge don't matter, and people who matter don't judge."

The relationship I built with my sponsor was something I had never shared with any man. Not with my father or brother. I was not at a place to be able to open up with anyone in my family about the changes I was going through. To them, the fact that I was clean, going to meetings, and not fucking up seemed sufficient. And I was okay with that.

I went to one or two meetings per day. One day per week, I answered the Narcotics Anonymous phone lines from 8:00 p.m. to midnight. I volunteered in Juvenile Hall every Thursday and performed my weekly duties, emptying ashtrays and making coffee, at meetings. I did my best to stay busy.

Slowly the quiet homeboy with the mean attitude started to open up. Other people noticed the change before I did. People would say, "Wow, you are so different now."

I would smile shyly, feeling somewhat embarrassed, and say, "Well, I got off drugs."

CHAPTER 17

I was around six months clean when Hope and I broke up. I spent one year abstinent. After that, I felt ready to explore my sexuality and allowed myself to date both men and women. I was comfortable hooking up with both for a while. A few months before my twenty-first birthday, when I was just over two years clean, I met someone and decided to try a gay relationship. At that point I started to identify as gay.

One month before my twenty-first birthday, Amá tried to raise the subject about me being gay in a roundabout way, though it was not like her to beat around the bush. "Jesse, I want to talk to you about something," she'd begin. Then she would pause and say, "Well, nah, forget about it. Maybe later." I knew what she was trying to do, but rather than help her I wanted to see how far she would take it before she actually asked.

This went on for a while. Then one day while she was cooking breakfast and I was getting ready to go to work at the hair salon, she said it again: "Jesse, I want to ask you something but am not sure how you're going to react and how to even ask. But . . ." And then she said, "Nah, forget it. Just forget it. I'll ask you later."

I was annoyed that she still didn't have the courage to ask me straight up, and disrespectfully I said, "What? What do you want to know? What are you afraid of? Do you want to know if your son is a fag? Well, yes, I am a fag. I don't know why you can't just ask me."

This was the moment I let my mom in. I was ready. My mom had kept trying to ask, and it was about time I let her in after pushing her away for so long.

But in Spanish it sounds much worse. "¿Qué? ¿Qué chingados quieres saber? ¿Si tu hijo es maricón? ¿Si me gustan los hombres? Pues sí. ¡Sí, lo soy! Soy puto. Sí, soy maricón. No sé por qué chingados no me preguntas directamente y dejas todo este rodeo."

The topic of conversation quickly went from me being gay to the disrespectful way I had spoken to her. I hadn't disrespected her like that since I'd gotten clean.

"Don't you ever speak to me like that again, cabrón! I'm your mother and I've tolerated way too much disrespect from you. It better be the last time you speak to me like that," she said as she motioned to throw the large wooden spoon she was using to stir the pot of beans at me.

"I'm sorry. I'm sorry," I told her. And I meant it; I was remorseful. I went up to her and hugged her.

"I love you no matter what. I don't give a shit if you're gay, but you will not disrespect me like that again," she said. She was livid.

Later that night, when I came home from work, she hugged me super tight and said, "I love you a lot. Please be careful and take care of yourself. You're perfect as you are. I'm just afraid for you. Please, please promise me you'll take care of yourself."

"I promise, Amá."

I never disrespected Amá like that again. I was blessed to have Amá's unconditional love, even though I never told my father that I was gay. He passed years later without ever officially knowing.

△▽△

As graduation from community college approached, my community college counselor said to me, "Now that you're done with the cosmetology program and have nearly completed your prerequisites to transfer, have you thought about what universities you want to apply to when you graduate?"

"I have no clue," I told her. "I don't even know how many credits I have left before I can apply to transfer to a four-year college. I'm here because I gave you my word that I would stay in school," I told her.

"Shut the door. I want to talk to you seriously," she said.

I did as she asked and then sat back down in my chair. For an instant I realized how my demeanor had shifted over the years. I no longer slouched. Instead I sat up and leaned forward, attentive to the people around me.

"I want you to consider leaving San Diego to go to school. If you could pick anywhere in California, where would it be?"

I decided on UC Berkeley. I had visited Oakland and the school once, and I remembered loving the oddball environment of misfit nerds I found there. They were like me, I felt.

"Well, it is a UC school, and you do qualify for the IGETC program," she said.

"What's that?" I asked.

"IGETC is a series of courses that California community college students can take to satisfy general education requirements to transfer to most major California colleges and UC campuses. I will get you a waiver for the application fees; your part will be to complete the application process. Is that a deal?" she asked.

"You got it, and don't trip. Just tell me what I need to do and I'll do it," I told her.

△▽△

One day a huge envelope from UC Berkeley arrived in the mailbox. I opened it with Amá sitting next to me. It was my acceptance letter. We jumped up together and cheered as she pulled me into a tight hug and kissed me all over my head.

"Congratulations! I know it's the school you've been wanting to go to, so go for it!"

The day I left for college, Amá made one of my favorite Mexican breakfasts: chilaquiles con carne deshebrada with coffee. She walked me out to my car—no longer the car I'd bought at fourteen but a white 1995 Nissan Sentra. Amá cried and gave me her blessing: "Que Dios te bendiga, mijo. Estoy muy orgullosa de ti."

I got into my car and drove off. I stared into the rear-view mirror as her reflection got smaller. This was my first road trip alone. It was August 1996. It was nice driving alone, windows down, music blasting, reflecting on both good and bad times, thinking of my family's history, and tripping at how far I had come. I had gone from living in poverty and dealing drugs to performing sex work for money. And now here I was, leaving one life behind to build a new one.

As I drove by the homes near campus, I saw cars double-parked with families helping freshmen unload boxes. Mothers hugged their kids while dads carried boxes. For a moment I felt envy that my leaving-for-college experience did not resemble the way American culture painted it. Then I realized I didn't have to compare myself to other students. The trek both I and my family had to take for me to be there had required bravery and strength. The way I saw it, my family had built a man of me, one with the support to handle the road trip, and the transition, alone, with courage.

I pulled up to the house where I was going to be living. It was smack-dab in the middle of fraternity row. It was the Chicano/Latino house called Casa Joaquín Murrieta (aka

Casa). I had heard about this house through the admissions process, applied to live there, and been accepted. My room was in the basement, and I had my own entrance through the back of the house. It was large with two twin-size beds, one on each end of the room. The beds sat on top of wooden boxes with drawers; there was a dresser next to each bed, along with two bookshelves and two wooden study desks with lamps on top. It was going to be tight for two people. And because it was in the basement, it felt cool and damp compared to the rest of the house. The back end of the room had a door that opened to a dark hallway leading to a small bathroom with a stand-up shower, which would be shared with two other rooms along the hallway.

At least I'll have lots of privacy, I thought. I tried to look at the positive, though it felt lonely unpacking by myself.

The door was open, letting in a cool breeze and light from the backyard patio. As I was unpacking, a woman with dark shoulder-length hair knocked, looked in, and said, "Hi! Are you Jesse?"

The woman before me had a very soft, loving, and nurturing voice that immediately made me feel welcomed and safe.

"My name is Mayra, and I am a resource for anything you need during your stay here at Cal. I work at the Academic Achievement Division, which is a resource center for students transferring from community colleges. Stop by first thing on Monday morning and we can discuss your education plan and any questions you might have about financial aid, work-study programs, and the support systems available to you."

We talked for a bit and then she left me to continue my unpacking. After a while, I went to move my car out of the driveway to the street. When I got back to the house there were five people—two guys and three girls—who I recognized waiting for me. I had met them before, at a Narcotics Anonymous convention, and we'd stayed in touch. I had mentioned that I was moving to Berkeley and told them when, but I was shocked to see them standing there. They ran up to me, screaming, "Congratulations, man. You made it to Cal."

My heart grew big with love.

"Come on, let's go," they said. "You can finish unpacking tomorrow."

I went to my room, changed my clothes, threw on some cologne, and took off. First we went to a meeting in the Haight District. Then we went dancing in the warehouse district of San Francisco. We hit a club called DV8 under a highway bridge. It was unlike any club I had ever been to. It was diverse, with straight, gay, Black, white, Latino, Asian, and transgender people all dancing to the most intense deep house music and underground hip-hop. Then they took me to an after-hours party at a megaclub called Universe. I lost myself in the deep soulful gospel house music and danced away the rest of the night with them. Years later I would do the same in New York City, partying and dancing clean, losing myself to the music at the Limelight, the Roxy, Twilo, the Tunnel, Crash, Esquelita, Monster, the Warehouse, and the Octagon and having a blast of a time doing it.

I thought we were going home when we left Club Universe, but they took me to another called the End Up, which was open nonstop from Friday nights until Monday mornings. We didn't wait in line and didn't pay any covers. I asked my friends how they had it like that, and they explained that a few of them danced at the clubs as go-go dancers and that some bartenders and doormen were in recovery and went to meetings, too. From day one I had a strong support system in Da Bay.

It was daylight by the time I got back to Casa. I looked around at all the stuff that I still had left to unpack and smiled. As I lay in bed, I reflected on the past twenty-four hours. Just yesterday I had pulled out of San Diego in my white Nissan Sentra and driven all the way up to UC Berkeley by myself. I may not have had family drop me off at college and hug me with dramatic goodbyes like other students, but I had something that I am sure so many others wish they'd had their first night away at college, and that was a support system and a community.

As I fell asleep, I thought about my family and about stories of my grandparents and great-grandparents. In particular I thought about the women in the family and the struggles they had to endure so that their children could have better lives. I didn't want my mother's struggles to be in vain, so I knew I couldn't give up—no matter what. Stories of resilience, family histories, and folktales filled me with pride and helped me fall asleep.

△▽△

Late 1800s—on the road between Nayarit and Sinaloa, Mexico

"*Vieja*," said Antonio, "*the road is too quiet. It's not normal. Keep your gun close.*"

Antonio and his wife, Silveria, were on the road from Tepic to Villa Unión to find work. Pregnant Silveria had the gun tucked in the wrap that held her infant son, Little Antonio. She'd taken the bullets out the day they left Tepic because she hated guns. Guns mixed with alcohol had left too many young widows in her Huichol and Cora family.

"*Be quiet, you old fool,*" said Silveria. "*No one's going to rob us.*"

A half mile down the road, they were held up. Antonio yelled at Silveria for the gun, but that only warned the robbers of the useless weapon she carried. One robber shot Antonio dead. Another yanked pregnant Silveria off her mule. She hit the dirt hard, and the baby rolled out of the wrap. One bandit yanked a leather pouch from around the dead Antonio's neck, which contained the little silver and gold Antonio had, and the robbers took off with their mules.

A group passing by stopped to help Silveria, who lay in the dirt road, crying, holding a child in one arm, another in her belly, and Antonio's head in her lap. They escorted her to a church in the center of the town of Villa Unión.

There, Silveria wailed to the priest, "I am seven months pregnant. I have a baby in my arms, no money, nothing to trade, and nowhere to go. Please help me, padre."

The priest agreed to bury Antonio and to allow Silveria to sleep in the pews until the baby in her belly was baptized—both on the condition that she clean the church after every service. Silveria's sadness and despair induced her labor that night. Her daughter, my grandmother Susana, was born premature. The priest arranged for a married couple to be the baptismal godparents of Little Antonio and baby Susana. Silveria and her kids would be allowed to live with the couple and their family as long as Silveria agreed to be an unpaid live-in nanny. She spent the rest of her short life in servitude. Neither Susana nor Little Antonio were allowed to go to school. Antonio worked in the family's sugarcane fields until the age of thirteen; when he hit puberty, his godparents told him that he was old enough to start his own life and had to leave. Silveria couldn't protest. She died two years later, when Susana was fourteen. Susana was forced to take over her mother's responsibilities. She thought she would never see her brother again.

One day when Susana was shopping for food at the mercado, a young man handed her a piece of paper and whispered to her, "Please read this note. My name is Miguel, but they call me Chino. I am a friend of your brother, Antonio." Then he ran off.

Later that night, Susana, who couldn't read, asked the nanny of a neighboring family to help her read the note. But the nanny, too, was illiterate. She offered, "When we go to the mercado tomorrow, we will ask my cousin, who can read, to tell us what it says."

The next day they learned the note read, Your brother Antonio will meet you in the town square tomorrow before the dinner hour.

Before sunset that same day, Susana used the excuse that she needed a few more things to prepare dinner and ran to *the town square to meet Antonio. The young man from the mercado, Miguel, was with Antonio, and he and Susana were formally introduced.*

"I was prohibited to come find you. I've been living in Mazatlán, working at a beer factory, which is where I met Miguel. He offered to help me come get you. Leave with us for Mazatlán at midnight," said Antonio.

Later that night, Susana left and never looked back.

The golden sand beaches of Mazatlán, with its three islands visible in the distance, captivated her. Within a year, Miguel declared his love for Susana, and they were married. Another year passed before their first daughter, Maria, was born. Those early years in Mazatlán were Susana's happiest, even though Miguel's parents didn't approve of their marriage. (Miguel's parents had arrived in Mazatlán due to the US Chinese Exclusion Act, where, upon entry, they were forced by Mexican authorities to change their names to Spanish names.) Miguel, wanting a boy, rushed Susana to get pregnant again. The second baby turned out to be a girl, as was the third, and the fourth. Susana spent the first decade of the marriage pregnant and bearing children. Miguel's frustration at her birthing only girls turned to anger. In drunken rages, he'd beat her. He forced her to have a total of ten children—all girls. Only their firstborn, Maria, and their youngest, Esperanza (Espi), survived beyond age five. The rest died from malnutrition.

Espi, my amá, was born premature, at a gestational age of seven months. The doctor, who helped Susana deliver Espi at home, gave Susana a shoebox and two hot-water bottles as a homemade incubator to keep the baby warm. A month later, a few days after Espi's baptism, Miguel left Susana for another woman.

When Maria turned thirteen, she married a man twenty-seven years older than her and left home. During her lifetime, Maria had a total of twenty-three children, fifteen of whom lived to adulthood. In those days, the more children a family had, the more income could be earned, because children were put to work at age five.

Susana took Espi out of school in the fifth grade because she was constantly fighting, defending herself while other poor kids bullied her.

"But, Amá, they are picking on me for being poor when they also are poor. Just yesterday I taught them how to tear off pieces of the freshly poured chapopote (black tar) from the street to dip in honey for chewing gum. Now they are picking on me, telling me I'm going to lose my teeth and be a molacha for the rest of my life. I won't let anyone make me feel bad for being poor. Please don't take me out of school," begged Espi.

"You will help your sister raise her kids when you're not helping me make tamales to sell. At your age I had to work with my mom just to have a roof over my head," said Susana.

Susana raised Espi with a firm hand. If she caught Espi playing games like marbles with neighborhood boys instead of taking care of Maria's kids, she'd drag her into the house by the hair, pour rice on the floor, and force Espi to kneel on it while holding hot rocks heated on the stove. When Espi was fourteen, Susana found her a job as a live-in nanny for the doctor who'd delivered her at birth. The life of being a nanny, which Espi's grandmother and mother also endured, repeated itself. Espi spent years raising rich people's kids—until the day destiny plopped my dad, Ricardo, into her life.

Espi was covering a restaurant shift for her niece one evening when Ricardo walked in to eat. He stalked her. Found out where she lived. Spoke to Susana. Seven days later, Susana forced them to get married. That's how my father and Amá met. It was 1970. She was twenty-eight years old. He was sixty-three. They left Mazatlán. One year later, they had a healthy boy. In 1972, in Tijuana, Espi, only seven months pregnant, gave birth to a premature girl who suffered from anal malformation. The baby needed multiple reconstructive surgeries as soon as possible or she could die. The doctor at the hospital refused to operate unless they paid for the surgeries up front in cash. Ricardo wasn't able to get the money, so desperate Espi returned to work less than forty-eight hours after giving birth. She convinced her boss at the restaurant to pay her daily instead of weekly. Each day after work she'd run to the hospital to see her baby and put money down, each time feeling a glimmer of hope that she'd be able to save her baby girl. Then one evening she arrived at the hospital only to find her twenty-eight-day-old daughter dead.

"Your baby died today. I left her body in that bathroom over there," said a nurse, pointing in the direction of a restroom next to the nurse's station.

Espi ran to the bathroom and found her dead baby girl wrapped in a blanket atop the toilet seat. Horrified, she grabbed the body and fell to the floor, crying. An hour later, Ricardo arrived. The nurse walked up to him and said, "We put the baby's body in there so your wife could have time with her; otherwise the hospital would have taken the body to the morgue and not allowed you to see it until the hospital bill was paid. I did what I could."

For one week, Ricardo did not come home. He left Espi with nothing other than their one-year-old son (my older brother). On the seventh day of Ricardo's absence, Espi decided to leave Tijuana and return to Mazatlán. She was resigned to the fact that her marriage was over and that Ricardo had left her, abandoned her in Tijuana, after the death of their second child.

Almost one year later, Ricardo showed up in Mazatlán and demanded that my mom return with him to the United States. He threatened to kidnap her. In fear, Espi reluctantly agreed. It was 1973. Ricardo would make sure that Espi didn't see her mother for ten years. He never changed.

CHAPTER 18

Living at Casa Joaquín Murrieta was an ideal way for me to transition into UC Berkeley. I was with the most talented, intellectually stimulating, politically active young Latinos. Many have become leaders of change in their spheres of influence. A few were Aztec dancers and invited me to participate with dance groups. We'd have drumming circles in the backyard, where other Native students would join in and we'd teach one another traditional songs from our respective lineages. After the drumming, some would stay and share stories about our families' journeys to this country, and others would share stories of life on their reservations. We each had stories of legends, journeys, mysticism, struggles, and above all—hope.

This piqued my interest in stories of immigration from other ethnicities, so I was able to study under great professors in ethnic studies, education policy, and sociology who encouraged me to pursue my research and learn as much as I could to create my own major focused on social policy and social movements in the United States. My research skills were taken to new levels, as I was able to combine my

years of volunteer work and experiences around the spread
of HIV to write my undergraduate thesis on HIV in the US
prison system. I conducted research on the pathologiza-
tion of homosexuality; the impacts of criminal justice policies, such as three-strikes laws, on communities of color;
the creation of the prison-industrial complex; and the
historic housing and urban renewal policies that concen-
trated poverty in urban areas by eliminating the political
and economic strengths of communities of color across the
country.

Then one day I met her. Nia. One day Nia walked into
my basement room at Casa to meet a friend of hers. As she
stood in the doorway, she asked, "Hi, are you Jesse?"

I was struck speechless when this beautiful half-Latina,
half-Filipina woman asked for me. Smiling, she repeated,
"So . . . are you Jesse?"

I responded, "Y-y-yeah. I-I-I am," as I blushed and
smiled, feeling dorky and giddy at the same time. She told
me she was meeting her friend, whose hair I was going to
cut. I shook her hand nervously, awestruck by the confidence and beauty this woman exuded.

Obviously I had met smart and beautiful women in the
past, but there was something about Nia that threw me for a
loop. Nia was like a character from a spy movie, like Ange-
lina Jolie or Jennifer Lopez. Nia was the first of many such
friends I met while at UC Berkeley, friends who taught me
how to strategically maneuver through a male-dominated
world with success while also remaining true to myself.
They taught me how to fight for social justice wherever
opportunities lie.

Nia became my coach, my ally, my mentor, and my homey. She was in her senior year and politically active. She helped me research internships, fellowships, and scholarship programs that I would have probably never heard about on my own. I knew I wanted to have an impact on the lives of youth and give hope to others with backgrounds like mine. Nia connected me to people who worked at the Criminal Justice Consortium, where I got a job helping inmates transition out of prison and helped organize the first conference on the prison industry at UC Berkeley called Critical Resistance, with activists and other towering figures like Angela Davis.

Nia encouraged me to apply for the Public Policy and International Affairs (PPIA) Fellowship, or what was formerly known as the Woodrow Wilson and Sloan Fellowship. I was accepted into the 1997 summer institute of PPIA at UC Berkeley. It provided me with an immersion in public policy and international affairs with rigorous assignments, group work, and case studies. It gave me a framework for quantitative and qualitative analysis for public policy, through which I learned how to use numbers and data to tell a story. When fellows completed the fellowship, the program provided funding toward a graduate degree, which I had never considered before. My plan had been to move back to San Diego after graduating from UC Berkeley.

After completing the 1997 PPIA Junior Summer Institute I went home for one week to put my stuff in my mom's garage and sell my car. Being home was nice. Amá made dinner, and my brother came over with the kids, but I spent most of my time getting ready for my trip. I was going to

Spain for an entire academic year. I had applied to the Education Abroad Program to study in Madrid. I had decided on Spain because I spoke Spanish fluently and could use the country as my home base to travel throughout Europe. Before I left, Amá told me, "Mijo, quiero vivir la vida por tus ojos." *My son, I want to live life through your eyes. Send me photos of all the places you visit, and remember I am always by your side.*

Amá's support helped me feel enthusiastically happy about my first-year experience in Cal and my decision to study abroad. She understood that a part of me felt guilty for having moved to Berkeley to go to college. I felt I had abandoned the family. And here I was crossing the Atlantic Ocean to live in Europe. For privileged people, this experience is just a matter of course, but for me, it presented a major conflict. Neither my mother nor my father had ever had the chance to travel that far. Yet Amá had encouraged me to continue my journey.

Together with a group of other students, I boarded a plane for the first time at LAX. I sat like an excited child when the plane took off but became terribly afraid during turbulence, holding on to my seat as if my life depended on it. I stared out the window and wondered, *Why me?* I didn't feel special. I didn't have a magic secret to life. Why was I getting these opportunities while others I grew up with did not?

While gazing out the window on the plane that day, I realized that persistence and resilience were key. I never gave up. And I had an amazing support system and a community that never gave up on me.

△▽△

My trip was full of joy until we got to customs at the airport in Madrid. My embedded fear and anxiety due to PTSD from being a Chicano raised by the border were resurfacing. My heart beat fast and my palms grew sweaty. I told myself the same shit I told myself every time I crossed the US-Mexico border: *Dude, don't trip. You're a United States citizen born in the USA. You have no drugs on you. You're clean and have no reason to be nervous.* It didn't work. I was the only student in the entire group who was searched. As I walked out, I yelled, "Oh hell nah. I did not leave the US just to have to deal with this bullshit here, too. Colonizing, racial-profiling motherfuckers!"

All the other students started laughing, even though I wasn't trying to be funny.

When we arrived at our dorms, I sat patiently waiting for my bags to be taken off the bus. They weren't. They'd been accidentally sent to Granada on another bus. I had not yet been in Spain one full day and already I had been racially profiled by customs and had no clothes to wear other than the ones I had on. Feeling bad, one member of the program staff took me to a local store called Zara, where I bought myself underwear, socks, pants, and a T-shirt.

By the time we got back, the students had already had dinner. I ate alone. Then I went upstairs to call my mom and tell her I had arrived safely. I told her I was happy and that everything was perfect. After we hung up, I called the Alcoholics Anonymous hotline for Madrid. They told me where there was a meeting and how to get there. I ventured into the city on my own and caught the Metro.

I arrived just as it was starting. Everyone looked much older than me. People nodded to me as a sign of welcome. I sat and listened to people share in their Spanish accents, which made me laugh inside because I felt like I was in a Pedro Almodóvar movie, and I remembered how far I had come from being stuck in a trailer in East LA, cooking meth and watching *Women on the Verge of a Nervous Breakdown*. During the meeting, the chairperson called on me to share. I told the group that it was my first night in Spain, that I was four years sober, and that although it felt amazing to be living the dream, I was afraid I would fuck it all up. I explained that I was the first in my family to ever travel this far. After the meeting, a few people invited me to dinner and offered to take me home. It was magical to be driven through the city on my very first night in Madrid by strangers who were part of a larger community that I was connected to.

At the restaurant I looked at the menu; although I spoke and read Spanish, I didn't understand a thing on it. I had no clue what *champiñones*, *mejillones*, *patatas*, *murcia*, or *jamón serrano* were. We used different words in the barrio. Then I saw *tortilla* and said, "They sell tortillas here?"

I ordered a tortilla with patatas, which I assumed would be a potato taco. When my order came out, it was a thick egg-and-potato omelet with red peppers and onions. "What is this? This ain't no tortilla," I said. The joke was on me. We ate outdoors in a tiny plaza surrounded by medieval buildings, talking and laughing all night. I got home at around 2:00 a.m. having made new friends.

That year I traveled throughout Europe. In every city I visited, I made it a point to go to a meeting, especially because what better way is there to be introduced to and shown around a city than by the alcoholics and addicts who know its ins and outs?

I took weekend trips to towns like Segovia, Toledo, Cuenca, Tarifa, and Cádiz and to large cities like Barcelona, Málaga, and Sevilla. My first weekend trip was to Málaga and a small beach town called Torremolinos. That trip changed my life forever. Another student and I visited a gay club. At the club I met a Spanish man on the dance floor. We hit it off, laughing and dancing till late. After the club I agreed to hang out with him for the night. He got us room at a hotel.

Given my sexual history, I was typically the partner with experience, but he laid me back gently and provided some of the most intense pleasure my body had ever felt. He had me explore things I never thought I would. I let go of my perceptions of manhood and machismo and went with the flow. It was ecstasy.

When I put my clothes back on, he put his arms around me, turned me around, and said, "Here, look into that mirror."

I looked into the floor-length mirror he'd pointed me to and asked, "What? What am I looking at?"

"You're beautiful, and you're even more beautiful when you let yourself go. You don't always have to be in control. Right now you're dressed, ready to go back to your hostel. Why? You don't have to go. Will you stay the night with me?" he asked.

I smiled. I stayed the night.

He woke me up in the morning with a cup of Spanish coffee and toasted bread with butter. "You were asleep and I didn't want to wake you. I hope you like coffee," he told me.

I was full of anxiety and angry with myself for allowing myself to be vulnerable and to sleep so deeply that I wasn't aware of my surroundings. For an instant I wanted to say, *Aight, playa, you good, homeboy*. But I didn't. I slid up on the bed, leaned against the headboard, and drank the coffee he'd made me, happy about the night we had just shared.

As I was getting dressed, he said, "Why do you hide your beautiful body behind all those baggy clothes? I'm taking you shopping today."

I laughed and said, "I'm not rich, bro. I didn't bring money for shopping."

"I ain't asking you for any money. I am a fashion stylist. Trust me, I know people here. They'll hook it up."

I went with the flow. I tried on fitted jeans and shirts that contoured my body. It was awkward to feel the material pressed so close to my skin. The pants constrained me. My lover bought me four different outfits that I could mix and match and two pairs of shoes. He convinced me to wear one outfit out of the store. It was a pair of fitted, low-rise, straight-leg black pants with a belt that had a nice silver buckle and a slim-fitting long-sleeve blue shirt.

Before walking out of the store, I told him, "Man, I don't know. I don't feel comfortable. This shit feels gay. I look gay."

He responded, "No. You look sexy and classy with European swag. Haven't you noticed that most guys in Europe look gay, anyway? Get over it."

I looked into the mirror one more time, and there I was. It was another, different Jesse looking back. And I looked good as hell, too. But I felt stripped of my armor.

On the way back to my hostel, we ran into my straight friends drinking Spanish coffee at a café. It was as if they couldn't believe their eyes. "What the hell?" they said. "Damn. Look at you."

I laughed in an embarrassed, childlike way and introduced my new friend to the group, and he asked them, "So what do you guys think? Don't you think he looks good?"

"Yeah, he looks good, and totally different," said one.

My lover looked at me and said, "You have my number, call me."

I put my hand out to shake his, but he pulled me close and kissed me on the lips in front of all my straight friends and in the middle of the street while people walked all around us. He whispered in my ear as he held me, "Relax. Let go. No one gives a shit." He then walked off, saying, "Call me."

Life was changing. I was changing. It felt great being way across the world, where no one knew me and I could be whoever I wanted to be. I was being pushed outside my comfort zone. I was living the fantasy. Living the dream.

Back in Madrid, one morning at around three thirty, walking home from a gay bar called Black and White in Chueca, I stopped to eat Chinese chicken and rice made by a Chinese immigrant woman on Gran Vía. She made arroz con pollo and sold it in aluminum boxes that she'd packed in a cooler. She was out there every morning from 1:30 a.m. to 6:00 a.m.

As I ate, a group of guys stopped to buy a soda from the

woman. One said, "Hola, guapo, where you headed?" as he smiled at me. He looked familiar. When he introduced himself as Pedro, my mind made the connection.

I asked, "Are you Pedro Almodóvar? The movie director?"

He said, "Yes."

Giddy, I told him I'd been introduced to his movies in the States when I watched *Women on the Verge of a Nervous Breakdown* and that it was an honor to meet him in person.

He said, "Thank you, thank you very much, but we are rushing to meet some friends at a bar in Chueca called Black and White. Why don't you join us?"

I thought to myself, *Fuck, how many opportunities will I get to party with Pedro Almodóvar?*

So off I went with the movie director and his friends to the bar I had just left. I sat at their table while drag queens came and went. He talked to me about his new movie, *Carne trémula*, which was then just about to release. He was funny, innocently flirtatious, and easy to talk to.

I went home with a huge smile on my face, astonished by how much my life had changed in such a short period of time.

Being abroad helped me to better understand myself. I didn't feel constrained, as I had most of my life, to be a certain way. I began to find my authentic self far away from cultural, ethnic, familial, and friendship ties. I experienced walking in castles and monasteries, down narrow alleys in Moorish neighborhoods lined with hookah bars. I hung out with the Romani until sunrise playing sevillanas and flamenco in the alleys of Cádiz during Carnival. I experienced Northern Spain's emerald-green landscapes and was mesmerized by the entrance of the Cathedral of Santiago de Compostela, where I gazed in a silent meditative state at the Tree of Jesse carved on a pillar at the portal of the cathedral, which millions of people had touched over hundreds of years as part of their spiritual pilgrimage to the site. I hiked up mountainsides and walked into ancient caves and touched cave paintings from civilizations long disappeared in Altamira. I couldn't believe I was standing in caves that were inhabited tens of thousands of years ago and touching the same cave paintings that I had seen in *National Geographic* magazines as a child.

I was living my life.

CHAPTER 19

The final days of my year abroad in Madrid were bitter-sweet. In less than one year I had grown and changed so much. Madrid was where I first came out publicly as gay. And although my brother and mom had met one or two insignificant boyfriends, I had never imagined that I would be as out as I was in Spain. I was anxious about my return.

After landing in LA, I started to criticize everything American. I experienced culture shock, and I felt I didn't belong anymore. The pretentiousness, hypermasculinity, and bro culture at the airport seemed so overwhelming that I immediately wanted to revert right back to it, yet it irritated me. People were rushing everywhere about me. My heart raced again with anxiety and fear while I passed through customs, and in spite of traveling to Turkey, Germany, Switzerland, and France, I hadn't experienced that since my first night in Spain. I realized that this new me—who enjoyed buying vegetables and fruits at corner stands and eating healthy meals in open plazas while drinking coffee and discussing worldly topics—was going to be hard to find back in the United States. I annoyed the shit out of Ariyel, who picked me up at the airport.

"Um, hello. Welcome to LA. You'd swear you've been gone like ten years."

"It just feels weird. I feel out of place. Even how I'm dressed."

"Yeah, you do look different. That's for sure. But get over yourself."

Knowing me as well as she did, she went to a drive-through taco shop and ordered me a carne asada burrito with a large agua de tamarindo. It was heaven. Immediately I was happy to have come home.

That summer of 1998, before returning to Berkeley, I took a job in Los Angeles at the Wall Las Memorias Project, working on HIV and Latino communities in East LA. My anger started to resurface as I encountered the injustice of how resources for the HIV and the LGBT communities were being dominated by white gay organizations in West Hollywood. Very few resources were going to communities of color, where rates of HIV were skyrocketing. The executive director of the organization became my mentor. He introduced me to leaders in the community, knowing I was hungry to meet other openly gay Latino activists advocating for our community. And although the organization did not focus on human trafficking and sex work, I was finally able to meet others who had lived lives similar to mine. Many had been forced into sex work as I was. I wasn't unique, and I connected to a community of Latino gay men who understood me as I understood them.

△▽△

My last year in Berkeley, I lived near the corner of Telegraph and Durant, the epicenter of Berkeley "hippieness," in a tiny one-bedroom apartment with my old roommate from Casa. My roommate was a muscular straight Latino from LA who was also raised in the barrio and who accepted me as I was from the moment we met. He'd found the place, which was known as the Chicano apartment because it had been passed down for years from Chicano to Chicano to keep the rent control for students who couldn't afford market-rate rents in the area. I slept in the bedroom, and my roommate slept on the couch in the living room. I got a job at a hair salon on Telegraph that allowed me to work around my class schedule. I also cut hair in the apartment for people who didn't want to, or couldn't, pay salon prices. Once again I was working full-time, going to school full-time, and trying to make money on the side to survive. More than ever, I was focused on graduation.

I wanted to finish my bachelor's degree so that I could return to San Diego and get a full-time job at City College working with other community college students. At least, that was the plan.

But that plan didn't unfold. Once again, life took me down an unexpected route.

During my first few months back at Berkeley, Nia kept urging me to consider graduate school. She wanted me to take advantage of the graduate school fellowship funds made available to me by the PPIA Fellowship. She said, "Jesse, you need to apply to the top ten public policy and international affairs schools in the country, and that includes Harvard."

Every time my professors and mentors saw me, they would ask, "How are your grad school applications going?" It was as if they were all conspiring to help me.

At one point I broke down while on the phone with Nia and told her, "I don't think grad school is for me. I don't think I can make it."

Nia said, "Just apply, Jesse. You have nothing to lose. Your application fees are waived, and if you are worried about the GRE, then walk into the financial aid office and ask for a waiver for the GRE prep courses. You have no excuse."

Later that day, I walked over to the office that handled GRE prep course fee waivers and got mine immediately. I didn't want to apply to a bunch of schools only to get rejected. I was also nervous about what would happen if I actually got selected by one. What if everyone in graduate school saw through my facade and realized I was simply a hood, formerly homeless, drug-addicted male sex worker who didn't belong with them?

I was overwhelmed with fear of success in addition to fear of failure. I went down to the Oakland Pier to meditate one night. On the way there, I looked at all the male sex workers I was passing. They were out in droves. I slowed down in my car, and each one whipped out their dick to show me the merchandise. Most if not all were Black men. I was instantly reminded of where I'd come from and the life I'd lived. I parked the car, walked back, and talked with two of them. Both were Black cis gay men. Each time a car approached, I would back away so I wouldn't disrupt their business. Once the car passed, we'd continue the conversation.

"Man, I don't know what the fuck I'm doing. What's it been like out here?" I asked.

"Man, you fuckin crazy. Stay the fuck in school. This shit is fucked up out here. Cops are constantly fucking with us. And the competition is steep. Times are hard. If you got out, stay out," the older man told me.

And then the younger man said, "When's the last time you been to a meeting or called your sponsor?" and started laughing.

I said, "What? How you know?"

He quickly interrupted and said, "I seen the tag on your car keys. They from NA meetings. Yo ass better get back to handling your business and doing step work or you goin be out here right along with us. I had nine months clean, and it was the best nine months of my life. Now look at me, back on the stroll."

This was the reality check I needed. I went back home and thanked God that my life had dramatically changed in only a few short years, and then I went to a late-night meeting where I shared about my fears of the unknown and how the familiar, no matter how dangerous or bleak, always seemed like the easier, softer way. But it never really is.

△▽△

When I walked into the GRE test prep course at Kaplan I noticed that the people there were mostly white and Asian. The only other Latino in the class was my roommate, because I'd forced him to get a waiver and take the course with me. I judged everyone. I thought, *Rich white mother-fuckers. Of course they do well on these tests, because the tests are biased and their families can afford to pay for test prep courses.* Not once did I consider that maybe the white or Asian students in class held the same insecurities I did, nor did I consider that maybe they were also there because of a fee waiver. Either way, I recognized at that moment that I was judging others in exactly the same way I didn't want people to judge me.

The prep courses taught me a lot. The biggest thing I learned was that these kinds of tests did not measure my intelligence. It was all about strategies for taking the test and how to dissect each question so you can score higher. I took the GRE on the last date it was administered with pencil and paper. I knew I was only able to be there taking the test because other people had helped me along the way and pointed me to this path. But I was proud of myself, too.

I applied to Harvard, UC Berkeley, the University of Chicago, Georgetown, Princeton, the University of Washington, and the University of Michigan in Ann Arbor. At first I didn't want to apply to Harvard because I thought there was no way they would ever accept someone like me. I felt it would be a waste of time to apply only to get rejected. But Nia insisted. "It doesn't hurt to apply. The worst they can say is no. But you will never know unless you try."

I agreed and set an appointment with the admissions

person at the Goldman School of Public Policy at UC Berkeley first, since that's where I was physically located. He also happened to be a Latino, so I figured he would provide positive guidance. When I showed up he wasn't there, and I had to wait thirty minutes because he was running late. When he finally showed up, he was curt and made me feel like I was bothering him.

"Jesus?" he asked.

"Yes. Hello. My name is Jesus. Nice to meet you."

As I put out my hand to shake his, he walked past me without introducing himself and without acknowledging that I was reaching out to him. He just said, "Come on, follow me."

When we got into his office, he handed me his card and asked, "So you want to get your master's degree in public policy here? What are your GRE scores?"

I told him what they were.

"Well, I recommend you look into other schools. Where else did you apply?" he asked.

"I applied to Georgetown, Michigan, Harvard, and—"

He interrupted me midsentence: "All good schools, but I highly doubt you will get into any of them, either, especially the Kennedy School at Harvard. Not with your GRE scores. We are a school heavily focused on quantitative analysis, and your scores indicate you lack in that area. Now, I have a lot of work to do, but thank you for coming in to see me." He put his hand out to shake mine without getting up from his chair, indicating it was time for me to go.

I put my head down and walked out. I felt like a kid glumly kicking rocks in disappointment. When I got home, the only person I knew to call was Nia. I picked up the receiver, stared at the numbers, and thought, *Why bother, dude? She probably doesn't believe in you, either.* My eyes filled with tears, and I wanted to slam the phone down. But I pressed the numbers instead. As soon as I heard her voice, I exhaled and a tear came down my face. I told her what happened.

Nia said, "Listen, doll, I need you to stay focused and not pay attention to the noise. Berkeley's loss will be someone else's gain. So don't let that asshole dim your light of hope. He's not worth it. Fuck him. Keep doing what you're doing."

△▽△

About six months after applying to grad schools, I received a big yellow envelope from Harvard in the mail. *No way! This can't be,* I thought as I stared at the envelope, holding it tight. My heart started racing. I took a deep breath and slowly began opening it with shaking fingers, eyes wide in anticipation and hoping for the best. I read the cover letter. My first reaction was *Oh hell nah, this can't be true.*

My second thought was *Hell fuck yeah, I'm going to* Hahvuhd!

My third was *Oh shit! How do I tell Amá?*

I sat there in shock for a minute. I remembered where I'd ended up on my last night using, how horribly I was brutalized and raped. Visions of being thrown down the stairs, naked, and into the cold night flashed into my head. I began to cry uncontrollably, then reached for the phone and called my mom. Through hard-core sobbing, I kept saying, "Amá, I love you. Amá, I love you. I am so sorry."

"¿Qué pasa? ¿Qué te pasa?" she kept asking, scared and worried, until I recognized I was scaring her.

"Amá," I said, "I am so sorry, but I got into Harvard, which is the school I really wanted to get into, but it means I'm not going to be able to move home to be close to the family. I am so sorry, Amá."

"Ya, mijo. No llores. Todo va salir bien. Ya verás. Ahora, ¿explícame que es eso?" she said as I kept crying. *It's okay, my son. Don't cry. It will all work out. Now, explain to me what that is.*

She didn't comprehend what Harvard was. I felt horribly guilty and selfish for choosing to go to Harvard. I'd dreamed of buying my mom her own home and living with her in it. This would have to be postponed. My life was taking a different path.

CHAPTER 20

A few weeks before my graduation, the Education Abroad counselor asked me if I wanted to study in Cuba for the summer. UC Berkeley was sending a pilot group of fifteen students. The turnaround time was quick; I had less than three weeks to apply—and to work out my paperwork with the State Department, too. One week before graduation, my approval letter came.

Prior to leaving, a few Cuban friends I'd made in Spain gave me the numbers of their friends and family members in La Habana. They made sure I had people I could trust in Cuba to look after me should an emergency arise. We were allowed to take two large suitcases on the plane, and my friends' family members asked that I fill one with old clothes I didn't mind giving away. The items that were especially desirable were jeans (Levi's were a commodity and good for trading); shorts (lined surfer shorts, ideally); dress shoes, sneakers (Nike and Converse), and sandals; shirts, underwear, tank tops, and socks; and any electronics I could carry, like a Walkman or a CD player.

In the second suitcase I was asked to bring rolls of toilet paper, individual female sanitary napkins (Kotex) and tampons (Cuban customs would not take them away as long as they were unboxed), condoms (unboxed), washcloths, bars of soap, toothpaste, toothbrushes, Neosporin, cotton balls, medical tape, latex gloves, pencils, pens, notebooks, and writing paper. These items were not readily available in Cuba, and much needed. I was told I should hold on to these items throughout my stay and give them to people I grew close with. Given that I was traveling with the goal of researching difficult topics such as the spread of HIV, male sex work, and HIV prevention strategies, these items would help get people to talk to me.

At Cuban customs, they asked if I wanted my US passport stamped. I told them not to, to avoid any possible problems I might have reentering the United States in the future. After they reviewed my documents, they searched everything. They tried to take my Walkman and my CD player, but I argued like crazy. They did, however, take my music tapes and CDs; my two Anne Rice books (*Interview with a Vampire* and *The Vampire Lestat*), as they were considered capitalistic propaganda; all my new pencils and pens; and loose papers from any items that I could use to spread capitalistic propaganda.

When the customs woman saw the sanitary pads and tampons, her eyes opened wide. She pulled one out and asked what I needed them for and why I had so many. With a friendly smile and a wink, I told her I'd brought them for my friend's daughter, but that if she needed some to please take a few. She looked back at her female supervisor, who gave her an almost unnoticeable smile. The agent turned back to me, winked as she grabbed a handful of pads and tampons, and announced in a sharp, stern voice that I was not allowed to take that many into Cuba. Then she handed them to her supervisor.

I was excited to have the opportunity to visit Cuba. I wanted to experience it for myself. I had no familial or emotional ties to the island. I believed in the stories of equality in Cuba, where revolutionary heroes stood up against imperialism and systems of oppression caused by racism and classism. Yet because I had met enough Cuban and Cuban American friends whose viewpoints differed dramatically from the ones I had been buying into, I wanted to form my own opinions.

I learned from those friends that I was naive in thinking that Cuba's form of socialism was great. It was a dictatorship. I realized the United States was allowing me to go to Cuba to form my own opinions, even if those opinions went against official US policy. I decided I would resist buying into one dogma or another. Most important, I made a decision not to allow anyone to silence my ideas.

On my first full day in Cuba, I and a few others in my group walked to the beach directly across the street from the hotel. We were going to enjoy the weekend before classes started on Monday in La Habana. I could not believe how clear and warm the water was. As I swam in the ocean, I thought, *Dear God, recovery is good. Thank you for allowing me to swim at beaches that I could see only in the pages of* National Geographic *magazines. God is good.*

I told two of my fellow students—Sherry, a Latina of Korean descent who was raised in LA, and a skinny Latina from Fresno named Laura—that I had heard there was a gay section of beach called Mi Cayito and that I wanted to check it out. They agreed to go with me. As we walked, a group of four men approached us. The closer they got, the more intense the staring became. I told Laura and Sherry in English, "You better be flirting! Smile!"

"We are smiling, fool," they replied.

After we passed the four men, we all turned to look. They had stopped and were standing, looking at us. They laughed and walked back toward us. They were gorgeous. One had cutoff jean shorts that reminded me of ones I'd worn as a kid. Another wore board shorts, and the last two were wearing male bikini briefs. They asked if we spoke Spanish. Sherry quickly responded, "Sí, claro." *Yes, of course.*

We introduced one another and the usual tourist-type conversation ensued about where we were from, welcome to Cuba, and blah blah blah. Their flirtatiousness toward us—including me, in a heterosexual-bromance, friendly, masculine way—felt natural and at the same time erotic. They asked where we were going, and Sherry said, "To a beach called Mi Cayito."

They all looked at one another and asked, "Are you two lesbians?"

Sherry and Laura quickly hugged up on each other, and in a sexy voice Sherry said, "Yeah, we are. We just want to go somewhere where we can lie close on the sand without anyone giving us problems."

They didn't look shocked at all. "Well, let us walk you guys," they said.

The girls laughed, and Laura said, "Nah, we aren't together. We're just kidding. But we're going because our friend here is gay. We're keeping him company to make sure he's safe on our first day in Cuba."

The guys looked at me and said, "Really? You're gay?"

I laughed awkwardly at being totally outed and said, "Yeah, I'm gay." It felt powerful, taking ownership, but I was nervous to do so in a place with a history of cruelty toward the LGBTQ+ community.

When we got to Mi Cayito, it became obvious that we had arrived at the gay beach. There were queens galore. We sat on the sand, talked, laughed, and enjoyed one another's company. After about thirty minutes, I called to a group of gay guys who kept looking our way. I introduced our group and began to ask questions about the gay scene in Cuba.

They taught me how to scan the environment from the perspective of Cuban subculture, which was somewhat similar to the down-low subculture in the United States, except that in Cuba people got arrested for being openly gay. They explained that most gay parties in Cuba were underground and rotated between bars, people's houses, and the occasional mansion in Siboney or a house belonging to a man named Papito, in a neighborhood called La Víbora. Papito threw parties that were famous among global celebrities, who flew to La Habana to attend them.

Toward the end of the day, the group of guys we'd met

walked us back to our hotel. Sherry and I waited with them at the bus stop directly in front. The guagua (bus), also known as el camello, the camel, didn't follow a schedule; it came when it came. While we waited, the guys told us we should go that night to a town called Guanabacoa, which was hosting an annual celebration in honor of their patron saint. The town, they explained, was founded in the early 1500s and was at the center of the syncretism of the African religions and Catholicism still practiced today. We couldn't be in Cuba and not experience the fiesta of Guanabacoa, they said, especially when we were so close to the town. They spoke freely with us until another group of locals showed up to wait for the bus. Quickly they shushed one another and changed the conversation. They couldn't speak freely for fear of being labeled dissidents and traitors.

"Chivatos are everywhere, so watch who you talk to. I am sure you will be watched while in La Habana," I was told. Chivatos were snitches. "Given your interests, people will not be willing to talk to you until they've seen you around for a while and gotten to know you. Take the time to get to know others, build relationships, and form your own conclusions. Most tourists don't get the opportunity to see the real Cuba. And pay attention to how Black and white Cubans live here. It's not the Utopia you think it is."

That evening at around eight o'clock, Sherry, Laura, and I hopped on the guagua to go to the patronal feast of Guanabacoa. The bus was crowded and hot. By the time we got to Guanabacoa, it was dark. Bands were playing in the center of town, and people were dancing in the streets. We walked down narrow streets that dated back centuries.

In Guanabacoa, I first encountered the contradictions of the island. It was like being in an area where the yin and the yang are constantly pulling against each other. Its culture and beauty tugged at its gory history of slavery and abuse. Being there was an unforgettable bonding moment for us. We stopped, breathed in the Caribbean air, and stared at the shining stars above. As I gazed at the sky, I felt connected to something greater.

△▽△

Two days later, after our first class in La Habana, the phone rang as we were getting ready for dinner. On the other end of the line was a friend of my friend Ricardito, from Spain. "Yesi. Soy Castrico, amigo de Ricardito de Madrid," the caller said. Ricardito had told his friend where I was staying. "Get ready, a group of us are coming to pick you up in fifteen minutes. We know the building," Castrico told me.

Downstairs, Castrico and two others picked me up in a taxi, an old '50s bomb. We talked, and they pointed out key landmarks, the entire way. "This, the Cine Yara, is the center of what you need to know. This is the gay center of Cuba. Across the street there is Coppelia, the famous ice-cream shop from the movie *Fresa y chocolate*. Down that street you will run into the Malecón. We'll introduce you to some people you should know."

We tried to get a coffee in a hotel lobby, but a security guard wouldn't allow my new Cuban friends to come inside.

Before 2008, Cubans lived in a system of economic apartheid, where people weren't allowed to stay in hotels, rent cars, or enjoy facilities designated for tourists. At that time, only select Cubans were allowed to stay at hotels and only with explicit government permission.

On the Malecón, we ordered coffee at a counter-cafeteria place called El Fiat. As we sat on the seawall, they started to school me on what I needed to know. "First, you need to lose the Mexican accent. We heard you come from a poor family, so you better learn the Cuban accent, papi, or you're going to be hustled out of every penny you have. Cubans pay one American dollar for a taxi ride while tourists pay eight. You will have to pay five or ten dollars to get into a club while a Cuban pays one or two. We hustle for everything here, so get ready to play the game. Don't worry about getting robbed, mugged, or beaten up, because at the end of the day you, as an American, have more rights than we do. No one will harm you. But as you just experienced, there are rules in place to keep the population from mixing with foreigners."

Where was the equality? The Malecón was crowded with gay people and sex workers. Castrico and his companions introduced me to some of their friends and told them to keep an eye on me. El Mexicano became my nickname. I entered a new chapter of my life in La Habana.

CHAPTER 21

The staff at Casa de las Américas, where we were studying, coordinated a site visit for me to Los Cocos, an infamous camp where people were quarantined if they had or were suspected of having HIV/AIDS. HIV in Cuba was a somewhat different issue than in the United States, as many in Cuba viewed HIV as a tool of biological warfare that had infected Cuban military soldiers from the war in Angola. The first HIV infections in Cuba were found in heterosexual, not homosexual, individuals.

HIV doctors taught me about the epidemiology of the virus in Cuba and the various forms of treatment. Residents at Los Cocos allowed me into their homes but spoke openly about their experience of living with HIV only as we walked the compound's perimeter; they feared their homes were bugged. In 1999, though people with HIV were no longer explicitly forced to live at Los Cocos, many felt coerced to do so anyway because, at the time, HIV medication was distributed only at centers like Los Cocos. Back then, one-pill-a-day medications did not exist, and ease of access was important for treatments that needed to be administered multiple times a day.

I couldn't help but compare life with HIV in Cuba to life with HIV in Mexico. In Mexico at the time, the government had doctors document cause of death as "unknown" or "cancer" for people dying of HIV/AIDS, to avoid having to expend resources on the issue and causing many more to die.

△▽△

Cops stopped me at least three or four times a day to ask me for my carnet de identidad, or identification card, while other Americans watched. It was like clockwork. I got stopped on the way to school in the mornings, in the early afternoons after class, on the way to do my research at Coppelia, the Cine Yara, or El Fiat on the Malecón, and on the way home.

After enduring two weeks of this kind of harassment, I'd learned to have my passport copy and California ID in my hand when a police officer approached. I'd extend my hand toward them. "Before you ask," I'd start as they looked over my documents, "I'm American. Yes, I speak Spanish. The original passport is locked in a safe. I am not a jinetero." Jineteros were male sex workers.

Growing up as a man of color in the United States, I was used to being harassed by police officers, but this was different. In the United States, what I experienced was simple racism and prejudice. In Cuba, I felt I was part of a system of suppression created to make everyone feel like they were constantly being watched.

One night two cops stopped me near the corner of my apartment building. One said, "So, Mexicano? Why do you enjoy hanging out with all the gays and pingueros on the Malecón? ¿Eres maricón?" *Are you a faggot?*

"How do you know my nickname? And why do you ask if you already know why I hang out with all the gays and male prostitutes?" I responded.

"How is your research going?" asked the same cop.

"It saddens me how big sexual tourism is here in Cuba. But why are you all of a sudden interested in talking to me? You have been complete assholes to me since I got here. What do you want?" I said curtly.

"It disgusts me that tourists like you come here with so much while we have so little. But what angers me most is how you have more rights than my people do. And yet my job is to protect you."

"What's that got to do with me? You don't know shit about me. And I don't need your protection—as a matter of fact, y'all cops have been fucking with me more than anyone else on this island."

He ended the conversation by walking away.

The next night the same cop approached me again and opened up about having a wife and a thirteen-year-old daughter. He asked if I had any toiletries I might be able to pass along to his wife and daughter.

I went upstairs and grabbed two rolls of toilet paper, ten sanitary pads, and two pairs of socks.

He graciously accepted them and said, "As of tomorrow, no other cops, at least in this neighborhood and in the Malecón, will pull you over to ask for your ID or bother you, regardless of the time of day." Then he proceeded to tell me about what life in Cuba was really like, to his eyes.

He told me how he wasn't able to leave the country because he didn't have any family outside of Cuba. A few of his friends had died trying to escape. He talked to me about how prevalent both racism and classism are in Cuba. Black Cubans were worse off than white Cubans. Those with money had more power. And many white Cubans were able to leave the island and live better lives abroad. "Listen to what people are really telling you," he told me. "Don't buy into the lie."

That night I wrote in my journal for a long time. I had a hard time falling asleep. This cop's words had got me thinking about my own ideologies. I'd come to Cuba because I was a socially conscious community organizer and a radical; I wanted to change the world. Now I felt a part of my identity was shattering. I felt naive and ignorant. There was no promised land, and I felt I was at a crossroads again.

△▽△

The next night I was at a local hangout where groups of gay men and trans women hung out in cliques waiting for news of where the next party was going to be that night. I saw a group of feminine gay teenage boys argue about who was going home with a high-ranking Spanish diplomat driving up the street. They knew his car well. A skinny twelve-year-old who got paid three dollars for the night ended up being selected. The boy had been a sex worker for his family's food since he was ten years old.

"Someone needs to contact the newspaper and report this pedophile," I said.

"Don't waste your time. He has diplomatic immunity. Besides, don't come here imposing your self-righteous, imperialist, American moralistic views on us. He has to work just like the rest of us. This isn't America, papi," a blond transgender woman in our circle of friends clapped back at me.

I didn't know what to say. I hadn't expected this in a country that I had imagined as a place of equality and more-equal distribution of wealth. But there was no equality or equal distribution of wealth in Cuba. Cubans looked over their shoulders for fear of being watched and overheard. Friends turned friends in to the authorities for anti-patriotic behavior, like selling food, fans, or air conditioners from their homes. I was saddened to learn that racism and poverty pervade life even in socialist countries.

Still, I took advantage of the remainder of my time in Cuba as best I could. I couldn't deny that I was blessed to be there. I sat with elders who had lived in prerevolutionary Cuba during the rule of Batista and in postrevolutionary Cuba during Castro. I loved listening to their stories, and I learned a lot. I allowed my values to be shaped by my own experiences and enjoyed the bittersweetness of this island of contradictions, which had changed my life forever. Cuba made me challenge my beliefs and stop moralizing other people's behaviors. Just as I didn't want to be judged for the life I'd lived or the things I'd had to do to survive, it wasn't meant for me to place judgment on others, either.

CHAPTER 22

Each weekend group trip in Cuba—to Matanzas, Varadero, Pinar del Río, and Viñales—was breathtakingly magical in its own way. In Matanzas we visited the large, bright yellow concrete home of a famous santera, a Yoruba Lucumi priestess named Star. As we arrived, the elderly woman stood in a large wooden doorway to greet us, smiling and waving at us to come in. Star had on a long flowy white dress with a white head wrap and long colorful beads around her neck. I learned that the necklaces were called elekes and that each necklace represents a different orisha, or deity, of the religion that enslaved people brought to Cuba. We were not allowed to enter any area of Star's home before first entering her altar room, which we also could not enter without her washing our hands in a glass bowl of perfume, flower petals, and holy water that sat atop a table outside the entrance. We waited in a line. As she washed each of our hands, she gave us brief spiritual readings.

When it was my turn, she took my hands. Hers were wet and wrinkly, with age spots. She guided my hands into the cold scented water and delicately rubbed them with the flower petals. Her upper body trembled, as if she'd gotten a chill, and I felt a weak electric current pass through me. She smiled and said, "You are on this island for a reason. You thought you came for one purpose, but in reality, your ancestors brought you here for another. You will know when it happens, but you will not leave here the same as you came. Your spirits will guide you."

She led us into her altar room. It was filled with altars to the various orishas. Some orishas sat on shelves and atop pillars. Brightly colored cloths draped from the ceiling. A multitude of fruits, cakes, other desserts, and vases with roses, sunflowers, gladiolas, and carnations sat on colorful straw mats. And two large white lit candles stood in the middle of the floor. The walls were painted a light sky blue. It was beautiful. She briefly explained to us the purpose of the altars and the meanings of the fruits, desserts, and flowers. They were offerings from believers who'd visited the home of her orishas. We were guided out a different door than the one we came through and found ourselves in a large cement yard. Chairs were lined against a concrete wall that separated us from a garden of fruit trees.

A group of Afro-Cuban dancers, drummers, and singers performed for us the dances and songs of the orishas. The dancers wore beautifully decorated outfits, each resembling a different orisha. Some orishas' dances were warrior-like, while others were sensual and fluid. After the performances, Star told the director of our program that she would have someone drive me back to the hotel because she wanted to speak with me privately.

When we were alone, Star led me into another room in

the house, where a woman friend of hers was placing a vase of white carnations on a table. "Hi, my name is Rosa," said the woman with a friendly smile. She had the same colorful elekes around her neck that Star wore.

This room was painted off-white, but the walls were chipped in areas. There was a small round table with a white cloth and seven clear glasses of water placed in the shape of a square U, open toward the front of the table. The largest of the glasses, at the center of the U, had a big silver crucifix inside. At the front of the table was a large white candle. At the back was the vase of carnations that Rosa had just placed. On the floor in front of the table was a white bowl of light blue water and white flower petals, and next to it was a bucket filled with herbs and branches. The table had a chair on each side, and one chair sat in the middle of the room facing the table. There was a clear glass of water and a small candle under the chair that faced the table.

Rosa and Star asked me to sit on the chair in the middle of the room. "Are you comfortable?" asked Star.

"Yes."

Star sat on the left of the table I was facing, and Rosa on the right. "Don't get scared, no matter what happens," Star instructed. "Don't cross your legs or arms, and keep your hands on top of your knees, facing upward." I nodded as she continued, "Don't get up from the chair, no matter what, unless told or moved to." I didn't know what she meant but nodded as I listened. "Only answer yes or no to our questions." I nodded in acquiescence, and they gestured to the glasses of water. "Focus on the glasses. If one in particular catches your attention, focus on it. Or if the flame of the candle is what catches your attention, focus on that. The important thing is to stay focused on the energy in the room. The candle is a light for your guardian spirits and ancestors, the glasses of water are for clarity, and the white flowers are for purity."

Rosa lit the candle under my chair and then the candle on the table. They began to pray and invited me to join along. The words to the Lord's Prayer, the Hail Mary, and the Apostles' Creed filled the air. When they finished, Star opened a booklet and began to recite prayers I had never heard before. As the minutes passed, I focused on the glasses of water and on the candle. I felt a shift in the energy around me; it grew still and calm.

At the end of the prayers, Star placed the booklet on the table and began to sing. Her voice was light, and melody filled the room. Rosa pulled a small, skinny bottle of perfume from under the table and opened it. She came to stand on my right, poured some of the perfume into her hands, bent down and grabbed flower petals from a bowl of water, and passed her wet hands over her head, neck, and body. She then waved her hands over the glasses of water on the table.

When Star sat back down, she told me to do the same. As I repeated her movements, I felt a rush of energy flow through my body. I shook. I didn't understand what was happening. Star and Rosa laughed, and Rosa kept singing. Star then repeated the same ritual with the petals and water, saying prayers in a language I didn't understand while Rosa sang. Star sat back down, lit a long fat Cuban cigar, and started talking.

She told me things about myself that I had never told a soul and mentioned things about my personal life that she had no way of knowing. How did this woman know so much about me? In a low voice, I told her that everything she'd described about me was true.

"So you were supposed to be the priest of the family, huh?" Rosa said. "Your life took a different path. You did not live the life of a priest. A trauma took place that changed your life's course."

"¡Luz!" said Star loudly. *Light!*

Rosa's body shook as she sat in her chair; her hands flailed in the air and her voice grew louder. "Your streets became your home. Am I right?"

"¡Luz!" exclaimed Star again.

"Am I right?" Rosa asked again, this time in a louder voice. "Speak up, boy, I can't hear you."

"Luz," I responded awkwardly.

Then Star joined in. "Then your life changed again. It was as if your body became a skeleton. But you were angry because of sadness. Clean yourself again," she ordered.

I got up from my chair and once again cleaned myself with the scented water and flower petals from the bowl. Once again, for an instant I felt a rush of energy through the cells of my body, through my veins, like a surge of electricity.

"Stay standing there, and you sit when I tell you," Star commanded. She slouched over with her elbows on her knees, rubbing her hands together and rocking back and forth. She held the large cigar with her teeth. "He doesn't know."

Star went on, "You blamed your mother. You all blamed her. You left. And you tried to escape at a young age. Now you can sit down."

I obeyed the order, unsteady on my feet. Rosa then turned to Star and said, "This boy has been blessed to live many lives in one. He can't even imagine where he's going. Don't you think?" They spoke to each other in this way as if I weren't even there.

"Oh, my child. It is no wonder you were delivered to our doorstep. Your ancestors brought you here to learn how to listen. And, most important, to learn how to heal."

Star continued, "You have lived a double life. You demonstrated one thing to the world that surrounded you, your family and your friends, when in reality you were something else. You have hidden who you are for most of your life. So much so that you went to bed with many women to cover up that you like men."

I stared at her in shock.

Star went on, "You were confused for a very long time. You hid in your books. But someone took advantage of you and took your innocence. That sweet innocent child was gone. What came next were dark years. Your life was taken from you. Your power was taken."

Star's words hit me like a wave. "Luz," I said as tears rolled down my face.

Star continued, "People came into your life to help you, but they didn't know how. You were thrown into a chasm of darkness and anger. You went down a path of destruction.

But there is one person who is a sister to you and who has always been by your side."

"Yes. Ariyel," I said through the tears.

"Stand up and clean yourself again."

Tears ran down my face as I did what Star ordered, and again a blast of energy coursed through my body. The last thing I remember was my eyes feeling like they were moving upward in my head, like I was leaping out of my body—and then I blacked out. Then I felt a beam of light push me back into my body, and I opened my eyes. As I came to, I found myself sitting in the chair again. I sat there, powerless and confused but released from the grip of a deep darkness. I felt light, truly light, for the first time in years.

At that exact moment, Star fell back into her chair, shaking dramatically. She spoke in a language I didn't understand—as if in tongues. I looked at her and then at Rosa, who gave me a reassuring glance.

Suddenly, speaking Spanish again, Star asked for forgiveness, her voice dark and deep. "I am sorry. I am sorry," she said over and over.

Star's chest lifted as her body arched in the chair. The energy in the room became very cold. Star fell back in her chair and opened her eyes. She was breathing heavily as she came to. The door opened, and one of the men who had performed in the backyard stood there, staring. "Is everything okay in here?" he asked.

"Yes, everything's okay. We are wrapping up. But before you close the door, tell this young man what you see," Star said.

The performer walked into the room and closed the door behind him. He looked steadily at me. His voice was deep but calming. "This young man is destined for greatness. He's had to live many lives in one. He's played many different roles. He wants to affect the lives of others but doesn't know how. He needs guidance."

He stopped there, gave me a warm smile, and walked out of the room, shutting the door behind him. Afterward, Star and Rosa sat and talked with me about my life. I was in such a faraway place, and yet I felt understood by these two women who were complete strangers to me. I felt healed and spiritually awakened, and I was floored by their ability to see into my very core.

Before we wrapped things up, Star told me that my mother had severe heart problems. She said that when I returned from Cuba, I had to go home directly to be by my mother's side, because her health was deteriorating fast.

She went on, "You come from a long line of medicine men and women who knew how to communicate with their ancestors. Your culture honors the dead and the spirits of those who came before you. Their experiences flow through your veins. Gather strength from them and you will make a difference."

I broke down into uncontrollable sobs as I took her words into my heart.

"You are a warrior. Like the women and men who came before you, whose histories and lives flow through your veins. Honor them. And honor yourself. Learn to listen."

We stood up, and Star recited a closing prayer. They

hugged me. I cried in Star's and Rosa's arms. For the first time in a very long time, my shoulders felt like there was no weight pressing down on them. Cuba really did change my life forever; it led me toward healing. This beautiful island of contradictions. I was a new Jesse, fortified by the combined strength and experiences of all those who came before me.

EPILOGUE

My favorite family story is the one of an encounter with La Llorona, the Crying Woman. Every Mexican family has a La Llorona story. My father's version went like this:

We saw La Llorona a lot when we were children up in the Sierras. We spotted her along the rivers and lakes, searching for her drowned children. Once I was riding horseback with my uncles Manny and Agusto. I was about ten years old. We came to a very narrow and dangerous trail along the river and had to dismount from our horses.

As we were leading our horses, my uncle Agusto at the front and Uncle Manny behind me, we stopped dead in our tracks. There she was, La Llorona, sitting on a rock at the edge of an arroyo, crying. We were approaching our pueblito of Cebollitas. The river current was very strong that night. Uncle Agusto urged me over and over to be brave, to keep walking, and not to look La Llorona directly in the face. She was just sitting there on the large rock, staring into the water, crying. As soon as

Agusto walked past her with his horse's reins in hand, she glanced sideways at me and then at Uncle Manny. I asked Uncle Manny to stay near me. We inched closer to La Llorona as she stared.

Then, in a flash, she was standing. We couldn't see her feet. It was as if she was floating there in front of us, staring at Manny as the river flowed behind her. Her dress blew in the wind, glowing like the moon. She shifted her gaze to me. I froze. Her arms remained at her sides, but she floated so close to me, it seemed our noses were touching. Everything went silent, but I heard a voice in my head telling me to follow her. Time stood still until Uncle Agusto grabbed my arm and pulled me toward him. Her spell broke.

Once we passed La Llorona, the world returned to normal. Once again we could hear the water of the arroyo, the night birds, and the crickets around us.

Growing up, my father was an amateur boxer and fought against some of the most famous Mexican boxers of the time, like el Kid Azteca. When I was nine years old, he forced me to spar with my brother. My brother beat the shit out of me, so I grabbed his arm and bit him hard. My father pulled me off my brother and told me that a man doesn't bite. I was so angry with him for forcing me to spar, I said, "Fuck you," and spit in his face. He punched me straight in the nose. I was laid out flat on my back. When I came to, my brother was laughing.

My dad was a man of contradictions—mean, but loving in his own way. He was miserly with his money but spent it *lavishly on other women. He refused to help my mom but was quick to help a stranger. He was quiet and reserved yet could speak viciously. My father told lots of stories but never shared his feelings with me. He died, and I never got to know his favorite color or his favorite song. At the end, I was the one who closed his eyes when I found him. I will never again hear his stories about the old days in Mexico, about magic and mysticism, about living with the land in the mountains, about the revolution and the survival of generations long gone.*

△▽△

I called my mom as soon as I landed at the San Francisco airport. She was in cheerful spirits and happy to hear my voice. I said good night and that I would see her in a few days. Less than twelve hours later, my brother called: "Amá is in the hospital. She had a heart attack."

I drove to San Diego and canceled my plans for the rest of the summer to stay by her side. Although Amá's health slowly returned, it was obvious that the stresses in her life had taken a toll on her heart. She had rheumatoid arthritis in her hands, spine, and legs. Her fingers cramped and locked in painful positions. I would help her wrap them in hot washcloths to unlock them and relieve the pain. Amá was getting old. Yet, one week after her heart attack, she was up at 4:30 a.m., catching the five-thirty bus to prepare food for the kids at school.

One morning I woke up and discovered she wasn't home.

I got scared. I called the school and learned she was there. Amá hadn't told any of us that she was going back to work. The doctors had recommended she rest at home for several weeks, and I was worried for her. I drove to the school to plead and demand she come back home, but Amá refused. "I need to work to pay the rent. I'm sorry, mijo, but I have to work."

I didn't know what to do other than tell her I'd pick her up from and drive her to work every morning while I was staying in San Diego. When I picked Amá up that afternoon, I told her, "I won't go away to Harvard if you need me to stay home to take care of you."

"No," she said, "I don't want you to resent me more than you already do. You promised me I would see the world through your eyes. Remember?"

I felt the prick of tears in my eyes and then the warmth of them rolling down my face. "Amá, I don't blame you. I don't resent you. And I'm sorry for all the mean things I've said to you."

I knew that no matter how many amends I made to her, no matter how many cards, letters, hugs, or times I told her that I owe my success to her and that I am proud of her and her strength as a mother, she did not believe it inside.

I lost control of myself. I was crying so hard that I couldn't see the road and had to pull off. I reached over and hugged Amá and cried. She held me and comforted me like only a mother knows how. She said, "I love you, mijo. You have to be strong and enjoy living your life. Look at me. If you have to go away to Harvard to get a better life, then move forward, my son. Don't look back."

So I did.

I was picked up from the airport in Boston by the woman who was to be my new roommate, Maya. We pulled up to a run-down four-story building on Norfolk Avenue in Cambridge. It was up the street from a Blockbuster and a restaurant named the Middle East in Central Square. Our building looked haunted. The front entryway was dark, the streetlights were off, the paint was chipped away, and the door didn't lock. I didn't say anything because I was grateful to have an affordable place to live.

When we walked into the building, we saw a man in a hoodie standing in the lobby, clearly selling crack to another guy. The buyer ran past us and out the door, almost knocking Maya down. I put my suitcase down and walked up to the man. I looked at the dealer and said, "Look, holmes, you need to get the fuck out of my building. We live here now, and you ain't running your nickel-and-dime operation out of my lobby no more. You hear me? I don't want this shit at my crib." My fists were clenched, ready to throw blows. He stared at me and didn't say a word.

We both stood there staring. Maya looked back and forth from him to me. An eternity passed. Eventually he said, "Aight yo. I'll take it elsewhere. We good?"

"Yeah, we good," I said.

I put my hand out, we gave each other the short version of the street handshake, and he walked out of the building. Maya silently walked to our apartment, which was just off the lobby on the first floor, and opened the door.

Once we were inside, she broke the silence. "Well, that was interesting," she said. "Not even fifteen minutes in our new building and already you're picking fights with our neighborhood dealer." We both started laughing.

She showed me my room. It was the size of a large closet. There was no bed and no place for me to put my clothes.

That tiny room became my home for the next two years. That first night as I slept on the floor, I thought, *What did I do?* The air in the city smelled like fish, my room was doll-house size, and there I was, sleeping on the floor.

I forced myself to write a gratitude list. At least I was indoors, lying on a carpet with a suitcase full of clothes and waiting to start classes at Harvard University. This was my dream. So if my biggest problem at that moment was telling a crack dealer not to sell drugs in the lobby of the building I was living in—well, my life really wasn't going so badly.

At school, I was surprised by and grateful for the support system that the financial aid office, the admissions office, the career center, and the academic dean's office at the Harvard Kennedy School all provided to me. Everything I needed for my classes had been taken care of. My only job was to show up and do the work.

Once classes started, however, I felt myself an outcast again. I showed up, participated in class discussions, completed assignments, and worked in the computer lab. Yet aside from a very small handful of people, I couldn't connect with other students. I felt different. I didn't want to let people in for fear of being judged. I couldn't talk to others and would often shut down. In a controlled group setting, like a classroom, I was okay, but one-on-one conversations petrified me.

My old insecurities came flooding back the night a group of us Latino students got together for dinner at a restaurant, to get to know one another. I was not as refined and polished as the others portrayed themselves to be. I thought I could talk authentically among them as I would back home with my friends in the neighborhood or among my close friends at UC Berkeley. I assumed that being Latinos would automatically bond us.

At one point, the entire table went silent when I asked another student if he was gay. Looks of shock and disgust passed over their faces while I cowered in my chair. My question was considered inappropriate, uncouth, and a clear sign of a lack of decorum and good upbringing. The student I'd asked responded with a mean look and a sharp "No, I am not gay," in a tone of disbelief that I would ask him that. He went on, "I think you're the only gay one here tonight."

I felt horrible. I had no ill intention and meant no harm. And who was I to out him?

Clearly, this wasn't my world. I quickly learned that my direct approach and my ability to make new friends, which had taken me years in recovery to develop, were not going to work at Harvard, not even among my own. I began to doubt whether I belonged, whether I was good enough to be there.

Harvard was not difficult for me academically. Hardest were the social interactions—the small talk between classes while waiting for the professor to arrive, during lunch, or at happy hours. I didn't use big words like the other students, and I spoke in a more animated manner than most. At the time, I didn't equate this to race and class, but there were clearly some divides that were going to be difficult for me to bridge.

My inability to connect with others turned into disappointment in myself. It was downhill from there. If anyone made an effort to get to know me, I didn't notice. I felt so low about myself that I thought Harvard had made a mistake in admitting me. I was terrified others would find out I was not smart enough to be there. I believed everyone thought I was too ghetto to be there. I became jealous of my roommates and of others because I thought they had been prepared to socially interact with people at Harvard while I hadn't.

They had done internships in government and at think tanks, while I, when not cutting hair, had been working directly with extremely low-income communities and with incarcerated individuals.

My problem was not that my work was less than that of others; my problem was that I believed the lie that somehow I wasn't good enough. I didn't see the value I could add to every discussion. Instead I felt ashamed of who I was.

Eventually I became angry. At NA and AA meetings in Cambridge and Boston, I felt misunderstood. At times I felt too embarrassed to share that I was struggling to adapt to life as a Harvard student when others there were struggling to get off dope.

One evening during the walk home from a meeting near Harvard Square, on Massachusetts Avenue, the police stopped me. This was the fourth time I'd been stopped since living in Cambridge. In a car, they turned on their sirens and shined a spotlight on me. Over the megaphone, they told me to stop. My heart raced with rage.

I dropped my bag to the ground, turned to face away from the street, put my hands behind my head, and spread my legs without even arguing. I resigned without a fight. The police asked where I was coming from. They asked for my ID, which, I explained, was in my pocket. I told them I was a Harvard student and that I was heading home. They patted me down and searched me. They pulled my cards and money out of my wallet, but when they saw my Harvard University ID, they paused.

They had received reports of people getting held up in the area and were just doing their jobs, they said.

I didn't respond. All I said was "Can I go now?"

I stood between Central and Harvard Squares and watched the car drive off, my hands clenched into tight fists by my sides and a mixture of anger, defiance, and defeat in my eyes. After standing in the cold darkness with no one around for what seemed an eternity, I bent over, picked up my bag, and continued on my walk home.

I became increasingly isolated and left my room infrequently. I was depressed. For a month I refused to get out of bed and skipped all my morning classes. My roommates would knock on my door to wake me, but I refused. I was paralyzed with fear of failure. I fell into a downward self-destructive spiral fast. I was too afraid to get high, I was too afraid to face the world, and I was too afraid to kill myself, so all I could do was stay in bed, wrapped in the safety of my blankets.

Then one day a Latina student named Faith invited me to

her house for dinner. I said yes. After dinner she told me she was worried about me, concerned I was messing things up for myself. She said, "What are you doing? You have gone through too much to let a place like this paralyze you. If you fail or get kicked out, you will be doing exactly what is expected of you. Is that what you want?"

That conversation was the first time someone had shown me they could see into me since I'd arrived at Harvard. She knew who I was and the path I was on.

The same week Faith had me over for dinner, a few mid-career students from my classes began to show an interest in me. The Kennedy School offers a one-year master's degree program to individuals who have been in the workforce for some time and who are ready to take on new challenges. I was fortunate to have courses with a substantial number of mid-careers.

A few mid-careers invited me to coffee and made it a point to tell me that they'd appreciated my comments in the classroom. They also gave me suggestions on how to be more effective. I felt they understood me better than my own peers. It was easier to have conversations with them without pretense. I accepted their feedback and guidance because it didn't feel patronizing. They would talk about situations in their lives and how they'd overcome challenges. And that made a world of difference for me, just like in the rooms of AA and NA, where personal experience is relatable. I listened to these mid-careers' experiences, and I took their suggestions. I slowly started practicing having short conversations with my classmates.

A blond white gay man from Nebraska who worked at the Harvard church with Harvard's openly gay African American minister; a blonde woman from Finland who'd worked in places like Kosovo and Yemen on peacekeeping missions; a man from the Virgin Islands who was in politics; and a man who worked in finance for the State of Israel—all took me under their wings separately and mentored me on basic time-management and networking skills. It was the small networking lessons that mattered most to me. They explained that I shouldn't order chicken or well-done steak at expensive steak houses. They taught me how to properly place a napkin on my lap and how to dab my mouth with it. They suggested I order cranberry juice with club soda and a slice of lime during business meetings at bars.

Mid-career women and men with military backgrounds who I'd thought I had nothing in common with showed me they were just as human as me and had feelings similar to mine. They shared with me that they too had moments of insecurity and that they too often felt disconnected from other students given their military service. They took time to get to know me when I felt other students weren't reciprocating my efforts. Their authenticity and vulnerability helped me build lifelong bonds.

I started once again, as I had early on in recovery, to identify my own prejudices and fears. I started to understand how my issues around identity and self-esteem, coupled with my life experiences, prevented me from allowing others to get to know me, or me them. I analyzed why certain people bothered me, and what they represented to me. In this way, I grew up.

I began to see the value of Harvard beyond the degrees and the academic rigor it offers. I didn't realize at first that people pay to go to Harvard for the professional and social networks they'll gain. No one sat me down and said to me, "Okay, while at Harvard, you need to make sure to take time to build relationships with your fellow students, because they will open doors to opportunities for the rest of your life."

I also didn't want to be that strategic. I enjoyed hanging out with the employees at the cafeteria in between classes; I felt at home with them. But, slowly, I began to attend social events and build friendships with other students. I came to understand that Harvard allowed me the space to create friendships with people from extremely diverse economic and racial backgrounds, from all over the world. In the classroom and when in working groups, class divisions were blurred—or so I told myself. They were forced to deal with me, and I had to deal with them, at least for the duration of our time there. For me, Harvard was an invaluable experience.

Little by little, I let my guard down. I recognized that I had built meaningful relationships with a small group of allies. I focused my energies on the positive and on the people I was connecting with. Those people turned out to be lifelong friends.

△▽△

During my second year at Harvard, I was a changed person. I hit the books hard and committed myself. I had a sense of purpose. I went to the gym in the evenings and made commitments to eat healthfully and to take care of my body.

I enrolled in a class on adaptive leadership. It was the one course everyone raved about at the Kennedy School. I sat in one of the largest classrooms at the school with worldwide leaders, like the former president of Ecuador, who was ousted by a military coup; the then future, and now former, president of Mexico; a future governor of the US Virgin Islands; and numerous other individuals who would eventually hold elected positions in the United States and abroad. The class was unconventional and controversial, and it pushed comfort levels while maintaining an atmosphere of productive disequilibrium.

In that environment, I spoke up about issues of race, class, gender, and sexuality. I had no idea what I was in for. Being outspoken and liberal at UC Berkeley is one thing. But being outspoken and liberal at Harvard is another. In leadership terms, I was killed off immediately. The manner in which I spoke, my body language, my demeanor, my tone, the language I used, my posture, the color of my skin, how I dressed, my tattoos, the fact that I spoke up and always participated; you name it—everything about me reminded others of "those" people, the kinds of people who those in positions of leadership have to "deal with"—or who they actually, many times, don't deal with by killing off, discrediting, and shutting out.

I learned in that classroom that I will always represent a segment of this population to others. And I felt it was my duty to speak to issues of race and inequality as matters that need to be addressed up front and not treated like add-ons or second thoughts in the creation of public policy.

I learned there that being the success story comes with both a benefit and a curse. I can always speak firsthand about being a beneficiary of social programs that had a positive impact in my life. But sometimes people interpret my success as that of an individual who pulled himself up by his own bootstraps, as opposed to my success being the product of a network, of the efforts of many people, some of them total strangers and at different touch points in my life, who made sure I did not fail. For me, there were no bootstraps.

I did not acquire my success on my own. My family played an enormous role. Even in my darkest moments, my family was there for me. In spite of how vicious and mean I became in my addiction, they never turned their backs on me.

My life experiences made me grateful to be an American. I was afforded opportunities to challenge my own ideologies and political beliefs, which were not always pro-American. The grass isn't always greener elsewhere, I learned. It is greener where I tend to it.

△▽△

As I walked off the stage at my graduation from Harvard on that muggy June day in 2001, I ran to where Amá, Ariyel, and Joy were standing, cheering for me. I pulled my mom into my arms, hugged her close, and cried like a baby.

"Yo sé, mijo. Yo lo sé. Te amo mucho mucho mucho," she whispered to me. *I know, my son. I know. I love you very, very, very much.*

Ariyel and Joy joined in on the hug as we all cried together. They were proud of me. Even after all I had put them through. With a giant smile across her face, Ariyel said, "I love you, Nerd."

I love you, too. Thank you for not giving up on me.

As I held Amá, I looked around at the crowd of people and understood that my future, much like my past, would be a series of triumphs and failures. But I knew that my inner strength, my ancestors, and those in my life who supported me would get me through. For an instant, I felt a higher power extend a hand to me and say, *Here it is. Do you want it?*

Deep inside, I heard my spirit respond, *Yes. I want it. I want to live my life today.*

I remembered my final night spent high. I remembered how I didn't want to live anymore. And here I was now.

I buried my head in my mom's shoulder, allowing her to hold me as her son. "Gracias, Amá. Te amo mucho."

"Yo lo sé, mijo. Yo lo sé. Yo también te amo." *I know, my son. I know. I love you, too.*

ACKNOWLEDGMENTS

The journey that led to this book's publication was definitely a roller-coaster ride. Many times I wanted to get off the ride and quit writing. I kept telling myself that no one wants to read my story. But many people along the way encouraged me to not give up, cheered me on, and showed me unconditional love and support, both inside and outside the rooms of recovery.

In writing these acknowledgments, it occurs to me how blessed I am to have so many people in my life who genuinely love me for me, just as I am. I've tried to mention every one of you, but when I got to page five, I realized my editor would most likely force me to cut it down due to space limitations. So please know that even if your name isn't listed here, you are important to me. Whether I met you in the rooms of recovery, in a live meeting, or on Zoom during COVID-19; whether we broke bread beyond a surface level and encouraged each other in high school, community college, UC Berkeley, Harvard, or UPenn, or on our professional paths—you matter to me, and I want to thank you for believing in me. I couldn't have done it without you. You know exactly who you are. Thank you for picking up the phone, day or night, and sharing moments of sadness, frustration, anger, joy, hope, and laughter with me. Most important, thank you for reminding me that I have a story to tell, that I am worthy of telling it, that I am deserving, and that—in spite of everything—I am not broken. I hope my story encourages others to not give up and to dream again.

First and foremost I want to thank my mom, my Amá, for constantly seeing the good in me and, in spite of life's circumstances, for continuously clutching on to hope, freely sharing your smile, and finding joy and laughter in everything you do. ¡Te quiero mucho mucho mucho! To Linda Sierra, my second mom, I know you are here celebrating with us in spirit. To my best friend, Andrea Sierra, *Y-A-T-W-B-M-W*. To my godfather, Ricardo Rosario, Ochungumi, vale más. Quiéreme. To my apá, thank you for doing for me in spirit what you couldn't in life.

To Alfonso, for loving this confused young boy unconditionally and helping me become a man. You never judged me. To CJ, for loving La Leona. To Danielle, I never thought meeting you would change my life forever. You're an angel sent by the heavens. To Izzy, for watering the seeds of education and believing in our youth. To Gracie, for taking care of me during my surgeries and being my travel buddy. To Shawn, love you, bro!

To my siblings, we may not be perfect, but we're not broken.

I started writing this book on Lanikai Beach in Oahu, Hawaii, because of Stacie Olivares and Kieu-Anh King, who flew me to Hawaii with them after my dad died. I was hurting and felt lost. You both sat me down, opened up my laptop, and encouraged me to start typing the very first words of this book. Thanks for standing with me. To the friends who read my book prior to any formal edits and gave me honest feedback: Erica Gonzales, Kole Hicks, Sabine Awad, David Lawrence, Matt Forman, and Nyla Wissa. To Erica, thank you for being my homey, force-feeding me pizza at matchbox, and taking long evening walks with me along the National Mall . . . Priceless!

Gracias, Stephanie Barnett Sims—after all these years, since Carnival in Cádiz with Justin and Laura, you are still a great friend. Your email to Stacey Walker King at MACRO got the ball rolling to make this a reality. Stacey introduced me to Yira Valero, who put me in touch with Leopoldo Gout. He believed in me and my story enough to introduce me to my wonderful and brilliant agent, Lisa Gallagher! Thank you, Lisa, for holding my hand and guiding me patiently through the process, and for showing the manuscript to Cristóbal Pera, who first took a chance on my book and championed it internally at Penguin Random House until it reached my editor, Maria Goldverg. Maria and Cristóbal connected me with the magical Felice Laverne, who helped me find my voice again. After countless generic rejection letters from agents, who would have thought that one serendipitous email would change my life forever?

On the Vintage Books & Anchor Books team at Penguin

Random House, I want to thank my editor, Maria Gold-verg, and the *I'm Not Broken* team: Alex Dos Santos, James Meader, Sophie Normil, Lauren Weber, Annie Locke, and Lisa Kwan for your hard work, including showing me how to set up social media accounts like Twitter without laughing at me. You all went above and beyond. On the Penguin Random House Audio production team, Dan Zitt—¡gracias, amigo! On the Vintage Español team, thank you to Alexandra Torrealba and Kelly Martinez Perez.

To the authors who returned my calls and texts—Reyna Grande, Malin Alegria, Leslie Schwartz, and Ruben Navarrette—¡gracias! Your unbelievable generosity with your time was invaluable. I wish there were more like you!

I also want to thank my therapists. Mental health is a struggle for so many of us who have generational trauma. I have been blessed to continue working on mine via EMDR with David Ross, parts work with Joseph Jeffers, and mental health counseling with the amazing behavioral health team at the San Diego LGBT Community Center. Thank you to Dr. Michael Wohlfeiler and Aissa Avila for being blessings in the lives of thousands—including mine!

I am grateful to all my professional and educational mentors: Maria Padilla, Pedro Noguera, Gil Conchas, Marc Cosentino, Maritza Hernandez, Nolan Bowie, Miguel Garcia, Michelle DePass, Darren Walker, Debra Joy Pérez, Towanna Burrous, John Harper III, Augie Sandoval, Lisa Nunn, Hermila Rangel, and the rest of the financial aid and EOPS teams at San Diego City College—thank you for your words of wisdom and guidance.

Along the way, others encouraged to keep on writing by popping into coffee shops, where I'd write for hours, to check on me. In San Diego: Mark Wenham, Fred Sotelo, Victor Diaz, and Celia Berriel; in Washington, D.C.: Karen Andre, Mileydi Guilarte, Aaron Dorfman, Bibi Hidalgo, Thamar Harrigan, Valerie Piper, Liudmila Batista, Deidre Jackson, and the crew at BusBoys and Poets; in Miami: Diana Borrego, Jossfer Smith, Thamara Labrousse, Regine Monestime, Daniella Levine Cava, Gloria Romero Roses, Alex Sarabia, Nancy Negrón, Ayxa Fernandez, Rashmi Airan, and the Miami Fellows III crew; in Denver: Crystal Almada, Danny Rivera, and MJ Dailey; in Tallahassee: Sarah James, Bob Ward, Shawn Bankston, Max Saeman, Mike McKeogh, and DJ Buchanan; in Orlando: Jon Thomas; in Tampa: Rodrigo Sabec, Michael Dunn, Pedro Velez, and Doris "Dee" La Boricua.

Thank you to the UC Berkeley and Harvard crews: Quirina Orozco, Jennie Luna, Bernadette Vargas, Temo Arroyo, Karla Ek, Frank Trujillo, George Galvis, Otto Cocino, Mayra De La Garza, Roberto Rodriguez, Marisa Castuera Hayase, Maurilio León, Donald "Dondi" Walker Tunnage, Lynne Lyman, Dan Sanks, Taiya Smith, María Teresa Kumar, Dan Erickson, Michelle Sauve, Marta Pernas, Will Pittz, Paivi Nikander, Ken Mapp, and the many others who helped me make it through. You know who you are.

To the next generation: the world is at your fingertips, so, Child, Lil Jesse, and Bibiana—don't let anyone dim your light. Enjoy the ride and cherish your innocence. You are beautiful exactly as you are. Continue to laugh from deep inside your spirit. And no matter what—don't give up!

Last but not least, to everyone in the rooms of recovery who, over the past twenty-nine years, has continued to suit up and show up to be in service to others. You took an eighteen-year-old kid and showed him that a life without drugs was possible. From sleeping in Balboa Park to graduating from Harvard! Wow! I love you all!